SOCIETAL STRATIFICATION

A Theoretical Analysis

Jonathan H. Turner

New York Columbia University Press *1984*

Library of Congress Cataloging in Publication Data
Turner, Jonathan H.
Societal stratification.

Includes bibliographical references and index.
1. Social classes—Philosophy. I. Title.
HT609.T87 1984   305.5′12   83-7660
ISBN 0-231-05740-7
ISBN 0-231-05741-5 (pbk.)

Columbia University Press
New York   Guildford, Surrey

*Clothbound editions of Columbia University Press books are Smyth-sewn
and printed on permanent and durable acid-free paper.*

To Alexandra

CONTENTS

PREFACE

This is a book on human stratification. But I hope that it is much more. For the pages to follow also represent an effort to build theory. My goal has been to criticize existing modes of sociological analysis, to suggest an alternative strategy, and to illustrate this strategy with a detailed analysis of societal stratification.

No doubt what I say will be controversial for many, but I hope that the controversial portions of this work will incite constructive criticism rather than acrimony. Too often in recent decades sociological theorists have been afraid to theorize; rather, we have all spent too much time talking about and arguing over ideas of the first sociological masters. Moreover, we have allowed research protocols to dictate the way we develop theories. My desire, which I hope will increasingly be shared by others, is to climb back into my armchair and theorize. In so doing, I have drawn heavily from sociology's first masters—especially Marx, Spencer, Durkheim, and Weber. But I have tried to "stand on their shoulders," not in their shadows. Nor have I let concern with operationalization and measurement problems arrest my imagination. I trust that my concepts are sufficiently well defined that researchers can find ways to measure them; every key term in the theoretical propositions to be presented is conceptualized as a metric, as something which varies and which can be counted.

I apologize in advance to the mathematically sophisticated, since I have distorted the elegance of your notation system in an effort to simplify and communicate to the nonmathematically inclined. My simple propositions can be transformed back into more traditional notation, but such an effort would be, in reality, mop-up work. My point in the chapters that follow is to specify in simple equations the relationships among variables implicated in those diverse processes that sociologists term "stratification." It is *the general form of the relationship* among concepts that is critical, not the elegance of notation to express these relationships. I want to communicate to a broad audience, not just to "mathematical sociologists."

This book develops five elementary principles on what I conceptualize as the five constituent processes of stratification: (1) the unequal distribution of material wealth, (2) the unequal distribution of power, (3) the unequal distribution of prestige, (4) the formation of, and differentiation among, homogeneous subpopulations, and (5) the rank-ordering of these subpopulations. These five processes are all conceptualized as variables that can vary independently of each other. My theoretical task, then, has been to isolate, and then specify, the most generic conditions of the social universe under which each of these five processes varies. I borrow heavily from a number of theorists, including, besides the first masters listed above, Talcott Parsons, Kingsley Davis, Wilbert Moore, and Gerhard Lenski. In particular, Lenski's work in his *Power and Privilege: A Theory of Social Stratification* has provided me with much insight; and as will become evident, I have reanalyzed the different types of societies that he presented in an effort to illustrate with data the plausibility of my elementary propositions.

I am sure that I have made mistakes in this book. But I do not see this as cause for great dismay, for the development of theory involves formulation, criticism, and reformulation. I accept and welcome the criticisms as necessary to reformulation. Only in this way will sociology advance as a science.

> Jonathan H. Turner
> *Laguna Beach, California*

ACKNOWLEDGMENTS

First, I want to express my gratitude to my colleague, Robert Hanneman, who has spent many hours talking to me about the ideas in this book. Had his schedule permitted, he would have co-authored this book. Second, I am grateful to those who read all or portions of the manuscript, for they made useful comments and suggestions. In particular, I want to thank Robert Hanneman, Mark Gottdiener, Bruce Mayhew, and Gerhard Lenski. Finally, I wish to acknowledge the financial assistance provided by the Academic Senate, University of California at Riverside. Over the years they have provided needed financial aid for my theoretical work; I am most appreciative.

Chapter One THEORETICAL PROBLEMS AND PROSPECTS

Toward a Natural Science of Society

In his famous address in 1937 before the faculty of the University of Chicago, A. R. Radcliffe-Brown forcefully advocated a "natural science of society."[1] For Radcliffe-Brown, the phenomenal universe consists of "natural systems" which are distinguished by unique types of relations among distinctive entities. Social systems constitute one of the natural systems of the universe, the relations among individuals. And sociology is an identifiable science by virtue of its emphasis on these relations. The goal of social science is, therefore, the same as it is for all sciences: to articulate abstract "laws" about the properties, operations, and dynamics of natural systems.

Such a position was as controversial in 1937 as it is today. To argue that the laws of human organization can be discovered and articulated invites criticism and stirs controversy. Indeed, many in the social sciences denounce the search for such laws as foolhardy[2] and a waste of time. For those in this camp, there is "something different" about humans which makes a science of social relations not just a waste of time but also a contradiction in terms. And even among those who accept the legitimacy of a scientific approach and the need to develop theoretical statements, there is surprisingly little agreement over what the "laws of sociology" will look like.[3]

There is little in this book that I can say to appease those who believe that a science of human social relations is impossible. For they hold a position that is at odds with my goal in these pages: to develop some laws of human organization.[4] For those who accept a more scientific viewpoint, but who disagree over what a scientific law is, let me return to Radcliffe-Brown's address. As he stated, there are at least four conceptions of a "scientific law":[5]

(1) the Newtonian view that a natural rule is "imposed upon reality by God"
(2) the extreme positivist view that a law is a statement of an observed regularity
(3) the pragmatist's assertion that a law is something which, for the purposes at hand, is convenient to believe
(4) the pre-Aristotelian, Ephesian concept that a law is "immanent in the universe"

It is the last view which, Radcliffe-Brown insisted, should guide scientific inquiry, for with careful scrutiny, thought, and reflection, natural systems will reveal their laws of operation. Such laws will allow us to understand the relations among properties of a particular natural system. As the "natural science of society," sociology must seek the immanent laws that inhere in social relations among individuals. Such laws are not given by God; they are more than statements of empirical regularity; and they are not rules to be discarded as convenience dictates. Rather, laws inform us about the nature of key social relations among individuals and collectivities of individuals.

It is this view of a "sociological law" that will inform this book. As I will delineate more forcefully in the next chapter, sociologists have been too fearful of their armchairs. We need to go back to basics and ask some very simple and yet important questions: what are the basic properties of our "natural system"? What processes connect these properties? What are the dynamic qualities of these properties?

While this book is about "societal stratification," it is, in reality, a theoretical effort. My intent is to discern what constituent properties of the social universe converge to create a social form like stratification. Then, I hope to develop some abstract laws on these properties, and at the same time to specify the processes connecting them as well as the dynamics inherent in them. At this stage, these statements may seem vague, if not platitudinous. I hope to clarify them as I proceed in these early chapters.

Issues in Developing Social Theory

The "Objective" and "Subjective" Realms

Sociologists have often acted as if the development of the abstract laws of society is impeded by the fact that humans think, reflect, emote, and otherwise engage in a host of psychological and cognitive processes. Many of these processes constitute another "natural system" in the universe and are the proper subject matter of psychology, and at times, biology. But to the extent that psychological processes influence social relations among individuals, they are relevant to sociological theory. Yet, as many contend, such relevance is an impediment to developing scientific theory. Let me briefly review the arguments on this issue.

First, the phenomenological project as envisioned by Edmund Husserl[6] and as carried forward by a variety of scholars takes the radical position that since perception of the universe is mediated through the cognitive processes of the human mind, knowledge of the external world must await a theory of "mind" or of cognitive processes. This argument, it would seem to me, applies equally well to other sciences, but it is seen most often as an impediment to sociological inquiry. Since other sciences have been able to discern immanent laws of their respective natural systems without engaging in the phenomenological project of unlocking the laws of consciousness, there is little reason for sociologists to be dismayed over their prospects. Indeed, we should be hopeful and optimistic about a natural science of society, since other sciences have been able to overcome the obstacles inherent in perception through human senses.

Second, many would argue that the unique symbol-using capacities of humans make their actions and patterns of interaction indeterminate, and hence, not amenable to scientific inquiry in the natural science sense. Herbert Blumer,[7] among others, has persistently argued that people construct and reconstruct lines of conduct in ways that are fluid, flexible, and unpredictable. Society is symbolic interaction and is, therefore, inherently indeterminate. Such a view rests on a profound misunderstanding of sociological laws. The goal of theory is *not* to describe particular interactive processes in concrete empirical settings and then to predict what will occur. This is what a naive positivist might do, but it is not what science seeks. The goal of science is to discover the basic processes that link individuals and collectivities of individuals. One of these processes—indeed, one of the most fundamental—is symbolic interaction, and the goal of sociological theory is to discover how this process operates in general, not in particular cases. Herbert Blumer, like G. H. Mead[8] before him, has been instrumental in discovering the laws governing these processes.[9] In fact, the process of interaction, per se, is probably one of the best understood in the natural science of society. The goal now should be to understand other processes equally well.

Third, many believe that there are profound methodological problems in "humans studying humans" and that these problems limit our ability to develop and test theories about human interaction.[10] For as those of this persuasion argue, the subject matter of the "hard sciences" does not think and act in the same ways as those investigating it.[11] There can be no doubt that this argument is true and that there are methodological and theoretical problems in studying humans. But there are always methodological problems in a science; and those confronting sociology do not seem any more insurmountable than the ones faced by other sciences—say, particle physics.[12] In fact, I rarely see arguments that stress the great advantage that sociologists have over many other scientists. We have an intuitive understanding of our natural system, and this should, with due concern for biased perception (a problem in all inquiry), allow us even greater insight into the processes of our universe. Thus, rather than presenting an obstacle, one of the great advantages of being a sociological theorist is that I live and participate in the world which I am seeking to understand.

Fourth, ever since Max Weber[13] was interpreted to have split sociology into two sociologies, "verstehen analysis" and "objective causal analysis," we have acted as if sociology were a two-step process. First, we objectively look at externalities; second, we try to understand these externalities "at the level of meaning." This dualistic view of sociological inquiry is, I feel, not very useful in building a natural science of society. People's perceptions, thoughts, cognitions, and emotions are a property of social relations; and they should not be separated from each other in our theoretical efforts (there are practical methodological reasons for doing so, given the current state of our research methods—e.g., questionnaires and interviews). To the extent that people's "meanings" are shaping the nature of social relations, they are a property of those relations and should not be seen as separate—as something we think about before and after we hand out a questionnaire.

Thus, social scientists in general and sociologists in particular have too long adhered to an unnecessary dualism.[14] Instead of the "mind-body" distinction, we seem to have followed a kind of "mind–body social" dichotomy, as if people's inner experiences could not be an object of inquiry in the same sense as overt behaviors and interactions that we can see with our eyes. Indeed, we have acted as if these inner experiences constituted "another world." Rather, to the degree that an individual's cognitive functioning is related to ongoing relations among individuals, it is a subject of theory building but no more "subjective" than any other property of our natural system.

Micro vs. Macro Sociology

The theoretical principles that will be developed in this book will, no doubt, be labeled "macro," because they are about social systems at the level of the society. While these principles may also be applicable to other units of analysis, such as groups, organizations, communities, and even the world system, the present effort focuses on societal systems. Little effort will be made to discuss the interactive processes among individual people, thereby assuring that this will be called a "macro theory."

In science, there is often a useful distinction to be made between micro and macro analysis. But it is a distinction with which I feel uncomfortable, since it maintains the dualism between the "mind and the body social,'' or at least a partition between concern with individual people and ''emergent'' social structures. Sociologists have tried to deal with this separation in a number of ways.

First, they have become boisterous and chauvinistic reductionists, as is the case with Herbert Blumer's contention that ''society is symbolic interaction.'' All those other ''structures'' and ''emergent properties,'' critics like Blumer contend, are hypostatizations and reifications. Understanding of society can only be achieved by examining the actual behavior and interactions among real people in concrete empirical settings. A more sophisticated version of this line of argument is presented by Randall Collins, who argues that many sociological conceptions of structure involve reifications of more elemental properties, such as varying distributions of people moving about in time and space talking to one another in diverse ways. Yet, to the extent that we wish to talk about macro properties of social systems, it is important to ''sample'' the micro interactive rituals from which such macro dimensions are made.[15]

Second, many sociologists since Georg Simmel[16] have sought to understand the basic forms of social relations without paying a great deal of attention to the nature of the units—individuals, groups, nation-states—implicated in these relations. Network analysis[17] is an example of this strategy; so are Richard Emerson's[18] exchange theory approach and various general systems theories[19] good illustrations of theory that concentrates on extracting the common forms underlying social relations among diverse types of social units.

A third approach to the micro-macro split is the most dominant and begins by addressing elementary behavioral and interactive processes; and then as ever more complex patterns of interaction are analyzed, new concepts are successively added. Talcott Parsons' ''action theory'' exemplifies this strategy as he moves from ''the voluntaristic theory of action'' to ever more complex systems—the social, the overall action system, and finally, ''the human condition.''[20] More modestly, Peter Blau's[21] exchange theory also exemplifies this strategy in that he begins with elementary exchange processes and then adds concepts, such as ''mediating values,'' to account for more complex exchange relations. (Blau's exchange theory also reveals elements of formal sociology, since the same basic processes—attraction, exchange, competition, and differentiation—operate for all social relations.)

A fourth approach is self-assertedly macro and simply ignores interactive processes, people's cognitions, and other processes typically viewed as micro. Peter Blau's more recent "macrostructuralism"[22] follows this strategy, and in so doing, abandons his earlier exchange approach. In such macro approaches, properties of structure—differentiation, hierarchy, ecological dispersion, homogeneity of subpopulations—are examined without reference to people, behaviors, cultural orientations, definitions of the situation, and the like. Even when interaction is a key concern, as it is in Blau's new theory, it is the overall "rates of interaction" that are conceptualized, not the actual processes of interaction.

There is merit in all these approaches, since each has yeilded much insight into the operation of the social universe. Blumer's advocacy and others' substantive works[23] have certainly helped unlock the mysteries of social interaction among individuals in diverse structural settings. Collins' analysis of ritual interaction chains certainly adds to our understanding of the processes that sustain systems of authority and complex organizations. Network analysis and other efforts to understand the basic forms of organization offer the hope that the underlying forms of all transactions can be isolated. The various attempts to move from micro to macro analyses have given us an appreciation for the underlying interactive dynamics of complex social relations, as well as an appreciation for the need to develop concepts and propositions about emergent properties. And assertedly macro approaches can provide us with some laws of these emergent properties. Yet, despite the apparent usefulness of all these approaches, the micro-macro debate and the implied discontinuity in the social universe continue unabated.

It can be asked, then, what the theory-building approach of this book will do to resolve the micro-macro debate. From my perspective, the micro-macro debate has been somewhat counterproductive; and the sooner we abandon the metaphysical and ontological baggage attached to the words "micro" and "macro," the better will be our theoretical efforts. The position argued in this book is that humans do all sorts of things, such as sleep, think, talk, fight, gossip, give orders, take them, and otherwise engage in a host of things that are interesting to observe. In all their activities people also form groups, build organizations, construct cities, consolidate into nation-states, go to war with other nations or at least exploit them, and otherwise elaborate interesting social structures which consist of regular and stable patterns of social relations. Of course, these structures are composed of micro-actions, but is it always necessary to address these? I think not, but the really important point is not to become committed irrevocably to a "micro" or "macro" position. For the goal of science is to understand all processes in the universe; and as sociologists our goal is to develop an understanding of those processes that involve the creation, maintenance, and change of social relationships. This much seems obvious, but the equally obvious implications of these simple goals are not fully appreciated by a discipline still arguing over the primacy of micro over macro, or vice versa, and over dualism in the social universe. For me, all of this argument seems to ignore the central task: to extract at the most abstract level possible the immanent laws of our universe. Such laws will state the most generic relations among properties of the sociological universe—that is, of our natural system. Some of these will certainly concern the properties of interaction per se; others will specify the unique properties of interaction among specific units, such as individuals and those collective units where the nature of the unit *makes a difference* in the nature of the social relation; still other laws will focus on the properties of specific relational processes, such as exchange, conflict, differentiation, group formation, mobility, and the like.

In other words, we should begin to visualize our universe as complex and as evidencing many distinctive processes about which laws can be extracted. Labels like "micro" and "macro" are merely heuristic devices for grouping principles; they are not statements about what is "really real." Sociological theory, therefore, should not consist of gallant ontological assertions about the ultimate nature of reality, but rather, it should be a storehouse of elementary principles which we draw upon, in different and varying combinations, to understand events that, for the moment at hand, are interesting to us. If war between nations is of interest, we draw from our storehouse certain useful principles; if behavior in public places is what presently fascinates us, we take from our storehouse a different set of principles. Each of these empirical events is equally "real," but they evidence distinctive properties and require the use of diverse laws if we are to understand their operation.

Theoretical Strategies in Sociology

Much of what is termed "theory" in sociology involves such activities as tracing the history of ideas, presenting intellectual biographies of the great thinkers, or making philosophical statements about what is real. None of these activities, for all their merits as history, biography, or philosophy, is theory. And therefore, these will not be addressed here.[24]

Yet, there are a number of activities in sociology that can more rightfully claim to be "theoretical." One of these is the process of concept formation. Many theorists in sociology spend a great deal of time defining concepts, and then arguing over these definitions. As a result, there is a huge literature on such concepts as alienation, anomie, self, role, authority, power, class, interaction; and there is at least a small literature on virtually every concept in the sociological lexicon. There cannot be an argument over the virtues of careful definition; the real question is: do we need endless arguments over most concepts in sociology? Unfortunately, these arguments do not lead to more precisely defined concepts; and too infrequently does debate revolve around the *relationship* among concepts—a much more interesting theoretical issue.

Another strategy for theory building in sociology is to make empirical generalization theoretical. Fairly low-level empirical generalizations are often dressed up as theoretical statements. The result is the proliferation of what I have called elsewhere "theories of ———" (fill in any substantive area in sociology).[25] We have theories of such things as marital stability, gang delinquency, modernization, ethnic groups, status attainment, and virtually any area of empirical inquiry in sociology. Such theories are, in reality, explicanda in search of an explanas; that is, they are empirical generalizations in need of theoretical principles. They are what we should seek to explain; they are not explanations.

Yet another theoretical strategy in sociology is taxonomic in nature. Much theorizing in sociology involves the development of classification schema. Such schema can order facts for us and point to regularities that stimulate a theoretical explanation. But taxonomy per se is not theory. Whether the Linnaean classification system, the periodic table, one of Max Weber's ideal types,[26] or almost any portion of Talcott Parsons' "system of concepts," a taxonomy does not make a theory. Like the empirical generalizations approach, what is to be explained is confused with the theory that explains. That is, the order given to events by the taxonomy is what requires explanatory principles.

A final strategy for building sociological theory revolves around model building. A model analytically accentuates important properties of an empirical process, or a set of related empirical events. Models are useful because they often tell us what is important in a setting. Moreover, they indicate the connections among important features of an empirical process. Models can, therefore, be very useful in creating theories, and conversely, in ordering empirical events so as to facilitate the testing of more abstract theoretical statements. But they themselves are not theory. Yet, sociologists frequently act as if theory and model were synonymous. Moreover, the difficulty in using models is that they are most powerful in closed systems, where the elements are known and where relations among them can be specified. As systems become open and admit many unknown and unmeasurable variables, or innumerable additional variables, modeling becomes tenuous and loses isomorphism with what is to be modeled. Thus, even as empirical descriptions, models lose much of their usefulness in the kinds of systems of most interest to sociologists.

In recent years, "causal models" have come to dominate much sociological discourse. Let me digress for a moment on these, since understanding their deficiencies will help clarify my own theory-building strategy. Like all models, causal models are inherently descriptive. The basic goal is to isolate the "cause(s)" of some empirical event in terms of variations in an antecedent event or events.

Such models are refined descriptions, to be sure; and they are useful in tracing the flow of the empirical world around us. But they are not theory; they are too tied to the empirical world. And, any effort to make them more abstract begins to obscure causality among events— the very reason for developing a causal model in the first place.

Yet, as will become evident, causality is a critical concern in developing theory. The problem with causal analysis in sociology has been its ritual coupling with multivariate statistical techniques and computer technology. With such coupling, the temptation to add yet one more empirical index, indicator, or scale to a regression equation seems to dominate intellectual activity. Instead, if we are really interested in causality, we need to think more abstractly and generically than is typically the case in sociology. If we seek to develop an abstract principle on a property of the universe, this principle usually states the conditions under which this property varies. There is an implicit causality in such a statement, but it is not the causality of the "path diagram." Causal connections among the generic terms in the theoretical principle can only be sorted out by delineating those processes that connect the "conditions" to the property that is the focus of the principle. Such causal connections are often reciprocal, involving direct and indirect feedback processes, as well as lag and simultaneous effects. These kinds of relations are not easily incorporated into a series of arrows with correlation coefficients. Or, if these kinds of relations are represented with coefficients, what is theoretically interesting gets lost in the process of reporting empirical regularities.

Thus, as theory seeks to explain *how* events in our natural system are *connected,* causality becomes a prominent issue. We may want to develop a model of such connections, but this model will not resemble that typically produced by the marriage of Pearsonian techniques with computer software. It will be abstract, incorporating concepts that denote generic properties which are connected to each other in complex causal relations. Yet, despite my reservations about the logic of causal modeling, it still has a limited role to play in developing social theory, which I will explore in later chapters.

In sum, then, while concept formation, empirical generalizations, taxonomy, and modeling are all implicated in the scientific process, they are not theory. They can help us develop and explicate theoretical principles, but they cannot serve as a substitute for those principles. In light of this fact, we need to develop a clearer conception of what theory is and what it can be for sociologists. There are three alternative forms which, following Lee Freese's[27] labels, can be termed systematic theorizing, formal theorizing, and axiomatic theorizing. Each of these is discussed below.

SYSTEMATIC THEORIZING. In systematic theorizing, ordinary language is used to link concepts conceptualized verbally. Such verbal propositions usually take the form "all other things being equal, x varies with y"; "the more x, then more of y"; "x is a positive function of y"; "if x, then y"; "x is an additive function of a, b, c"; and so on. Most theories in sociology are formal; and despite the fact that they are often somewhat loosely constructed, they have provided considerable insight into the operation of social phenomena. The strengths of systematic theories are severalfold:

1. They tend to be robust in the sense that their empirical application and implications are clear.
2. They do not require expertise in a formal (and for most sociologists, a foreign) language, such as mathematics; hence, they can be more readily understood.
3. They are less likely to fall prey to the tendency in sociology to become so consumed with the formal calculus that substantively important phenomena are lost in technically elegant, but vacuous, theoretical manipulations.

Yet, there are severe limitations to systematic theories, including:

1. They do not contain a logic, or calculus (save for the grammar of language), with the result that deductions cannot be precise.
2. They tend to be filled with empirical content which limits their level of abstraction, and hence their usefulness in different empirical contexts.

AXIOMATIC THEORIZING. Much systematic theorizing in sociology is called "axiomatic," but few of our theories can meet the requirements of this strategy.[28] Axiomatic theory cannot use ordinary language, for it must have a formal language that can denote "exact classes'' and that can be precisely manipulated in terms of the syntax of a formal calculus. Axiomatic theory can, therefore, be deductive, but its higher-order propositions cannot be empirical in the sense of summarizing, modeling, mirroring, or otherwise being connected to substantive empirical events. For axiomatic theory is a closed logical system in which all terms must be conceived as quantities and deductions made in terms of the logic of the formal calculus.[29]

The great weakness of axiomatic theorizing is that it is most useful in explaining events in highly controlled situations where the weights of those variables of interest are known and the influence of other variables is excluded. Sociologists are rarely able to study closed empirical systems, or to control events in the empirical world. We are forced by practical, political, and moral considerations to deal with events in the natural world; hence, it is unlikely that we would be in a position to test very often a truly axiomatic theory. While there may be some applications for axiomatic theory, and while some argue for its suitability in sociology,[30] we must recognize that sociologists cannot create the equivalents of highly controlled experiments in the physical sciences; and hence, axiomatic theory is not likely to be very useful for most of the problems of interest to sociologists.

FORMAL THEORIZING. A formal theory is, in many ways, an attempt to move beyond systematic theories, on the one hand, and to incorporate a more precise calculus of axiomatic theories, on the other. The most typical formal theory translates into logic or mathematical equations a verbal statement.[31] Such a translation does not make the theory more abstract or axiomatic, but it typically does force more careful definitions of concepts and precise statements of their relations to each other.

Often formal ''theories'' are little more than modeling, or simulation. Such efforts can be useful in exploring the relations among variables, but they are nonetheless limiting. First, models are inherently descriptive. And second, the more formal they become and the more they rely upon the formal calculus of mathematics, the more they describe a hypothetical world. Economists, physicists, and others have used such modeling techniques to practical advantage; sociologists can do the same. But these efforts will not, I feel, greatly facilitate the development of theories, since we must deal with open, complex systems.

Yet, formal theories offer the best strategy for sociologists. We need to begin to state relationships among abstract concepts more precisely; and the use of verbally defined concepts that are linked by the calculus of mathematics offers the best strategy, I feel, for developing sociological theory. Such statements will never be so abstract as those in axiomatic theory, for they will still be imbued with empirical referents. But if we seek to formulate concepts about only the most generic dimensions of the social universe and to state the relations among the concepts with greater precision, then we can begin to extract the immanent laws of our natural system.

Chapter 2 A PROPOSAL FOR DEVELOPING SOCIOLOGICAL THEORY

The Lost Vision

The strategy that I propose for developing sociological theory owes its inspiration to Auguste Comte—an often maligned and ridiculed figure in the social sciences. It is strange that the titular founder of our discipline should be held in such low esteem; and it is certainly a reflection of how we have failed to profit from the insights of our predecessors. Despite the prejudices against Comte, I would like to open with a few remarks on our founder. For we would all do well to review his early works.[1]

As is known, Comte preferred the title "social physics" over the current name of our discipline. For Comte, the term "physics" had multiple meanings, since in his time it had not been wholly usurped by the present scientific discipline of that name. In the most general sense, physics means to study the "nature of" phenomena; and for Comte, social physics was to involve the study of the nature of society. Comte also wanted to emulate the physical sciences in both methodology and theory construction. In particular, he drew inspiration from the Newtonian revolution and firmly believed that social phenomena are subject to invariable natural laws. Such laws, he emphasized, could not be either causal or functional; that is, they could not be about origin or purpose. Rather, sociology's laws must examine the "circumstances" of phenomena and to "connect" them by their "natural relations of succession and resemblance." As he forcefully argued in the opening pages of *Positive Philosophy:* [2]

> The first characteristic of Positive Philosophy is that it regards all phenomena as subject to invariable natural *Laws*. Our business is,—seeing how vain is any research into what are called *Causes,* whether first or final,—to pursue an accurate discovery of these Laws, with a view to reducing them to the smallest possible number. By speculating upon causes, we could solve no difficulty about origin and purpose. Our real business is to analyse accurately the circumstances of phenomena, and to connect them by the natural relations of succession and resemblance. The best illustration of this is in the case of the doctrine of Gravitation.

Sociology did not draw great inspiration from these words. Our nineteenth- and twentieth-century forefathers went on a functional orgy from which we have only recently recovered; and we are still obsessed with causality, whether one of the mechanical and ponderous "determinisms" of Marx (or some other figure) or one of the diagrammatic spiderwebs with arrows that typify multivariate causal analysis. Comte saw the folly of these approaches; contemporary sociologists still, on the whole, remain oblivious to the problems of both causal and functional analysis.

What I propose is that we follow Comte's advice and develop laws about the nature of social relations that are not overly concerned with either causes or functions. These laws will simply state the "natural relations" immanent in the social universe among generic variables. Causal analysis is for historians, engineers, and ethnographers; functional analysis is for politicians, theologians, and social philosophers. As scientists concerned with the invariable natural laws of our universe, our goal must be to extract from our observations and our analytical manipulations those properties of our universe that reveal "natural relations of succession and resemblance." As Comte emphasized: [3]

> We must distinguish between the two classes of Natural science;—the abstract or general, which have for their object the discovery of the laws which regulate phenomena in all conceivable cases; and the concrete, particular, or descriptive, which are sometimes called Natural sciences in a restricted sense, whose function it is to apply these laws

to the actual history of existing beings. The first are fundamental; and our business is with them alone; as the second are derived, and however important, they do not rise to the rank of our subjects of contemplation.

What Sociological Theory Cannot Do

Sociologists often force unrealistic expectations on themselves. Two of these have been particularly harmful: (1) the expectation that *theory should predict* events, and the corresponding dismay over sociology's failure to be predictive; and (2) the expectation that we should have *a theory of* this or that phenomenon. Let me review each of these in greater detail.

1. In open systems we cannot even known about the existence of every variable, much less describe with precision the respective weight of each variable. As a result, prediction becomes virtually impossible. Only when scientists can work in artificially controlled environments, or in ones where the number of operative forces is inherently small and where their magnitudes are great (say, for example, the gravitational pull of planets in a solar system), is prediction a viable scientific goal. But in the natural world, outside the closed laboratory there are typically too many operative forces, whose weights and interaction effects are unknown or only partially understood, to make possible statements about what will occur next. Whether the scientist is a physicist, chemist, biologist, geologist, economist, or whatever, prediction becomes untenable when dealing in the natural world.

Since sociologists must typically explore events in natural settings, it is unrealistic to think that our theoretical principles will be predictive. Too often, we see this failure to be predictive as a sign that laws like those in the natural sciences cannot be generated.[4] But if I took a physicist away from the vacuum tube or the accelerator, the chemist away from the laboratory, or any scientist away from artificially controlled experimental situations, none of them could make predictions of what would occur in the real world. But if an event occurred, such as an earthquake, an explosion, or the descent of an object to the ground, all could offer elementary principles that would help us understand how the natural event, which they could not predict, had occurred. We would not condemn them for their failure to predict, nor would we suddenly be convinced that physics or geology could not be sciences. Thus, sociologists should not apply a criterion to themselves that even the more advanced sciences could not meet.

2. Sociologists often try to develop *a theory of* some phenomenon. Some of these are trivial as theory, because they are, in reality, empirical descriptions. Theories of marital stability, gang delinquency, organizational control, ethnic antagonisms, and similar substantive fields in sociology are not very abstract, nor do they pertain to generic properties of the social universe. Other "theories of" seek to be more abstract and do deal with generic properties. For example, theories about conflict, exchange, norm formation, differentiation, hierarchy, ecological dispersion, and similar issues appear at least to focus on some universal property of human organization that transcends time and cuts across different empirical cases.

The main problem with these "theories of" is that they all proceed as if *a unified* theory of some topic could be developed. This is the wrong way, I feel, to look at theory building. Instead, what we need to do is view our universe as evidencing certain processes that operate in law-like ways. These processes often intersect and interact with each other in varying combinations. We cannot develop a theory of each intersection of forces; rather, we can only state the law-like operation of a given process. Many of the phenomena of interest to sociologists are not unitary but are congeries of more elemental forces and processes. One does not, for example, have *a* theory of stratification; rather, stratification is a term we give to a number of more discrete processes[5]—inequality, ranking, group formation, mobility, etc. In my view, theory in sociology should be a series of elementary principles that articulate the relations among the key properties of basic social processes. To understand stratification, then, we use a number of elementary principles in combination.

Theory should be a storehouse of elementary principles which we successively bring to bear, in varying combinations, to understand particular topics of interest—whether these be stratification, war, political centralization, ethnic antagonisms, etc. We should not have *a* theory of these and other topics, despite their frequency of occurrence. Instead, in our storehouse, we have a backlog of elementary principles that can be retrieved and combined to help us understand any of these or many other topics.

I should emphasize that I am not advocating "middle range" theory,[6] since this vision has helped legitimate in contemporary sociology "theories of" almost any substantive topic. As social theorists, we need to ask ourselves several related questions that are anything but "middle range": what are *the most* basic and generic properties of the social universe? What process accounts for the dynamics of these properties? How are these processes related? How can I express this relationship in an elementary way? How can these elementary principles be combined to understand a particular topic or event? These are the kinds of questions theorists should seek to answer.

Thus, in sociology and in the social sciences in general, we cannot have "a" theory that will be highly "predictive." Any such theory would be trivial and not relevant to the more pervasive and significant forces of the social universe. But this is not to say that a "natural science of society" is impossible. On the contrary, it has not always seemed possible because we failed to heed Auguste Comte's warning and because we have imposed unrealistic expectations upon ourselves. It is time to recapture Comte's vision.

What Sociological Theory Can Be

A natural science of society must begin by attempting to isolate the most basic processes of the social universe. It must then attempt to state the relations among properties of this universe that are implicated in these processes. Such propositions will be relatively simple and abstract; they will not seek to account for everything, just the process under investigation.

One way to develop such elementary principles is to select an area of major interest to sociologists, such as stratification. Then, we can ask: what constituent processes are involved in stratification as a social form? Can we develop some elementary principles for each of these constituent processes? This is the strategy of this book. I will seek to answer these two questions for a topic area—that is, stratification—which is considered important by all social scientists, and yet, which has somehow eluded complete understanding. The reason for this theoretical failure is twofold: theorizing about stratification has been excessively causal[7] and functional;[8] and theorizing has too often sought "*a* theory of" stratification.[9] I hope to avoid these pitfalls by developing propositions that place concern with causality into perspective and that stay away from the intellectual quagmire inherent in the notion of functions.

Developing Elementary Principles

What will such propositions look like? In all my earlier efforts to state abstract principles, I have employed ordinary language. These principles usually took the form: "the greater the degree of X, the greater the degree of Y."[10] Such propositions suffer from a number of problems. First, only two variables are incorporated into the proposition. I sought to correct for this problem by developing subpropositions that specified conditions influencing an increase or decrease in X. Thus, my early efforts took the following form which is similar to that employed by Blau[11] and others:

The greater the degree of X, the greater the degree of Y
  1a. the greater the degree of A, the greater the degree of X
  1b. the greater the degree of B, the greater the degree of X
  1c. the greater the degree of C, the greater the degree of X

And so on, until I listed all those conditions affecting X. This strategy is useful, but it is cumbersome. Moreover, it does not conveniently allow for the weighting of variables, nor does it lend itself to discussion of interaction effects among variables.

A second problem with this stragegy is that it does not allow us to talk about very many variables at the same time. In most theory construction, this is not a problem, since good theory should have only a few variables. Yet, even with four or five variables the strategy is awkward. To resolve this problem, I have adopted a different form in recent years to facilitate the incorporation of more variables, while at the same time, to avoid the cumbersome nature of the above illustration.[12] This strategy is similar to Collins'[13] approach which takes the following form:

Y is an additive function of X, A, B, and C

The major problem with this kind of statement is that relations are not always additive or linear. Most relations among sociological variables are nonlinear and multiplicative. Moreover, the problems of weighting variables and discussing interaction effects are not resolved by this format any more than by the previous one.

As I pondered these limitations, it became clear that a more formal language, such as mathematics, would be necessary. By using mathematics, it would be possible to handle several variables simultaneously in one proposition, to weight these variables, to state nonlinear relationships between them and the variable of interest, and to state multiplicative as well as additive relations. The major problem with "mathematical sociology," however, is that its practitioners are often chauvinistic, and at times, too pretentious. Those who are skilled in mathematics are often fascinated with the mathematics rather than with the processes of the social universe that mathematics can help us understand. With some obvious exceptions, the result has been that most sociologists cannot understand a great deal of mathematical sociology. I certainly cannot, not just because I am unschooled in, and unskilled at, mathematics but also because the sophistication and elegance of our current mathematical applications exceeds our substantive understanding of how the world operates. In short, we presently have more mathematical tools than we probably need. I propose to use only those that we need and that can be readily understood by those unschooled in mathematics. Moreover, I am going to bend the conventional notation system to suit my purposes.[14]

My use of mathematics to express relations will begin with the isolation of a generic process that I believe is one of several constituent processes of what sociologists term "stratification." Let us say that one of these processes is Y. My goal then becomes, in Comte's words, one of analyzing "the circumstances of phenomena." That is, what generic properties of the social universe are connected to Y.

If I perceive that Y is related to X, A, B, and C, then I will initially articulate an equation of the following form:

$$Y = f(X) \circ g(A) \circ h(B) \circ i(C)$$

where:

X = a defined property of the social universe
A = a defined property of the social universe
B = a defined property of the social universe
C = a defined property of the social universe

and where:

f, g, h, i = the presumption that Y varies with X, A, B, and C; the terms f, g, h, i indicate that the degree and form of this variation for X, A, B, C, on the one hand, and Y, on the other, are not yet known or have not yet been ascertained

$\circ$ = there are relations among such functions, but at this point they are unspecified

Such an expression merely states that Y is an unspecified function of X, A, B, and C and that I do not know at this point the respective weights of, or relations among, the variables. If I have a sense for the respective weights of the variables, I will add to the definitions of X, A, B, and C the following statement.

$$f(X) > g(B) > h(C) > i(D)$$

This weighting of functions gives us a hint as to the relative importance of X, A, B, and C for Y, but it does not specify the functions, nor the relations among the functions, as they affect Y. But this is where theory begins: we need to speculate initially on what processes reveal affinities and then weight these affinities in terms of their impact on some property of particular interest (in my illustration, Y).

The next issue is: why are certain properties of the social universe seen as related? That is, what processes operate to connect X, A, B, and C to Y? By having insight into these processes, it is possible to be confident of the weightings assigned to X, A, B, and C. Moreover, we can begin to specify the nature of the functions among X, A, B, and C as they affect Y. It is at this point that we may construct causal models of the processes that operate to connect X,

A, B, and *C* to *Y.* In many ways, of course, such a model may have implicitly or explicitly guided the selection of *X, A, B,* and *C* as related to *Y.* Whether the model comes before or after the equation $Y = f(X) \circ g(A) \circ h(B) \circ i(C)$ is less critical than the interaction between the model and the development of a more specific equation. It is likely, for example, that a crude or somewhat vague model guided the selection of variables for the equation, but once this preliminary equation exists, it forces the question: what is the relation of the variables to each other? An answer to this question requires refinement of the model of those processes connecting *X, A, B,* and *C* to *Y.* Out of such interplay between the model and the equation it becomes possible to specify the relation mathematically between *X, A, B,* and *C,* on the one hand, and *Y,* on the other.

Such an exercise probably begins with the question: does an understanding of the processes underlying the preliminary equation allow for, first, a weighting of the variables (if this has not already been done), and second, a determination of the relationship between *X* (and then, *A, B,* and *C* successively) and *Y* as linear or nonlinear? Assuming that the first has already been done, there are eight basic answers to the second: relations between *X* and *Y* (and then, *A* and *Y; B* and *Y; C* and *Y*) can be negatively or positively linear, logarithmic, exponential, and curvilinear. The types of curves, and formulas for creating these curves, are presented in figure 2.1.

I have provided the general formulas in figure 2.1, because I do not intend to use them later. Rather, my goal will be to state whether a relationship between two variables is linear (no notation necessary), logarithmic (log), negative logarithmic (−log),[15] positively exponential (exp), negatively exponential (−exp), positively curvilinear (cur), or negatively curvilinear (−cur). For example, if the relationship between *Y* and *X* is logarithmic, I will simply write $Y = \log(X)$; and if it is negatively logarithmic, the notation will be $Y = -\log(X)$. If the relationship is exponential, $Y = (X^{\exp})$; if it is negatively exponential, $Y = (X^{-\exp})$; if it is positively curvilinear, $Y = (X^{\text{cur}})$; and if it is negatively curvilinear, $Y = (X^{-\text{cur}})$. (In the equations to be developed in this book, however, no curvilinear statements are developed, although we should remain attuned to the possibility that later theoretical statements will reveal these forms.) The exact slope of the curve

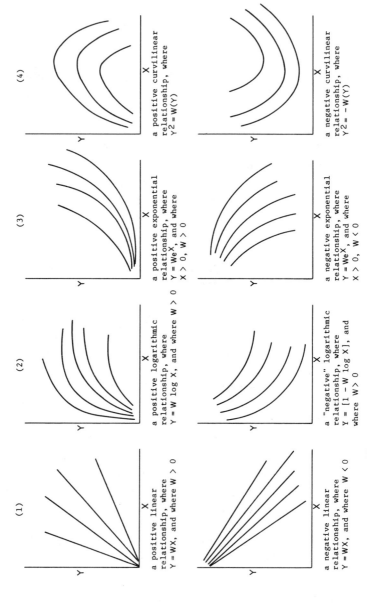

Figure 2.1 Basic Types of Relationships Between Two Variables

expressing the relationship between X and Y cannot be expressed theoretically, since it depends upon the empirical conditions for a given case and upon the weights of other variables in a particular equation. All that can be done theoretically, especially since we must operate in natural situations, is to state the general form of the relationship among variables.

After visualizing the nature of the relationship between Y, on the one hand, and X, A, B, C on the other, the next task is to weight the variables in terms of their impact on Y. This is done in the initial functional statement, but in its translation to a more precise equation I will use the symbol W to assign weights. To illustrate, I might state the following relationships among weighted variables:

$$Y = W_1 [\log(X)] + W_2(A^{-\exp}) + W_3(B^{\exp}) + [-\log(C)]$$

where:

$$W_1 > W_2 > W_3 > W_4$$

In this equation, X is weighted more than A, A more than B, and B more than C. Note also that I used the terms for expressing the nature of the relationship between Y and X, Y and A, Y and B, Y and C. In the above equation, Y is seen as an additive function of X, A, B, and C. But relations among many social processes are often multiplicative in their effects on a particular variable; and hence, the equations that I propose to develop can also reveal the following form:

$$Y = \{W_1[\log(X)] \times W_2(A^{-\exp})\} + \{W_3(B^{\exp}) \times W_4[-\log(C)]\}$$

The exact grouping can, of course, vary according to the theoretical stipulation; the above is only an illustration, but it indicates the general nature of the equations to be developed in later chapters. In the above example, Y is an additive function of the multiplicative effects of $\{X \times A\}$ and $\{B \times C\}$.

These examples present the language that I will employ in subsequent chapters. Let me illustrate further my approach by presenting a more substantive example (its accuracy is not being asserted) that involves all the elements discussed here. The initial statement would appear as follows:

$$P = f(TE) \circ g(DL) \circ h(NR) \circ i(N)$$

where:

P = level of economic productivity in a society
TE = level of technology in a society
DL = efficiency in the division of labor in a society
NR = level of natural resources available to a society
N = the size of the population in a society

and where:

$$f(TE) > g(DL) > h(NR) > i(N)$$

To translate, my initial sense is that societal productivity is an un-specified function of the level of technology, the efficiency in the division of labor, the degree of access to resources, and the size of the population. Moreover, I believe that, in terms of their effects on productivity, technology is more important than the division of labor; the division of labor is more critical than resources; and resources are more significant than population size. The next step is to be more specific in indicating first the nature of each relationship between P, on the one hand, and TE, DL, NR, and N, on the other; second, the relations among TE, DL, NR, and N in their effects on P; and third, the relative weightings of TE, DL, NR, and N. By specifying the processes that connect TE, DL, NR, and N to P, and perhaps by also constructing a causal model of these connections, it becomes possible to develop a more specific equation which, for illustrative purpose, might look like the following:

$$P = \{W_1[\log(TE)] \times W_3(NR^{\exp})\} \times \{W_2(DL^{\exp}) \times W_4(N^{\exp})\}$$

where:

$$W_1 > W_2 > W_3 > W_4$$

In this equation, P and TE are seen as logarithmically related, while the relations between P and the other variables (NR, DL, N) are seen as exponential (again, I am not asserting that such is actually the case; this is only a hypothetical illustration). TE and NR are viewed as multiplicatively related in their effects on P, as are DL and N. Then the products of $TE \times NR$ and $DL \times N$ are seen as multiplicatively related in their effects on P. And as the weights (W_1, W_2, W_3, W_4)

indicate, *TE* is weighted more than *DL* which is weighted more than *NR* which, in turn, is given more weight than *N*. Thus, while the mathematics involved in the above equation are obviously very simple, they do allow for the simultaneous presentation of several types of relations among weighted variables.

For this reason it is perhaps appropriate that we begin to translate verbal formats into mathematical statements. While others may prefer verbal statements, I feel it is time that we began to translate verbal propositions into a more precise calculus. This can be done without being mathematically sophisticated, chauvinistic, or arrogant. Yet, if one is offended by the notation offered here, it is relatively easy to translate the theoretical statements into conventional notation which, for me, is cumbersome but which may in the long run be necessary for communicating to a wider audience. For the present, however, I will stay with the unconventional notation.

Some Further Implications

As has been emphasized, sociological theory should consist of a series of elementary principles that state the relations among generic properties of the social universe. Such elementary principles are to be developed in two ways: the translation of the more discursive verbal efforts of past and present theorists, since there are enormous insights in these works; and with the benefit of these insights and our own intuition, the isolation of basic properties of our universe and the formulation of an elementary principle that indicates the relations among properties. This is what is proposed for subsequent chapters on those constituent properties that we sociologists loosely term "stratification."

But inherent in this effort is a longer-term strategy for developing a storehouse of elementary principles on human organization in general. This strategy consists of asking a simple question after presenting an equation like the one on productivity, or *P*. For each of the terms in the equation—that is, *TE, DL, NR,* and *N*—is it possible and desirable to construct an equation or elementary principle? That is, is there an elementary principle to account for the level of technology? Similarly, is there an elementary principle for *DL, NR,* and *N?*

The development of these additional equations moves beyond the issue of productivity to more general properties of social organization. Once one elementary principle is developed, it immediately suggests several others that need to be articulated. And these new principles will suggest additional ones that can be developed, and so on. At first glance, it might seem as if we could proliferate an infinite number of principles in pursuing such a strategy, but the expansion of principles ends quickly, since there is not an infinite number of generic properties in our universe. As a result, the same properties will keep reappearing (in varying combinations) in our elementary principles. For example, if we sought to develop an elementary principle for technology *(TE)* which, as will be recalled, was the most heavily weighted term in the elementary principle for productivity *(P)*, some of the same terms would reappear in different combinations and relations to *TE.* I suggest that *P* and *DL* would both be part of an elementary principle on *TE;* and if such is the case for other equations, a relatively small number of principles (less than fifty, I suspect) on social organization would be developed following this strategy.

As some elementary principles on the basic properties of stratification are offered, then, they represent a way to begin theorizing about social organization in general. That is, for each of the terms in the equations on stratification processes, it is possible to articulate additional principles. In turn, for each of the terms in these additional principles, yet another set of principles could be developed. In this manner, principles on stratification serve as a wedge, or starting point, for developing principles of social organization.

Anticipating Criticisms

Before this chapter closes, some of the inevitable criticisms of this strategy should be reviewed. Critics will probably say things like: "These principles are not very original, new, or earthshaking"; "They are awfully simplistic"; "The real world is more complex than that";

"How could you ignore ——— Process" (fill in the blank with your favorite topic); "How could you ignore ——— context" (fill in the blank with historical, empirical, cultural, temporal, etc.); "This is not explanation, but description." Each of these criticisms is examined below.

"These Principles Are Not Very Original"

Sociologists too often assume that our laws must be earthshaking—a bolt of lightning on the intellectual landscape. Or, we are often a bit snobbish about what would constitute a sociological law; that is, if a law sounds like "something that we already know," this fact alone disqualifies it from being an immanent truth of our universe. For reasons that are inexplicable to me, we act as if profound insights must be difficult to grasp and must include ideas about which we never before thought.

In reality, sociologists have already discovered many of the immanent truths of our natural system. This is why, I suspect, thinkers like Marx, Weber, Durkheim, Pareto, Spencer, and Mead are continually reread and reanalyzed. We sense that there are universal truths in their works, and we are certainly correct on this score, not only about them but about others closer to our time. As I have already mentioned, the propositions to be developed are not original. We have all used them, at least implicitly, for a long time. But familiarity should not breed contempt; otherwise we will fail to understand our universe.

"These Principles Are Very Simplistic"

Of course theory is simple; that is its goal, to simplify. The essence of theory is simplicity both in the number of variables included in a statement and in the connections among them. Sociologists have too long held a multivariate and descriptive bias which makes us feel that if we do not have many variables in our equations, we will not "explain enough variance." No one theoretical principle can explain everything in any universe all at once; and no proposition in any science can account for interaction effects of forces in complex natural settings. All that theory can do is help us understand some particular property of our universe; it will do so not by adding variables, but by taking them away and leaving us to consider relations among only the most basic and generic. If this seems simplistic, it should, since all theory seeks to simplify the seeming complexity of the natural world.

"The Real World Is More Complex Than That"

The real and natural world is always more complex than a theoretical principle. The natural world is filled with forces about which we know little and for which we often have no measuring instruments. But for a particular property of the universe, theory can tell us which forces are most important, and what their basic relations are, despite our inability to make precise measures or to know about other forces that influence the weights of the variables in our theoretical principles.

Thus, the world will always be more complex than our theories. Each new proposition simplifies, but it often points to other forces in the universe. Such is the nature of science; and if we sought to explain every dimension of our universe at once and with one theory, we would all still remain in awe of the universe and pray to gods to let us understand its ways.

"How Could You Ignore ———— Process" *(fill in the blank)*

Easily, out of either stupidity, ignorance, lack of concern, or a careful assessment that whatever it is you have in mind, I did not think it as critical as you. If critics consider a particular property of the universe to be given insufficient attention, then they can develop their own theoretical principles which can be tested against the offending ones. No matter which is correct, or even if neither turns out to be useful, science will have advanced. We will know more.

My goal in developing some elementary principles is to invite criticism. If I miss something important, I would like to know. Our theories can be improved by criticism; I challenge others to do better, for sociology as a science can only profit.

"How Could You Ignore the ——— Context" (*fill in the blank*)

Again, theory does not seek to describe. A natural science of society is not a science of specific contexts—capitalism, mobility between 1960 and 1980 in America, horticulture, or some other historical or empirical context. The goal of theory is to see what diverse contexts have in common, not what makes them unique. The laws of our natural system should be timeless and should be useful no matter what the context, as long as the processes denoted by a theory exist. Thus, one does not develop a set of theoretical principles about capitalism; instead, one develops principles of productivity. We do not have theories of kinship, but of organizational processes of subpopulations. We do not have theories of World War I, or war in general; we have propositions on conflict.

Our concern with context, I feel, betrays the descriptive bias of our discipline. It is reflected in our obsession with causality, with model building, and with explaining variance with multivariate statistical techniques. My goal as a theorist is to see what properties are common to all stratified societies, not those of a particular type or those in a specific historical period (as important as these may be for other intellectual purposes).

"This Is Description, Not Explanation"

This criticism may have some merit. Do the equations that are being proposed as the goal of theory simply describe empirical events with a new vocabulary? Do they explain *why* or *how* properties should be related to each other in the way specified in the equation? By themselves, the equations do not; when stated alone, they lack a "dynamo'' or "operator''—that is, a force or process that links properties of the world. This is why I believe that the analysis of the processes connecting properties included in an equation is necessary. For in describing these processes, and in developing causal models on them, we can get a sense for the dynamics underlying the relations specified in an equation.

Yet, this is far from an unambiguous issue. To illustrate, the notion of "natural selection" might be an example of a dynamic force that connects a number of properties of the biological universe and helps us understand one of its most fundamental processes, speciation. But the concept of "natural selection" could be accused of being descriptive because it is merely a term that denotes a descriptive scenario of hypothetical segments of a species adapting to the conditions of their environment. Moreover, is there a "dynamo" in the equation, $E = mc^2$, or is this simply a description of a basic relationship in the physical universe? Or, is an equation like $F = ma$ merely descriptive?

This issue boils down to the question of what we consider "explanation'' to be. It has already been argued that explanation does not always involve prediction; it is not taxonomy; and it is not causality. But what is it? Some have suggested that explanation answers the questions *why* and *how*. Why and how do events occur? But a description of historical events leading to the Russian Revolution answers these questions, and is that what we mean by theoretical explanation? In my view, explanation would occur if the Russian Revolution were seen to follow from a proposition, or set of propositions, on conflict processes. Such propositions would state the generic conditions under which violent conflict occurs, while at the same time being accompanied by an analysis of the processes connecting these conditions to conflict. But would such propositions, and statements on underlying processes, also be descriptive?

What about other forms of theorizing? In axiomatic theory, explanation has a precise meaning of rigorous deduction in terms of mathematics from abstract premises, or axioms, to empirical events, but as has already been shown, this mode of explanation is of limited use in sociology. So, we cannot impose a strictly axiomatic criterion of explanation on ourselves; otherwise, there could be little theory in sociology. Perhaps this is what some, such as Blumer, mean when they argue against a science of society. But I suspect that they mean much more: human social organization does not reveal invariant properties. My goal is to discover these invariant properties and to understand them, even if we must forgo the rigor of axiomatic theory.

In the end, it is perhaps wise to defer to the philosophers of science on the issue of what constitutes explanation. Or perhaps we can all begin to articulate for ourselves just what each of us means by explanation. This is what I have done in this chapter. Readers will have to decide for themselves if the elementary principles developed in later chapters have explanatory power.

Summary and Preview

In this chapter, a strategy for developing theory in sociology has been presented. Perhaps the case is stated in the extreme, but theoretical activity must overcome well-entrenched biases not just among researchers but also among theorists. In the next chapter, a review of the theories on stratification is undertaken. This review will involve a translation of various theorists' ideas into elementary equations. Thus, the review can serve as a preliminary illustration of the theoretical strategy outlined in this chapter. But equally important, the key concepts and many of the relations among these concepts that appear in later equations are borrowed from others' pioneering efforts.

My goal in reviewing others' work, then, is to follow up on points made in these first two chapters and to indicate the sources of key elements of the propositions developed in later chapters. For there is nothing earthshaking about these propositions; they represent an eclectic mix of ideas developed by others, ideas with which we are all familiar.

Chapter Three STRATIFICATION THEORY

Implicit in any effort to develop a new theoretical approach is a criticism of existing modes of theorizing. In this chapter I will review what I believe to be some of the more general problems of stratification theory, a critique essential in order to highlight why I advocate the strategy outlined in the last chapter. Then, a summary and translation of existing theorists' ideas will be performed. Most of the insightful substantive work on processes of stratification has already been performed by social thinkers over the last one hundred years. While the tone of this chapter may on the surface appear somewhat critical, my comments should be placed in a broader perspective and viewed as laudatory of those who have uncovered some of the key dynamics of the social universe. For as will become evident, the theoretical ideas in this volume owe their inspiration and substance to the scholars reviewed in this chapter.

Problems in Stratification Theory

The first great weakness of theory on stratification processes is that it is not truly theoretical. Rather, much of what is considered theory is descriptive; it involves an account of stratification in a particular type of empirical system. Whether Karl Marx's[1] description of the dynamics of capitalism, Marshall Sahlins'[2] analysis of stratification in kinship societies, Gerhard Lenski's[3] and Talcott Parsons'[4] analysis of societal evolution, Immanuel Wallerstein's[5] account of the world system, Max Weber's[6] separation of class, status, and power, Pitirim Sorokin's[7] analysis of social mobility, or any number of important works, there is a descriptive bias. Sometimes this is deliberate, as was the case with Marx, who did not believe that sociological laws could transcend historical epochs; at other times, abstracted descriptions of types of stratification systems—for example, feudal, kin based, capitalistic—are considered theoretical. They are not, for all their insight. Instead, they represent nice compilations of data that require a theory to explain why empirical events can be ordered into types of stratification systems. I am grateful that such difficult empirical work has been done, for it provides me with a sound data base for checking on the plausibility of my theoretical statements (and of course, those of others).

A second problem in the literature on stratification is that it tends to be excessively analytic. This may seem like an incredible statement, since this chapter is devoted to making a number of analytical distinctions. But in examining theory in stratification, one can easily observe a tendency to make distinctions and then argue over them. For example, it would be difficult to find a consensus on the definition of the most crucial concepts in stratification—say, for example, "class," "stratum," "caste," "power," "prestige," "rank," and others. In fact, much of the theoretical literature on stratification involves discussions of definitions and enumerations of typologies (such as types of power, rank, class, etc.). These discussions can be useful, as was Weber's distinction between class, status, and party, or as was Marx's distinction of a class "of" and a class "for" itself. Yet, at some point, we must do something with our analytic distinctions. We must convert them into variable properties of the social universe and see how they are related to each other. If we did this more often, analytical work would be greatly facilitated, since it is in working with concepts which have been incorporated into propositions that we will be able to fine-tune definitions and analytical distinctions. As long as theory in stratification consists of controversies over definitional distinctions, it will remain stagnant.

A third problem in theorizing about stratification is its causal and deterministic bias. Whether the analyst be Marx or Lenski, emphasis is on "the causes of" some property of the universe, such as class conflict, inequality, class consciousness, mobility, evolution from one societal type to another, the caste system, and other events of interest to stratification theorists. As I stressed in the last chapter, causal analysis is inherently descriptive when one *begins* analysis with a search for the causes of an event. Moreover, concern with causality invites other problems. One is an infinite regress of the form: *b* caused *a*, *c* caused *b*, *d* caused *c*, and so on. Where do we end such a regress? And when is the causal argument adequate? Causal analysis soon becomes complex when the reciprocal and feedback implications of events are explored; and as scientists working in the natural world where we cannot control for, or exclude, innumerable forces, we begin to add variables to our equations. The result is for causal analysis to be a jumble of arrows; or if complexity is abandoned for simplicity, then causal statements become a dogmatic and vague determinism, as is the case when scholars assert such things as the "means of production" causes this or that event. Of course, causal analysis is useful for descriptive purposes; and as I argued in the last chapter, it can often help us denote the processes underlying the connections among properties of the universe. But despite its usefulness, there has been far too much concern in the theoretical literature with the "causes of" a property of stratification system. In my view, this is not the way to initiate theoretical activity.

Yet another problem in theorizing about stratification is its functional bias. While the term "function" has been banned from the sociological dictionary, we still address the "consequences" of events. For example, the consequence of heterogeneity, says Peter Blau,[8] is to increase rates of interaction and societal integration. The consequence of class conflict in capitalism is to change society toward a less exploitive profile.[9] The consequences of mobility are to decrease class polarization[10] and hence to increase the integration among different social classes. While we no longer feel comfortable in talking about the functions of stratification or in developing propositions employing concepts like "survival problems," "system imperatives," and "system needs," sociologists still talk like functionalists. If we are not analyzing "the causes of" a stratification process, we will typically be caught assessing its consequences for ——— (fill in your favorite system requisite that you now call by another name). Analysis of functions takes us into the realm of evaluating what is good and bad, what is functional and dysfunctional, what is integrative or malintegrative, what is organizing or disorganizing, what is adaptive or maladaptive, and other distinctions that mask moral evaluations. Philosophers, theologians, politicians, and ordinary people should, and do, make these distinctions; and they are a part of the social universe and one of its more important dynamics. But as theorists, our job is to study "ethnofunctionalism," not to articulate some version of it.

A related problem is the self-consciously evaluational tone of much theorizing about stratification. Whether one is a Marxist, a critical theorist, or an old fashioned liberal, stratification is seen as bad. It hurts people; it limits their opportunities and chances for self-realization; it creates conflicts and tensions; and it does other bad things to the body social. Such considerations are irrelevant in theorizing. Our task is to understand how stratification operates, not to condemn it, preach against it, or construct utopias. We all do this with sufficient frequency in our personal lives; it can only cloud our understanding if we let it influence our scientific lives.

A final problem in theorizing about stratification concerns the fads and foibles of topics. Too much of our research and conceptual literature is topic oriented, as scholars move from "cold" to "hot" topics. For example, evolution was a popular topic in the nineteenth century, died in the early and middle twentieth century, and is now legitimate again as neo-evolutionism.[11] Mobility was explored in the early decades of this century, died for a while, and then reemerged with the wonders of multivariate analysis under the heading of "status attainment" theory and research.[12] Status crystallization emerged with Weber, died until resurrected by Lenski, and seems to have slipped into obscurity again.[13] Class conflict is now all the rage, but was less interesting three decades ago.[14] Community power studies[15] and speculation about "power elites" were everywhere two decades ago; now, they are recessive. The world system[16] is topical now, whereas it was less interesting two decades ago (actually, it was studied under different names, such as Western Civilization, Empires, Colonialism, etc.). It will be difficult to develop theory about stratification processes as long as we are hooked on this intellectual roller coaster. Our goal is to seek understanding of the invariant properties of the social universe, and it will be hard to do so as we hop around from topic to topic.

These, then, are some general criticisms of stratification theory. Despite these shortcomings, however, present efforts, and those of our predecessors, have isolated the basic properties of stratification processes and articulated some of the crucial relations among these properties. In the development of the elementary principles to be presented in subsequent chapters, my debt will be obvious. For the present, a review of the theoretical positions of prominent thinkers can highlight this intellectual debt.

The Ghosts of Marx and Weber

Karl Marx and Max Weber still haunt us in ways that are, I feel, unproductive. We still stand in the shadows of these giants and we appear reluctant to stand on their shoulders—lest we fall down. Sociological theory is still about persons, rather than about generic processes of our universe. We still have Marxian, Weberian, Parsonian, and Homansian theory. A theory textbook is a discussion of persons and perspectives, not a review of priniciples about the social universe.

I say this to set into context a warning. The present analysis will portray Marx and Weber in a way that offends "Marxians" and "Weberians." This is not an incantation over their sacred texts, nor is it a review of them line by line. My feeling is that, at best, Marx, Weber, and others of the last century and early decades of this century should now be footnotes. We should have extracted from these giants what is theoretically useful and moved on. We do not need yet another analysis of Marx and Weber. Rather, my goal is to state succinctly Marx's and Weber's theoretical contribution and move on— that is, I want to stand on their shoulders, not in their shadows.

To do this, several analytical steps must be taken. First, it is necessary to state ideas of Marx and Weber more abstractly than they would believe desirable. Second, it is critical to ignore "the silent dialogue" of Weber with Marx as well as other conceptual disputes revolving around these figures. Third, it is necessary to convert their causal arguments (both were overly concerned with causality) into less deterministic statements.

Karl Marx's Principles of Stratification

When Marx's ideas are examined at the most abstract level, devoid of polemics, ideology, utopian dreams, and other nonscientific aspects of his intellectual scheme,[17] two sets of theoretical principles can be observed. One involves statements about the nature of social organization where levels of technology, productivity, rank differentiation, power, and exploitive beliefs are seen as fundamentally related in the social universe. The other set revolves around statements on the conditions producing conflict and change in social systems. I have argued elsewhere[18] that it is in these two sets of elementary principles that Karl Marx's theoretical contribution resides. Obviously, he made other intellectual contributions in his description of capitalism and in his polemical/political arguments, but these are not theoretical.

The first set of elementary principles on social organization can be expressed in equations (3.1), (3.2), and (3.3) below:[19]

$$I = W_1(P^{\exp}) \times W_2\left[\log(C_{CP})\right] \qquad (3.1)$$

where:

$I =$ degree of inequality in the distribution of those resources valued by members of a population

$P =$ the level of production among members of a population (see my more elaborate definition in chapter 5)

$C_{CP} =$ the degree of concentration in the control of the means of production among members of a population

and where:

$$W_1 > W_2$$

Equation (3.1) states that the level of inequality in the distribution of resources is a weighted function of productivity and the concentration of control in the means of production. The relationship between productivity and inequality is exponential and given more weight than the logarithmic relationship between control of the means of production and inequality. The relationship between production and control of its means is multiplicative in its effects on inequality. Thus, in Marx's eye, productivity must increase substantially for inequality to increase, primarily because there must be someting to distribute unequally. But initial concentration of control in the means of production escalates inequality for any level of production. Of course, as the multiplicative relation between P and C_{CP} indicates, increased production will provide the resources for usurpation of control; and once in the control of a small elite, production escalates in response to the elite's desire to extract more resources for further control, thereby increasing inequality (I). In equations (3.2) and (3.3) below, I present my interpretation of Marx's view of the forces that influence the level of production and its control. These equations take us beyond the issue of inequality per se and into the realm of social organization in general. Yet, they are central to understanding Marx's view of stratification.

$$P = W_1\left[\log(TE)\right] \times W_2(DL^{\exp}) \times W_3(N^{\exp}) \qquad (3.2)$$

where:

TE = the level of technological resources available to a population, with technology defined as knowledge about how to manipulate the environment

DL = the extent and efficiency of the division of labor

N = the size of the population in a society

and where:

$$W_1 > W_2 > W_3$$

$$C_{CP} = W_1(C_{PO}) \times W_2(C_{MW}^{\exp}) \times W_3(C_{IM}^{\exp}) \qquad (3.3)$$

where

C_{PO} = the degree of concentration in a population of the capacity of individuals and collective units to control of the activities of other individuals and collective units

C_{MW} = the degree of concentration in the distribution of material wealth among members of a population

C_{IM} = the degree of concentration of the capacity for ideological manipulation

and where:

$$W_1 > W_2 > W_3$$

Equations (3.2) and (3.3), respectively, attempt to specify Marx's view on those forces involved in productivity and control of the means of production. Production is seen by Marx as a multiplicative function of technological resources, the division of labor, and population size. Technology is logarithmically related to production, while the division of labor and population size are exponentially related to production. As the weights indicate, the level of technology is the most critical variable, followed respectively by the extent of and efficiency in the division of labor and the size of a population. Control of the means of production is linearly related to the concentration of power and exponentially related to the concentration of material wealth and the instruments of ideological manipulation. As the weights emphasize, the concentration of power is a more critical force than material wealth or the capacity for ideological manipulation. I should note that equations (3.1) and (3.3) are partial tautologies, since inequality could be defined in terms of the concentration of power and material wealth. But this tautology exists in Marx's thinking, for he typically asserted that control of the means of production is related to the possession of power and material wealth, and vice versa, and that inequality is related to the degree of control of the means of production, and vice versa. To obviate this tautology would require at the very least separate equations for C_{PO} and C_{MW} that specify properties other than control of the means of production that are related to the concentration of power and material wealth. Marx does not supply these at a theoretical level. However, at an empirical level, he develops the "laws" of capital accumulation and control of the means of production in the "capitalist epoch."

Marx's other set of propositions concerns the generation of "class conflict." The basic proposition is summarized in equation (3.4):

$$CF = W_1(I^{\text{exp}}) + \{W_2(AI^{\text{exp}}) \times W_3[\log(WL)] \times W_4(PL^{\text{exp}})\} \quad (3.4)$$

where:

CF = the level of overt conflict between subpopulations in a social system, with conflict defined as actions by one party that are intended to prevent another party from realizing its goals

AI = the degree of awareness of interests on the part of subordinates, with "interests" being defined as those actions that are seen as increasing resources and with "subordinates" being defined as those who possess few resources and who do not control the means of production

WL = the extent to which subpopulations withdraw legitimacy from existing patterns of social relations, particularly social relations involved in production

PL = the degree of political organization among subordinates to pursue their interests

and where:

$$W_1 > W_2 > W_3 > W_4$$

In Marx's view, conflict is a weighted function of the degree of inequality in the distribution of resources, the level of awareness among subordinates, the extent to which subordinates withdraw legitimacy, and the degree of political organization among subordinates. Inequality, awareness of interests, and political organization are exponentially related to conflict, since it requires significant increases in these to generate conflict. The withdrawal of legitimacy, however, is logarithmically related to conflict, for once this process is initiated, conflict relations are likely to escalate rapidly.

As with Marx's view of inequality it is important to communicate his vision of those forces increasing I, AI, WL, and PL. I have already done this for I in equation (3.1). In equations (3.5), (3.6), and (3.7), I attempt to summarize Marx's thinking on the conditions affecting the weights of AI, WL, and PL.

$$AI = \{W_1[\log(AL)] \times W_2(DR^{\text{exp}}) \times W_3(MO^{-\text{exp}})\} \\ \times \{W_4(CM^{\text{exp}}) \times W_5(UB^{\text{exp}}) \times W_6(L^{\text{exp}})\} \tag{3.5}$$

where:

AL = the level of alienation from their productive activities among subordinate members of a population

DR = the extent to which established social relations among subordinates are disrupted by superordinate members of a population

MO = the rate of mobility among subordinate members of a population

CM = the level of communication among subordinate members of a population

UB = the degree to which unifying beliefs that articulate their interests can be generated among subordinate members of a population

L = the availability of political leaders

and where:

$$W_1 > W_2 > W_3 > W_4 > W_5 > W_6$$

In this equation, the awareness of interests among subordinates is viewed by Marx as a multiplicative function of alienation, disruption of relations, mobility, communication, unifying beliefs, and leadership. Alienation is seen as logarithmically related to awareness, because Marx saw alienation as violating basic human needs, and hence, as setting into immediate motion a questioning of environmental conditions. Disruption of relations is exponentially related to awareness, and mobility is a negative exponential of awareness of interests among subordinates. These three forces—*AL*, *DR,* and *MO*— are multiplicatively related to each other in their effects on *AL*. And in terms of their effects on *AI,* these variables are multiplicatively related to *CM, UB,* and *L,* which, in turn, are multiplicatively related to each other in their exponential effects on *AI*.

$$WL = W_1(AI^{\exp}) + W_2[\log(RD)] \qquad (3.6)$$

where:

RD = the degree of relative deprivation experienced by subordinate members of a population

and where:

$$W_1 > W_2$$

In equation (3.6), the withdrawal of legitimacy is viewed by Marx as an additive function of awareness of interests and relative deprivation. Awareness of interests is exponentially related to the withdrawal of legitimacy; in contrast, relative deprivation is logarithmically connected to withdrawal, since escalating deprivations immediately set into motion a rejection of conditions that generate these deprivations.

$$PL = \{W_1[\log(L)] \times W_2(UB^{\exp})\} \times W_3(CM^{\exp}) \qquad (3.7)$$

where:

$$W_1 > W_2 > W_3$$

In equation (3.7), the level of political organization among subordinates is visualized by Marx as a function of the multiplicative relation between leadership and unifying beliefs, on the one hand, and communication among subordinates on the other. Marx saw leaders, such as himself, as the critical force behind unifying beliefs, which, in turn, could help mobilize publics that are in communication. Leadership is logarithmically related to political organization, since initial increases in leadership are soon translated into political organization, especially if leaders can articulate unifying beliefs to populations whose members can communicate.

Equations (3.1) through (3.7) communicate, I feel, Marx's vision of stratification processes as they are influenced by basic properties of social organization. Obviously, in the construction of these equations, inferences about Marx's vision of stratified social organization have been made. Yet, if these inferences are later seen as incorrect, it is an easy matter to rewrite the equations. For these and subsequent equations, I extend an invitation to critics to revise my preliminary efforts. I also recognize that many critics consider the effort in the above equations inappropriate, if not outrageous. And I suspect that Marx would turn over in his grave, since he did not believe in Comte's view of positivism. Yet, it can be argued that much of Marx's substantive work involves an effort to demonstrate how the organization of capitalism increased the weights for the variables in these seven equations. And contrary to what Marx asserted, and what many contemporary devotees of Marx believe, the properties of the universe and their relations as specified in these equations mark a major contribution to scientific sociology. For the theoretical goals of this work, some of the generic variables in these equations will be used when the elementary principles of stratification are developed in later chapters.

Max Weber's Principles of Stratification

A great deal has been written about Max Weber's multidimensional conceptualization of stratification in terms of class, status, and power. Yet, as useful as this formulation is, it says little theoretically; it is simply a typology. In fact, if we carefully scrutinize Weberian sociology in general, it becomes clear that Weber was a taxonomist and what I have called an "institutional ethnographer."[20] He was at his best when analytically isolating the critical properties of empirical systems and describing their historical origin and present operation. As a theorist, however, Weber was less successful. He did not believe, or was not interested, in developing abstract theoretical statements. Thus, when one looks for his principles of stratification (as opposed to typologies and descriptions of stratification), they are hard to find. In my search for Weber's principles of stratified social organization, I found just a few principles, and they look very much like those developed by Marx on class conflict.[21]

$$CF = W_1[\log(WL)] \times W_2(PL^{exp}) \qquad (3.8)$$

where:

$$W_1 > W_2$$

For Weber, conflict between superordinates and subordinates (CF) is a logarithmic function of the withdrawal of legitimacy and an exponential function of the political organization of subordinates. Withdrawal of legitimacy by subordinates and their political organization are multiplicatively related in their effects on CF.

Much more interesting than the properties in equation (3.8), however, are Weber's statements on the conditions influencing the withdrawal of legitimacy and political organization.

$$WL = \{W_1(CO_{PO,MW,PR}^{exp}) \times W_2[-\log(NH)] \times W_3(MO^{-exp})\}$$
$$\times W_4[\log(L)] \qquad (3.9)$$

where:

$CO_{PO,MW,PR}$ = the degree of correlation among the respective distributions of power (PO), material wealth (MW), and prestige (PR)

NH = the number of social hierarchies organizing the activities of members in a population

MO = the rate of social mobility of individuals in terms of increasing their levels of PO, MW, or PR (see the revised definition of this term in chapter 10)

and where:

$$W_1 > W_2 > W_3 > W_4$$

Weber argues that the withdrawal of legitimacy by subordinates is an exponential function of the correlation between power, material wealth, and prestige; an inverse logarithmic function of the number of hierarchies in a society; a negative exponential function of the rate

of upward social mobility; and a positive logarithmic function of political leaders (in his term, charismatic leaders). And in terms of their
effects on *WL,* the correlation of resources, number of hierarchies,
and rate of mobility are multiplicatively related to each other, and
then as a whole, to the availability of political leaders who can mobilize sentiments that result from low rates of mobility in a hierarchical system where power, wealth, and prestige are correlated.

$$PL = \{W_1[\log(L)] \times W_2(AI^{\exp})\} \times W_3[\log(NO)] \qquad (3.10)$$

where:
NO = the number of organized subunits in a society
and where:

$$W_1 > W_2 > W_3$$

For Weber, leadership and awareness of interests interact and
increase the level of political organization *(PL),* with leadership being
weighted more and bearing a logarithmic relation to *PL* and with
awareness of interests evidencing an exponential relation to *PL.* But
as Weber emphasized in all his works, political organization requires
an organizational base in the society. This base is conceptualized as
the number of organizations *(NO),* and Weber appears to visualize it
as logarithmically connected to *PL* and as multiplicatively related to
L and *AI* in its effects on *PL.* That is, there must be at least several
diverse organizations in a society for political organization to ensue
as a result of the activities of leaders mobilizing subordinates' level
of awareness. But after an initial organizational base is reached, subsequent increases do not so dramatically affect *PL.*

In sum, equations (3.1) through (3.10) represent one way to in-
terpret Marx and Weber. Naturally, this is not the only way, but it is
a way that has been attempted too infrequently. If this interpretation
has misrepresented Marx and Weber, corrective efforts to rewrite the
equations would be appreciated.

It should also be emphasized that the plausibility of these ten
propositions has not been assessed. Later some of the concepts, and
their stated relations, will be incorporated into an alternative set of
elementary principles on stratification. For the present let me com-

ment on some of the properties of the social universe which Marx's and Weber's analysis leads us to expect as important. Obviously, conflict (*CF*) is seen as critical, and in fact, Marx's and Weber's theoretical statements (as opposed to their descriptive statements) focus almost exclusively on this process. They do so, however, to the detriment of understanding the more general processes implicated in stratification. Yet, their respective analyses of conflict highlight a number of properties of the social universe which, I feel, are important to understanding not just conflict but stratification in general. I should mention several of these.

As has already been emphasized and as will become more evident later, stratification is a series of discrete processes, not a unitary property of the universe. As such, inequality (*I*) and mobility (*MO*) are distinctive processes and need to be analyzed separately. Moreover, inequality is, as Weber emphasized, multidimensional and needs to be seen as involving discrete processes related to power (*PO*), material wealth (*MW*), and prestige (*PR*). Other critical variables implicit in Weber's work are the number of social hierarchies (*NH*) and the number of organizational units (*NO*) in a society, for these greatly influence, I suspect, some processes of stratification. The remaining variables in Marx's and Weber's schemes—*CF, AI, WL, PL, AL, DR, CM, UB, L*—are most relevant to the analysis of conflict in stratified social systems and less relevant to the understanding of other constituent processes of stratification.

The Forgotten Giant: Herbert Spencer on Power

One of the more regrettable events in the history of sociology is the neglect of Herbert Spencer's work in the twentieth century. For if we ignore his political philosophy, which appears separately from his more scientific efforts, he offered sociology some of its early insights.[22] Among these are statements on the conditions promoting the centralization and concentration of political power.[23] Since any formulation of stratification processes must seek to develop principles on the concentration of power, we would do well to express Spencer's view. This is done in equation (3.11).

$$C_{PO} = W_1\left[\log(ET)\right] + W_2(IC^{\exp}) + \left[W_3(IT^{\exp} \times W_4(P^{\exp})\right] \quad (3.11)$$

where:

ET = the level of external threat perceived by members of a social system

IC = the level of internal conflict among subpopulations in a social system

IT = the total volume of internal transactions among individuals and subunits in a social system

and where:

$$W_1 > W_2 > W_3 > W_4$$

In this proposition, Spencer argues that conflict within and among social systems increases the centralization of power. In particular, conflict with other systems (what is termed external threat) promotes centralization and concentration of political power in a society; and hence, *ET* and C_{PO} are viewed as logarithmically related and assigned the greatest weight. Internal conflict can, for a time, create dispersion of power as sectors of a society mobilize their resources, but the end of the conflict typically produces more concentrated power than existed before the conflict. Even without the effects of conflict, high levels of productivity and the related high volume of internal transactions require regulation. Such regulation, Spencer argued, comes from the expansion of the administrative units attached to the centers of political power. And thus, as production and internal transactions mutually encourage each other's expansion, administrative power becomes increasingly concentrated.

The origin of these ideas is often forgotten by sociologists[24] who have had to rediscover these and other insights of Herbert Spencer. While we have not failed to remember Marx and Weber—indeed, we continue to worship them to our detriment as a science—we have too readily ignored Spencer. We need to reexamine Spencer's work with a less biased eye, and then as we should for Marx, Weber, and others, we must move on. For as will become evident in later chapters, Spencer's proposition appears central, since it isolates some of the critical properties of social systems that can help us understand inequality in the distribution of power.

Contemporary Theorizing on Stratification

With the exception of Pitirim Sorokin's[25] conceptualization of mobility processes, theoretical work on stratification was recessive until its reemergence under the banner of "functionalism" and "conflict theory." Since contemporary conflict theory has involved few statements on stratification beyond those developed by Marx,[26] the works of prominent conflict theorists such as Ralf Dahrendorf[27] will not be analyzed. Instead, the functional work of Kingsley Davis and Wilbert Moore, as well as the analytical approach of Talcott Parsons, will first be discussed. Then, the neo-evolutionary approach of Gerhard Lenski, which, I feel, incorporates the useful ideas of Marx, Weber, and other contemporary stratification theorists, will be examined.

The Davis-Moore "Hypothesis"

Probably no single work on stratification has generated so much controversy as the famous Davis-Moore[28] hypothesis. The hypothesis is stated in equations (3.12), (3.13), and (3.14).

$$I = W_1\left[-\log\left(\frac{FI}{N}\right)\right] + W_2\left[-\log\left(\frac{AP}{N}\right)\right] \qquad (3.12)$$

where:
  FI = the number of positions in a social system that are defined by the members of that population as functionally important
  AP = the number of available personnel to fill positions defined as functionally important
  N = the size of the population in a social system
and where:

$$W_1 > W_2$$

Equation (3.12) states the basic hypothesis that the more functionally important a position and the less available personnel to fill that position, the greater the rewards associated with that position. But equation (3.12) translates the hypothesis so that it more clearly applies to

systemic inequality (*I*) by visualizing inequality as a negative logarithmic function of the ratio of functionally important positions (*FI*)
and available personnel (*AP*) to the total size of the population (*N*). In
those societies where there are relatively few positions defined as
functionally important and where there are relatively few persons
available to fill these positions, then inequality in the distribution of
rewards will be high.

In equations (3.13) and 3.14), I have tried to translate Davis and
Moore's argument on those forces related to *FI* and *AP* into elementary principles.

$$FI = FN \qquad\qquad (3.13)$$

where:
  FN = functional requisites of a social system

$$AP = (TA) + (TR) \qquad\qquad (3.14)$$

where:
  TA = the degree of talent required to occupy a functionally important posi-
      tion
  TR = the level of training required to occupy a functionally important po-
      sition

Equation (3.13) is like most functional statements in that it is a categorical assertion. *FN* is not a variable but a categorical statement of
functional requisites. It could be translated into a variable by visualizing the degree of salience of a requisite, but Davis and Moore only
provide a rough listing of functional needs without specifying their
respective weights. Equation (3.14) is at least a statement of relations
among variables. Davis and Moore appear to argue that the availability of personnel is a linear, additive, and unweighted function of the
degree of talent and training required to fill a functionally important
position.

The vagueness of this argument has been roundly criticized[29]
and need not be discussed here. Of more importance is the issue: what
makes this proposition so fascinating to sociologists, who have spent
a great deal of time debating and testing it? To argue that the hypothesis is mere ideology is to dismiss it for superficial reasons. Moreover, we would also have to dismiss Marx, Weber, and others if this

is our criterion of worth. In contrast with most who have criticized this principle, I think that it has some merit, but not without drastic reformulation. People do make distinctions about "functional importance" and they do assess talent and training. And such distinctions and assessments are relevant to inequality, but not all types of inequality. Davis and Moore have part of a principle on the unequal distribution of prestige; in later chapters, their ideas will be modified and supplemented with additional concepts in order to articulate an elementary principle on the subject.

Talcott Parsons' "Analytical Model"

The other functional approach to stratification is Parsons' analytical model.[30] In Parsons' approach, developing propositions that state relations among properties of the social universe is less important than isolating critical properties per se. Much like Weber before him, Parsons always adhered to a taxonomic strategy of theory building in which critical elements are analytically emphasized and placed within a larger classificatory scheme. Thus, much as was the case for equation (3.13) above, it is sometimes difficult to translate Parsons' ideas into propositions in which critical concepts reveal variability. And as is the case with the Davis-Moore hypothesis, the theoretical usefulness of Parsons' model will be determined by my ability in later chapters to translate his ideas into propositions of covariance among concepts.

For the present, Parsons' argument can be expressed in a simple equation:

$$I = \left[\log(CN_{VS})\right] + (DF_A^{\exp}) \qquad (3.15)$$

where:

CN_{VS} = the degree of consensus over "value standards" of a social system

DF_A = the degree of differentiation among the "properties" of actors in a social system

There are no weights for the variables in equation (3.15) because none are evident in Parsons' treatment. Moreover, Parsons' conceptualization of "value standards" and "properties" of actors have been translated into variables, since otherwise his argument would read: inequality is related to the properties of actors as they conform to the value standards of a social system. But such a statement is not a systemic statement; it applies only to the rewards that a given actor will receive. Thus, Parsons' proposition is translated into a statement that identifies properties of social systems—the degree of consensus on values and differentiation of properties among actors. As stated in equation (3.15), inequality (I) is a logarithmic function of value consensus (CN_{VS}) plus an exponential function of diversity in the properties of actors (DF_A). That is, in systems where there are clear and accepted value standards and differences in the properties of actors, these properties will be differentially evaluated and rewarded. What generates consensus over values and differentiates actors? Parsons' answer is functional, as is evident in equations (3.16) and (3.17):

$$CN_{VS} = CN_{FN} \tag{3.16}$$

where:

CN_{FN} = consensus over the functional needs of a social system

$$DF_A = (Q) + (PF) + (PS) \tag{3.17}$$

where:

- Q = the extent to which the "qualities" of actors that are relevant to meeting functional requisites are clearly differentiated
- PF = the extent to which the "performances" of actors that are relevant to meeting functional requisites are clearly differentiated
- PS = the extent to which the "possessions," or valued objects, of actors that are relevant to meeting functional requisites are clearly differentiated

As with the Davis-Moore hypothesis, functional needs are critical, but in Parsons' view, they determine the level of consensus on value standards that, in turn, influence evaluations of the qualities, performances, and possessions of actors. Thus, in Parsons' analysis inequality reflects the application of value standards to actors' properties. These value standards are developed in response to the survival requisites of a system; and actor properties will be evaluated in terms of those qualities, possessions, and performances of actors that meet these value standards. As Parsons states this argument, it has no variables; and in order to convert Parsons' ideas into statements containing variables, it has been necessary to distort his argument somewhat. But in his terms, Parsons' statements are theoretically vague and untestable. Moreover, a careful scrutiny of his "analytical model" reveals that it is not a theory of inequality but, at best, a principle of ranking. And once this is recognized, we are in a position to work with his ideas and incorporate them into a less grandiose, but nonetheless important, theoretical principle.

Gerhard Lenski's Synthetic View

Without the functional trappings of Parsons' work and with a clear recognition of Marx's insights, Gerhard Lenski[31] has proposed a neo-evolutionary model of stratification. His goal has been to articulate the variables most responsible for the unequal distribution of privilege in different types of societies—from hunting and gathering populations, through horticultural and agrarian systems, to industrial and postindustrial societies. While Lenski has presented his ideas in a causal format, the scheme can be converted into a series of propositions. In equations (3.18) to (3.21), I have sought to recast Lenski's model in a manner that will serve us in later chapters.

$$I = \left[W_1(P^{\text{exp}}) \times W_2(ES^{\text{exp}}) \right] \times W_3(C_{PO}^{\text{exp}}) \tag{3.18}$$

where:

ES = the level of the economic surplus relative to the size of a population
and where:

$$W_1 > W_2 > W_3$$

$$P = \left\{ W_1\left[\log(TE)\right] \times W_2(NR^{\text{exp}}) \right\} \times \left[W_3(DL^{\text{exp}}) \times W_4(N^{\text{exp}}) \right] \tag{3.19}$$

where:

NR = the level of natural resources available for productive activity
and where:

$$W_1 > W_2 > W_3 > W_4$$

$$ES = W_1(P^{\text{exp}}) \times W_2(NR^{\text{exp}}) \tag{3.20}$$

where:

$$W_1 > W_2$$

$$C_{PO} = W_1(P^{\text{exp}}) \times \{W_2[\log(ET)] \times W_3(LE_{PO}^{\text{exp}})\} \qquad (3.21)$$

where:

LE_{PO} = the degree of legitimacy attributed to those holding power

and where:

$$W_1 > W_2 > W_3$$

Equation (3.18) converts Lenski's causal analysis to a simple equation incorporating the critical variables in the theory. While Lenski does not present his formal theory in this manner, his actual discussion of specific cases in the text of *Power and Privilege* is more in line with the relations specified in equation (3.18) than his causal diagrams. Productivity (P), economic surplus (ES), the concentration of power (C_{PO}) are all seen as exponentially related to inequality (I).

Productivity and economic surplus are multiplicatively related to each other in their effects on inequality, with their product standing in a multiplicative relation to the concentration of power as the latter affects inequality. That is, productivity increases economic surplus, and conversely, surplus increases productivity when reinvested as capital. Surplus allows for its usurpation by those with power; and such usurpation is used to consolidate power. The result is increased inequality as production, surplus, and concentration of power increase.

Equations (3.19), (3.20), and (3.21) specify those forces influencing the weights of the critical variables in equation (3.18). Productivity (P) is seen by Lenski as a logarithmic function of technology (TE), and an exponential function of environmental or natural resources (NR), the division of labor (DL), and population size (N). Economic surplus (ES) is viewed as an exponential function of productivity and environmental resources. And the concentration of power (C_{PO}) is considered to be an exponential function of productivity and legitimacy of political authority (LE_{PO}) and a logarithmic function of the degree of external threat (ET). In these equations, some of the ''secondary variables'' in Lenski's analysis have been eliminated because they are not consistently employed and are more typically invoked to explain minor variations in the basic relations specified in the equations. Yet, for our purposes, these equations capture the essential relations among generic properties of the social universe that will prove useful in developing several elementary principles of stratification.

Conclusion

In this chapter, I have reviewed some of the weaknesses in the literature on stratification. In general, "theorizing" about stratification tends to be excessively descriptive, evaluative, definitional, causal, functional, and topical. Yet, there have been numerous important contributions to theorizing about stratification processes, and for the main body of this chapter, I have tried to summarize those from which I will draw key concepts and propositions. As will become evident, I will borrow from Marx, Weber, and Spencer; I will recast dramatically the functional argument; and I will use many elements of Lenski's synthesis. In particular, I visualize the effort in the next chapter as building upon Lenski's synthesis; that is, my goal is to take the next step in developing theoretical principles of stratification.

There are other works on stratification from which I have drawn, but they are redundant to those presented here. Moreover, as will become clear in later chapters, there are bodies of empirical research from which I have inducted concepts and propositions.

Thus, as I stated in chapter 1, this is a book on theory as I have visualized its goals. Within the parameters of the theoretical strategy presented in chapter 2, I have sought to be eclectic, in that concepts and propositions will be drawn from diverse sources. In addition, I do not feel compelled to drag with any concept or proposition other, less useful ideas. For example, I will take from Marx, but not be Marxist, since much of Marx is not useful in building theory. I will borrow from Weber and not be a Weberian. I will borrow from Spencer but not be Spencerian. I will extract what is useful from functional theory without being a functionalist. And I will take from Lenski, as he took from others, without being committed to all his assumptions or his causal strategy.

The remainder of this book, then, will consist of two types of activities. One will involve isolating the constituent processes that, when viewed together, are termed "stratification" by sociologists. The other will be to construct elementary principles for each of these processes. In the next chapter, I will offer my view of the constituent processes of stratification, and after this exercise, I will present some elementary principles on these processes.

Chapter Four

PROPERTIES OF
STRATIFICATION

"A" Theory of "the" Stratification System?

In developing theoretical principles about the social universe, it is necessary to specify just what part of the universe is to be the subject of inquiry. If one engages in only a cursory review of the literature on stratification, however, it becomes immediately evident that there is little consensus over what stratification is. True, similar words are used to describe stratification—words like class, inequality, mobility, rewards, privilege, power, prestige, poverty, class conflict, and so on. Also, most everyone agrees that stratification is multidimensional and that the economy is somehow very important in understanding the various dimensions of inequality and social class. And some authors have sought to break down stratification into its constituent processes, as in the case for Melvin Tumin[1] when he views stratification as composed of the processes of "differentiation and ranking," "evaluation," and "rewarding."

Yet, unlike Tumin, most authors lump various processes together and then seek to explain the operation of all processes simultaneously. Typically, after a number of analytical distinctions are made—say, between inequality, class, status, and power—everything that is separated gets thrown back together and "a" theory is developed about "the" composite phenomenon. For example, Lenski[2] provides an enlightening discussion of the "parts" of "distributive systems." Classes, class systems, mobility processes, conflict processes, and other "parts" of the distributive system are discussed in a most interesting way, but when "the theory" is summarized, it consists of one explicandum—"the nature of distributive system"—

and a series of weighted variables that "cause variation in" in this explicandum.

What is true of Lenski's analysis is even more true of many other theoretical efforts. Scholars seek to develop *a* theory about *the* stratification system, even after they have made a series of analytical distinctions about different properties of stratification. Instead of developing separate principles about each property, theorists tend to talk about stratification as if it were a unitary thing.

The result is a diversity of theories that implicitly address somewhat different properties of stratification. For typically, the theorist is interested in explaining one process more than others, even if this process is billed as "the" stratification system. One theory offers to explain distributive processes;[3] another is, in reality, a theory of mobility[4] or conflict;[5] still another examines class formation;[6] and so on. But each is seen as *a* theory of *the* system. This state of affairs generates much confusion, which can best be illustrated with reference to the infamous David-Moore hypothesis.[7] The basic hypothesis is that the unequal distribution of "rights and prerequisites" to "different positions" is a joint function of the degree to which a position is "functionally important" and "difficult to fill." This hypothesis was billed as *a* theory of *the* stratification system; and while its functional trappings were enough to get it into trouble, the more fundamental problem is that it is a hypothesis about only one property of stratification: the distribution of rewards. It says nothing about classes, ranks, class systems, mobility, conflict, and other properties of stratification systems. Moreover, as I hinted earlier and will argue in a later chapter, it is actually a proposition about only one kind of distribution—the distribution of prestige—and it is incomplete at that. I suspect that had Davis and Moore billed the hypothesis more modestly and accurately (say, "some principles of prestige distribution"),[8] it would have been better received, even with its functionalism. But my point here is to illustrate a basic tendency in sociological theory in general and stratification theory in particular. We tend not to develop theoretical principles about the constituent processes of phenomena. Instead, too often we develop theoretical principles that seek to explain too much and/or to explain a vaguely conceptualized property of the universe.

The goal of this chapter, therefore, is to outline basic properties that will be familiar, since they are the basis for organizing most textbook discussions about stratification. But my view is that "stratification" is only a name that sociologists give to a number of related processes for which we need to develop separate theoretical principles. Moreover, these principles are not just about stratification; they are principles about pervasive processes of the social universe that when viewed in combination become elementary principles of stratification, but when combined in other ways with additional principles become the elementary principles of some other property of the social universe. We cannot, I believe, have *a* theory of *the* stratification system. Rather, sociological theory will pertain to generic processes of the social universe which combine and interact with each other to generate different social forms. One of these forms is stratification, but it is not the only one.

Generic Properties of Societal Stratification

For present purposes, stratification is viewed as a social form consisting of three constituent processes.[9] These will be analyzed as (1) the unequal distribution of valued resources, (2) the formation of homogeneous subpopulations, and (3) the ranking of these subpopulations. That is, stratification is "composed" of these three processes, each of which needs to be defined and each of which needs to become the subject of its own theoretical principles.

The Unequal Distribution of Resources

The unequal distribution of valued resources is a critical dimension of stratification. Some individuals and collectivities in social systems receive more of what people value in a society than do others. Following Weber[10] as well as contemporary exchange theory,[11] we can visualize that valued resources are not all the same. There are different types and the three most generic are: material wealth (MW), power (PO), and prestige (PR). Each of these is defined below:

Material wealth (MW) = those material objects, or the capacity to purchase such objects with money, that people in a society value and perceive to be gratifying

Power (PO) = the relative capacity of individuals or collective units in a society to control the actions of other individuals and collective units

Prestige (PR) = the respect, esteem, and honor that individuals bestow upon others in a society

These three types of rewards, I feel, are comprehensive in that other rewards are a special case of one or some combination of these. More important, it is imperative that we keep the distribution of these rewards conceptually distinct from other properties of stratification, such as subpopulation formation and ranking. Too often, these are analyzed together, as is the case for Weber, whose distinction of class, status, and party combines the issues of distribution with ranking and subpopulation formation. The processes are separable; and we confuse theory and research when we fail to develop separate principles for each.

Inequality of material wealth has often been conceptualized by comparing the actual distribution of material wealth, or one of its imperfect indicators such as income, to a hypothetical state of perfect equality where the total wealth is equally divided among all members of a society.[12] Figure 4.1 shows how such data are typically illustrated. From such diagrams, a Gini coefficient can be developed to indicate the degree of deviation from perfect equality. In this manner, comparisons between different societies, or of the same society over time, can be made. Such coefficients are usually visualized as an indicator of the degree of concentration (C) of material wealth, or C_{MW}—that is, how much wealth is in the hands of how few people. The other generic rewards of a society can also be conceptualized in this way, as is also illustrated in figure 4.1. Thus, C_{PO} and C_{PR} can be represented in same manner as material wealth. That is, the degree of concentration of material wealth, power, or prestige corresponds to the extent to which the actual distribution of these rewards deviates from a hypothetical state of perfect equality. Thus, we can conceptualize distributional inequality in terms of the respective degrees of

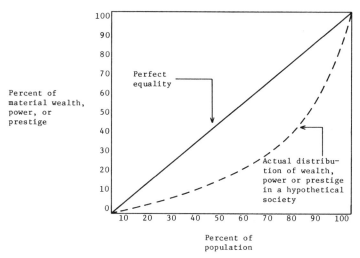

Figure 4.1 The Concentration of Material Wealth, Power, and Prestige in Society

concentration of material wealth, power, and prestige. That is, societal inequality (*I*) can be defined in the following manner:

$$I = W_1(C_{MW}) + W_2(C_{PO}) + W_3(C_{PR})$$

where:

$$W_1 > W_2 > W_3$$

In this equation, the degree of inequality in the distribution of resources is defined as a weighted and additive function of the degree of concentration in material wealth, power, and prestige. As the weights indicate, I view C_{MW} as more critical than C_{PO}, which I am, in turn, defining as more important than C_{PR}.

The relative weightings of C_{MW}, C_{PO}, and C_{PR} reflect certain theoretical considerations. Figure 4.2 presents these in graphic form. My basic argument is that system size, level of differentiation, productivity, and perhaps other interrelated forces determine the relative concentration of these resources. In a small, relatively undifferentiated system, prestige (*PR*) is more relevant than material wealth and power in understanding the operation of the system. As a system increases in size, however, the distribution of material wealth (*MW*)

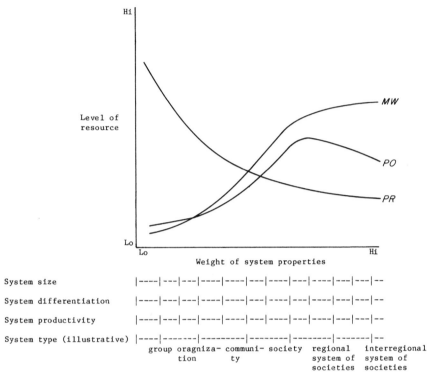

Figure 4.2 The Relative Importance of Resources in Different Types of Social Systems

and power (*PO*) becomes increasingly relevant in understanding the dynamics of the system. At the societal level of organization (in terms of size and differentiation), the relative weightings in the definition above are most likely to prevail. Of course, there can be deviations, as is the case with very small "societies" of hunters and gatherers who are little more than a small group; or there may exist particular empirical circumstances that explain deviant cases. But in general, especially for societal systems of most interest to sociologists, I suspect that these relative weightings are the most typical.

While my purpose in this chapter is only to define properties of stratification, I should add at this point several other theoretical observations. First, many of the acrimonious debates in the sociological and anthropological literature over which resources are most important for understanding stratification are placed into a new context. Depending upon the system referent, the salience of resources for stratification processes will vary. Second, the more recent arguments by Wallerstein and others over the varying bases for the "world system" can also be interpreted in this manner. Power reveals a curvilinear pattern in figure 4.2 because the administrative costs and logistical problems in its use increase with growth and differentiation; and at some point, C_{PO} becomes inadequate to maintain system integration. This point is increasingly likely to be reached as the unit of reference is a multiregional system of societies. Thus, political empires tend to be unstable; and as the scale and scope in a system of societies increases, material wealth (its concentration and exchange) becomes a more viable way to link systems together into a "world system." While these considerations take me beyond my current focus on *societal* stratification, it is important to recognize that there are theoretical reasons behind the weightings of C_{MW}, C_{PO}, and C_{PR}.

Ranking and Subpopulation Formation

In the literature on stratification, there is no more consistently used and poorly conceptualized term than "class" or "social class."[13] Moreover, there is a host of additional terms that appear to denote the same properties—terms like "stratum," "strata," "rank," etc. Definitions of these terms all vary somewhat, but they do, at the same time, pertain to a series of key properties of stratification:

1. The members of a society reveal differences in terms of their behaviors, attitudes, and possessions;[14] and these differences are related to at least the following:[15]
   a. economic position and material wealth
   b. access to political power
   c. possession of prestige
   d. educational attainments
   e. sex
   f. ethnicity/race
   g. age

2. The members of a society can be categorized in terms of their modal behaviors, attitudes, and possessions, with the result that one can observe identifiable "classes" of individuals who share common behavioral tendencies, attitudes, and possessions.
3. The members of a society can be rank-ordered in terms of their "class."
4. The members of a society can, therefore, be viewed as existing within a series of ranked classes which reveal variations with respect to at least the following:
   a. homogeneity of behaviors, attitudes, and possessions
   b. clarity of criteria of membership
   c. clarity of class boundaries
5. A society, as a whole, can be viewed as a system of ranks that reveal variability, at least with respect to:
   a. number of classes
   b. size of respective classes
   c. degree of inequality in possession of material wealth, power, and prestige among classes
   d. rates of mobility among classes
   e. clarity of rank-ordering among classes
   f. rates of cooperative and/or antagonistic interaction among members of classes

I am sure that additional features of "class" can be added, but the above listing is sufficient to make my point: one of sociology's most important metaphors is the notion of a society consisting of ranked subpopulations, or classes (or if one prefers, strata). Of course, as with most metaphors, we quibble over such matters as:

(a) Is that what Marx (or some other important figure) really meant by class?
(b) Is not class only one dimension of stratification?
(c) Is society really like layers on a cake or geological strata?
(d) Is class really a reflection of economic position, or some composite of criteria?

And so on. But in general, despite our recognition that there are wide variations within and between societies in terms of their "class structure," we hold to our metaphor. Some have criticized this metaphor as an extreme reification or hypostatization.[16]

Critics are both right and wrong in their charge that sociologists have reified the concepts of class and stratification. If we walk out on the street and look around, we do not see people organized like geological strata. But "people on the street" are still very much attuned to each others' "class" or "rank." As they confront one another, people categorize each other in terms of their rank. And in every society that I know about, there is an amazing degree of consensus over a person's "class." Of course, people do not make the fine distinctions that sociologists mistakenly enumerate—between upper-working and lower-working class or some such thing—but people ple can roughly place each other into upper, middle, lower ranks in terms of material wealth; and they can usually make further distinctions in terms of power and prestige. And this is real behavior; it is not a sociologist's reification. If anything, it is people in a society who reify, not the sociologist studying them. Thus, I see class as a useful metaphor—one which really makes a difference in terms of how people interact and in terms of what occurs in the society as a whole. Indeed, unless we wish to focus only on face-to-face interactions, we must begin to visualize the overall patterns of class that result from, and at the same time that constrain, people's actual interactions.

Like most metaphors, however, the notion of class is imprecise. We need to perform some definitional work that captures the properties of the social world denoted by the metaphor but that defines these properties more clearly. As with other concepts in theory and research on stratification, we have not fully appreciated the fact that the concept of "class" or "strata" embodies at least two distinctive processes: group formation processes and ranking processes. There may be more processes involved, but for the theoretical principles that I will develop, these two are the most relevant.

In my view, then, "class" and "stratum" are just terms to describe the additive and interactional effects between two distinguishable processes. One revolves around those forces that create a sense of identity among individuals as well as a high degree of homogeneity in behaviors, attitudes, and possessions among subsets of a population. This process is labeled "subpopulation formation." The other concerns the extent to which these subsets are differentially evaluated. This process is termed "ranking." It may be best to abandon words like "class," "strata," and similar terms, since they evoke so many diverse connotations. In their place, I propose to develop principles about ranking and subpopulation formation. More specifically, these processes will be conceptualized in terms of the degree of differentiation (DF) of homogeneous subpopulations (HO), or DF_{HO}; and the degree of linear rank-ordering (RA) of homogeneous subpopulations (HO), or RA_{HO}. The two basic concepts are defined below:

Differentiation of *Homogeneous Subpopulations* (DF_{HO})	= the degree and extent to which subsets of members in a society reveal common behavioral tendencies and similar attitudes so that they can be distinguished from other subsets of members in a society
Ranking of *Homogeneous Subpopulations* (RA_{HO})	= the degree to which homogeneous subsets of members in a society can be lineally rank-ordered in terms of their perceived worthiness

I have deliberately limited my focus in defining group formation processes. I think that the differentiation of homogeneous subpopulations (DF_{HO}) is only one critical property of group formation processes; there are certainly others, such as sense of common identification, political consciousness, economic and political organization, etc. But for this preliminary effort, a more focused point of emphasis on DF_{HO} is desirable. With respect to ranking of these homogeneous subpopulations (RA_{HO}), it is assumed that all people are constantly engaged in a process of evaluation and that in any society subsets of members can be ranked in terms of their "worthiness."[17] The actual standards or criteria of worthiness, and who imposes them,[18] are less important to our initial theoretical task than the simple insight that people rank-order each other. The theoretical task before us, then, is to specify the conditions increasing, or decreasing, the degree of homogeneity in subpopulations and the degree of linearity in the rank-ordering. Equally important, we must recognize that these processes are separable, although there are interaction effects between them.

That is, there can be homogeneity without dramatic differences in ranking; and there can be great disparities in rank-ordering of individuals but less homogeneity in subsets of individuals.

The failure to recognize that these are distinctive processes has,

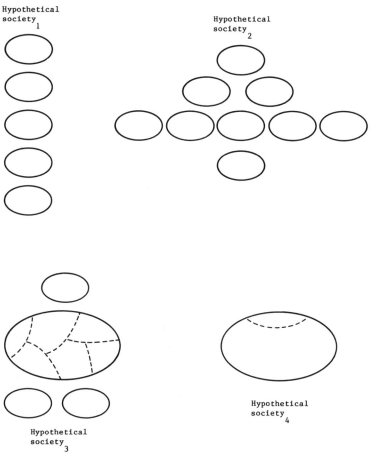

Above are some possible ways that RA_{HO} and DF_{HO} can covary. In Society$_1$, the solid lines indicate clear subpopulations and the linear ordering indicates that there is a clear ranking of these subpopulations. In Society$_2$, there are ranking distinctions among homogeneous subpopulations, but some of these subpopulations reveal a similar rank. In Society$_3$, there are three distinctive subpopulations—one clearly of high rank, two closely approximate low ranks. But the most evident feature of this society is the large amorphous middle subpopulation, which reveals only ambiguous degrees of DF_{HO} (as indicated by the broken lines). And Society$_4$ reveals low DF_{HO} and RA_{HO}. The point is that DF_{HO} and RA_{HO} can vary enormously; the issue is not one of "class" vs. "classlessness" but of varying degrees of DF_{HO} and RA_{HO}.

Figure 4.3 Ranking and Subpopulations in Different Societies

I feel, created much confusion in the stratification literature. For example, scholars have argued over such matters as whether or not there are "real classes" in modern industrial societies.[19] Even the way the issue is phrased is less than useful, since class becomes a nominal concept rather than something that can vary by degrees. But even more important is the failure to recognize that homogeneity and ranking can vary somewhat independently within and between societies. One society may differentiate several homogeneous subpopulations that are clearly rank-ordered; another may evidence considerable homogeneity of subpopulations but little rank-ordering among them; still another can reveal little differentiation of subpopulations but much ranking of individuals; or a society might reveal just a few homogeneous subpopulations that are ranked (say certain ethnic groups, the superwealthy, and the very poor) and show low homogeneity and moderate or low ranking for the rest of the population (see figure 4.3). Thus, as long as we talk in terms of nominal states (like "class" vs. "classless," or "class" vs. "caste"), we will not capture the actual dynamics of those multiple processes subsumed under the term "social class." Our goal as theorists and researchers should be to isolate generic properties of the social universe and to explain their varying states—not to argue over nominal categories that collapse distinctive and generic properties of our universe.

Conclusion

In this chapter, I have performed some of the preliminary definitional work for the theoretical principles to be developed in the remaining chapters. My intent has been to isolate the three most generic processes—the unequal distribution of valued resources, the formation of subpopulations, and the ranking of these subpopulations—that comprise that property of the social universe termed "stratification."

In the remaining chapters, the theoretical strategy outlined in chapter 2 will be pursued. Chapters 5, 6, and 7 will develop elementary principles on the unequal distribution, respectively, of material wealth, power, and prestige. Chapter 8 will explore the process of subpopulation formation and the conditions increasing the degree of homogeneity of such subpopulations. Chapter 9 will examine the process of ranking and seek to develop an elementary principle that states the conditions under which ranking is linear. In each of these chapters, I will try to illustrate the plausibility of the elementary principles by introducing data on different types of societies for each term in the equations on these constituent properties of stratification. These data will consist of composite summaries of the available information on hunting and gathering, simple and advanced horticultural, agrarian, and industrial societies. The presentation of these data should not be, in any sense, viewed as a "test" of the elementary principles, but rather, these data should be seen as my initial effort to illustrate the plausibility of the principles. I have selected the same basic types of societies as Gerhard Lenski in his *Power and Privilege* because I wish to emphasize the intellectual debt to this work. As I noted earlier, the principles to be developed and their illustration with ethnographic data build upon the conceptual and empirical base laid by Lenski.

Finally, in chapter 10, I will explore a topic that is usually considered essential to understanding stratification—social mobility, or as I will term it, *MO*. Indeed, many a critic will probably have wondered how I could have omitted such an important topic in my discussion of the generic properties of societal stratification. But as will become evident in chapter 8, I view rates of social mobility as one of the conditions influencing the degree of homogeneity of subpopulation formation. Yet, I recognize that for many sociologists, mobility is considered one of the most central topics in any discussion of stratification, even though I remain convinced that sociologists have, in general, focused entirely too much of their research and conceptual effort on it. In deference to those who feel this way, however, I will analyze *MO* in the same way that I will have done with the other properties of stratification in order to demonstrate how one moves from elementary principles on stratification to more general properties of social organization.

Chapter Five

THE UNEQUAL
DISTRIBUTION
OF MATERIAL
WEALTH

Inequality in the Distribution of Valued Resources

As I have stressed in the previous chapters, the term "stratification" does not denote a unitary property of the social universe. Rather, it is a word that sociologists use to denote the intersection of several component processes, each of which is operative in other than stratifying social contexts. One set of these discrete processes is the unequal distribution of material wealth (MW), power (PO), and prestige (PR). The issue of inequality (I) pertains to the degree of concentration (C) of these three valued resources. That is, what proportion of individuals control or possess what proportion of each resource? As was argued in the last chapter, then, inequality (I) can be defined as a weighted and additive function of the respective degrees of concentration (C) in material wealth (MW), power (PO), and prestige (PR). More formally, inequality at the societal level was defined in the following terms:

$$I = W_1(C_{MW}) + W_2(C_{PO}) + W_3(C_{PR})$$

where:

$$W_1 > W_2 > W_3$$

From this general definition, the theoretical task now becomes one of articulating the most generic conditions under which the concentration of material wealth, power, and prestige vary. In other words, what basic properties of the universe increase or decrease C_{MW}, C_{PO}, and C_{PR}?

In this chapter, a modest beginning on this theoretical work will be begun by developing an elementary and highly abstract principle on the concentration of material wealth, or C_{MW}.

An Elementary Principle on the Concentration of Material Wealth

Equation (5.1) states the generic properties of the social universe which, I feel, are related to the unequal distribution of material wealth in societal social systems.

$$C_{MW} = f(P) \circ g(NH) \circ i(NO) \qquad (5.1)$$

where:

P = productivity, or the total volume of products and services generated by the members of a society, with products defined as material objects created by the conversion of environmental resources and with services defined as activities that facilitate the production and distribution of material objects[1]

NO = the number of subunits in a society that organize people's activities

NH = the number of hierarchies that link organizational subunits in a society, with hierarchies defined as the vertical organization of units in terms of power

and where:

$$f(P) > g(NH) > n(NO)$$

In this proposition, the degree of concentration of material wealth (C_{MW}) in a society is visualized as an unspecified function (that is, f, g, and h) of the level of productivity (P), the number of organizational subunits (NO), and the number of social hierarchies (NH).[2] I have conceptualized productivity as the total volume of material objects and services generated in a society. This formulation is not far removed from standard notions of total GNP, but it is not the same as "productivity" measures in economics since it does not divide the total products by the number of workers. The concept "number of organizations" draws attention to a property of social systems that is too infrequently examined: the number of subunits in a system that organize people's activities. As will be argued, the sheer number of identifiable organizations accounts for many of the distributive dynamics of social systems. The number of hierarchies denotes the fact that organizational subunits in a society are linked together, to varying degrees, in terms of power and authority.

What is the rationale behind equation (5.1)? Productivity is emphasized because it is impossible to have inequality without a surplus of material goods (and money used to buy them) that extends beyond people's subsistence needs.[3] This idea was, of course, first given forceful advocacy by Karl Marx[4] and more recently by Gerhard Lenski.[5] As will be recalled from chapter 3, their respective formulations are:

$$(\text{Marx}) \ I = W_1(P^{\exp}) \times W_2\left[\log(C_{CP})\right]$$

where:

$$W_1 > W_2$$

$$(\text{Lenski}) \ I = \left[W_1(P^{\exp}) \times W_2(ES^{\exp})\right] \times W_3(C_{PO}^{\exp})$$

where:

$$W_1 > W_2 > W_3$$

From Marx's perspective, the level of inequality (I) is an exponential function of the level of productivity (P) and a logarithmic function of the degree of concentration in the control of the means of production (C_{CP}). From Lenski's viewpoint inequality (I) is an exponential function of productivity (P), the level of economic surplus (ES), and the degree of concentration in power (C_{PO}). I have phrased the argument somewhat differently from either Lenski or Marx, but the essential point is much the same. People will seek to extract as much surplus as they can; and as productivity increases, there is more to extract. To extract surplus requires power so that one can control other units; and once surplus has been extracted, it becomes a basis for consolidation of more power which can then be used to control other units in a system in ways that allows further extraction of surplus and consolidation of power. A modified version of Lenski's[6] view is diagrammatically represented in figure 5.1.

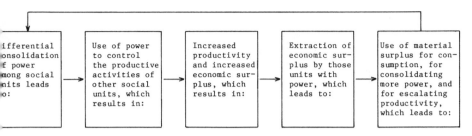

Figure 5.1 Productivity, Economic Surplus, and Power

As stated, potentially there could be no end to the cycle presented in figure 5.1. Power is used to extract surplus in ways that allows the powerful to encourage greater productivity in order to gain more power. In actual social systems, however, this does not occur. There are inherent properties in the consolidation of power that inhibit its unlimited consolidation. One such property limiting the consolidation of power is forces, such as the level of technology, population size, division of labor, and resource levels, which determine the level of productivity and the total amount of economic surplus that is available for extraction. Another limitation is the conflict-producing results of economic exploitation. For as Marx emphasized,[7] and as Dahrendorf[8] has more recently argued, subordinates eventually resist the efforts of superordinates through ideological mobilization, political organization, and conflict.

Yet another limiting factor is the set of administrative problems in using and extending a base of power. As greater amounts of power are consolidated and as efforts to expand the use of power are increased, problems of issuing, administering, enforcing, and monitoring directives escalate. How are initiatives to be given? How are they to be administered? How are recipients of orders to be monitored? How are pockets of resistance to be controlled? These problems are typically resolved by developing hierarchical chains of command and organizational units specialized in various administrative functions. And the more power that is sought, the more productivity must be extended if increased levels of resources are to be extracted; and as a result, the greater must be efforts to extend the scope of control by increasing the length of the chain of command and by proliferating more specialized administrative units.

In turn, as chains of command and organizational subunits are extended, they become themselves centers of conflict over authority, as Ralf Dahrendorf [9] and Randall Collins [10] have emphasized. With conflict, different segments and levels of the political hierarchy develop their own resources which, in effect, dilute the power of central decision-making units. Moreover, the existence of various layers and types of administrative units consumes, as overhead, many of the extracted resources, thereby decreasing those available for consumption by elites, for reinvestment in productivity, and for further consolidation of power. The processes are diagramed in figure 5.2.

These considerations led me to ask a more general question that included the dynamics portrayed in figure 5.2, and yet extended this line of argument beyond the political realm. What conditions *in a society as a whole* break the power-productivity cycle portrayed in figure 5.1? How can the dynamics portrayed in figure 5.2 be made more abstract and applicable to all realms of a social system? My answer to these questions was the concepts of *NH* and *NO*. That is, the greater the number of hierarchies (*NH*), the less concentrated power will be and the less power can be used to consolidate the material wealth that comes from production. And, the more the organizational subunits in a society, whether political, kinship, religious, leisure time, community, economic, or some other form, the more the resources that must be dispersed to sustain these organizations, and hence, the less concentrated are power and material wealth.

Thus, the number of hierarchies (*NH*) represents, I feel, a more general and abstract way to state Marx's and Lenski's insight: the fewer hierarchies, the more consolidated power; the more consolidated power, the greater the capacity to extract productive surpluses; and as Michels [11] noted, the more hierarchical the pattern of organization, the more material resources flow to the top of the hierarchy. But as the number of hierarchies increases, material resources will be more dispersed; and while they may flow to the top of the hierarchy, the existence of several hierarchies lowers the concentration of material wealth. Similarly, the greater the number of organizational subunits (*NO*) the more will be the material resources used to sustain

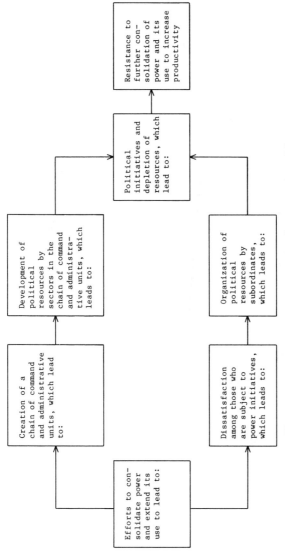

Figure 5.2 Inherent Limitations on the Consolidation of Power

them and the less will be the concentration of material wealth. Of course, if these units are organized hierarchically, then some of the dispersing effects of an increase in NO are diluted by a decrease in NH.

These considerations of the underlying processes that connect the variables in equation (5.1) allow for a more specific formulation, which is done in equation (5.1a):

$$C_{MW} = W_1(P^{\exp}) + \left[W_2(NH^{-\exp}) \times W_3(NO^{-\exp})\right] \qquad (5.1a)$$

where:

$$W_1 > W_2 > W_3$$

In this equation, the concentration of material wealth is viewed as a positive exponential function of productivity and as a negative exponential function of the number of hierarchies and number of organizations.[12] These relations are diagramed in figure 5.3. The major conceptual and empirical problem in visualizing these relations is that NH and NO counter the effects on C_{MW} of increases in P. The particular level of C_{MW} in a society will vary in terms of the exact level of

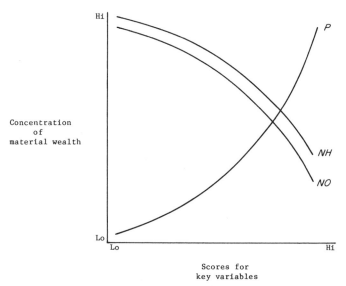

Figure 5.3 General Relationship Between C_{MW} and Each Explanatory Variable

P, NO, and NH; and over time, the degree of C_{MW} will shift in terms of the profile of the slopes for each of these three variables.[13] Equation (5.1a) merely represents my best guess as to the general weightings and relations among these variables.

In equation (5.1a), productivity (P) is considered to be more important than number of hierarchies (NH), which, in turn, is seen as more critical than number of organizations (NO) in their respective influences on the concentration of material wealth. I have multiplied NH by NO because an increase in one will increase the effects of the other on C_{MW}. There are, of course, causal effects among these variables, but these are more readily communicated when separate equations for P, NO, and NH are developed. Yet, at the end of the chapter, we will briefly consider some mutual causal effects. For the present, my concern is only with the impact of P, NH, and NO on C_{MW}.

The earlier discussion on the rationale for selecting these variables led me to construct equation (5.1a). For by exploring the dynamic processes underlying the association of basic properties in the social universe, it becomes possible to transform a rough equation like (5.1) into a more specific theoretical statement, as is the case with equation (5.1a). This transformation represents an important part of the theoretical strategy discussed in chapter 2—a point I wish to emphasize again before proceeding further. Statements such as (5.1) and (5.1a) might be viewed as "static" in the sense that they connect social system properties to some variable of interest—in this case C_{MW}. Critics can justifiably charge that there is little process in such statements; they are seemingly static and ad hoc. On the one hand, theory must begin to make such statements and simply connect basic properties of the universe, but on the other hand, it is desirable to specify the underlying processes among such connections. Thus, a major element in my theoretical strategy is to develop a descriptive scenario of the processes that underlie statements like (5.1) and like those that will appear later. In fact, it is consideration of these processes that enables me first to see certain properties of the universe as connected, and then to specify in greater detail their relations to each other.

In addition to these issues I want to stress again at this juncture another important element of the theoretical strategy being developed in this book. Conceptualizing C_{MW}, P, NH, and NO as *variables* obviates the unfortunate tendency among sociologists to argue in absolutes and categorical assertions. Any empirical case will evidence different scores for each of these variables, and thus the level of C_{MW} will vary. We do not have to argue over who exploits whom, over whether stratification is multidimensional or unidimensional, or over other issues that have consumed far too much of sociologists' intellectual energies. Rather, by viewing I as composed of C_{MW}, C_{PO}, C_{PR} and by conceptualizing as variables those social forces that influence any one of these, we are in a position to understand different empirical instances of inequality in terms of the same propositions. In the present case, we can recognize that C_{MW} is only one of three generic resources that are unequally distributed and that C_{MW} is connected to certain dynamic processes that inhere in P, NH, and NO. Equations (5.1) and (5.1a) represent my best effort to specify these relations, but I invite others to add variables and to rewrite the equation as well as to delineate additional processes that underlie the relations specified in the equations. Such a dialogue will have constructive consequences as opposed to the obstructive arguments that have typified so many debates on inequality.

The Elementary Principle Illustrated

In assessing the plausibility of equation (5.1a), different types of societies—hunting and gathering, horticultural, agrarian, and industrial—will be examined with respect to the varying weights for the variables in equation (5.1a). In table 5.1, I have summarized the existing data on hunting and gathering, simple and advanced horticultural, agrarian, and industrial societies with respect to productivity (P).[14] Obviously, a table like this is a composite of modal tendencies; actual societies reveal considerable variability in terms of their particular histories and empirical circumstances. I have described productivity in terms of five elements: technology, capital formation, labor, entrepreneurship, and land. *Technology* refers to the level of knowledge in a society about how to manipulate the environment; *capital* denotes the tools used to manipulate the environment (including money that buys tools and/or services); *labor* pertains to the size of the labor force and the diversity of productive roles; *enterpreneurship* points to the mechanisms by which economic activity is organized; and *land* refers to patterns of ownership and access to natural resources.[15] At the far right of the table, the total level of productivity stemming from the weights for these five economic elements is reported.

As can be seen by reading across the top row of table 5.1, hunting and gathering societies utilize a basic knowledge about hunting and plant life, in conjunction with simple tools such as the bow and arrow and digging sticks, to extract a subsistence level of existence from the environment. Typically, productive activity is organized in bands composed of several nuclear families, with bands ranging in size between thirty and one hundred persons. Females perform most of the plant gathering and account for about 80 percent of the economic production; males engage in hunting, and at times, help in the gathering. Such bands wander through a delimited territory in a semicircular pattern, moving on as they deplete the resources of an area. In such societies total productivity is inevitably low.

The second row summarizes the data on simple horticultural societies. These societies are composed of small communities that use their knowledge of plants and animals, in conjunction with simple tools, to cultivate tracts of land and to maintain small numbers of animals. Such societies settle in a region and are considerably larger than hunting and gathering societies. Moreover, they reveal a much more elaborate division of labor, with specialists in certain crafts becoming prominent. Such labor is typically organized in extended kinship units, linked together in a descent system, such as lineages (and at times, clans and moieties). Yet, because their gardening methods often deplete resources, they must resettle occasionally on new tracts of land. As a result, productivity is typically moderate, at best.

Advanced horticultural societies reveal a considerably more developed technology for planting and herding as well as more efficient and sophisticated tools than do simple horticulturalists. Their communities are much larger and more stable; they manifest a much more extensive division of labor; kinship systems are quite elaborate, extending at least to the clan level and often into moieties, and they are

Table 5.1 Productivity (P) in Different Types of Societies

	Technology	Capital	Labor	Entrepreneurship	Land	Total (P)
			Variables Influencing Level of Productivity			
Hunting and gathering societies	hunting techniques; plant seasons; crude tools and weapons	tools made directly from nature: wood, stone, bone	very small; division by age/sex	nuclear unit; band	communal ownership of territory; little control of resources	Low
Simple horticultural societies	hunting; domestication of animals; plant cultivation; simple tools and weapons	digging sticks	small; division by age/sex; occupational specialties; proto-slavery	community organization; headman; kin groups; trade specialists	community ownership of land tracts; kin ownership of plots; some control of resources	Low–moderate
Advanced horticultural societies	metallurgy; hunting; herding; domestication; plant cultivation; irrigation; fertilization	hoe, axes, knives; metal tools; storehouses	large; division by age/sex; extensive occupational specialization; slavery	community; chief; kin groups; merchants; markets	individual ownership; kin ownership; communal ownership; considerable control of resources	Moderate

...rian societies	plow, animal power; metallurgy; wheel; sail; plant cultivation; herding; domestication; water power; irrigation; fertilization; terracing	plow, beasts of burden; carts, boats; storehouses; money	large; division by age/sex; vocations; elaborate division of labor	shops, guilds, kin units; control by state	private ownership; state ownership; some communal; considerable control of resources	Moderate–high
Industrial societies	all of the above to a greater degree; inanimate power; mechanical production	machines; factories; storehouses; mechanical transport facilities; money	large; division by age/sex; professions/vocations; elaborate division of labor	shops, factories, bureaucracies; state management of corporate entities; unions, professional organizations	private ownership; state ownership; enormous control of resources	High–very high

the primary basis for organizing productive activity. Moreover, the beginnings of new, nonkinship organizational forms are also evident—merchant specialists and markets being the most conspicuous. As a consequence, productivity ranges from moderate to high levels.

Agricultural societies represent extensions and elaborations of the base laid by advanced horticulturalists. This expansion results from a series of technological innovations: the harnessing of animal power with tools (the plow, for example); the development of metallurgy and the production of new, more efficient tools; the transformation of transportation with the use of carts on roads; the use of water and air as sources of energy; and the perfection of irrigation, fertilizing, and terracing techniques initially developed by advanced horticulturalists. The result of these innovations is the creation of new forms of capital such as animal-powered plows, carts, pumps; the expansion of trade; the building of elaborate storage facilities; and as the volume of trade increases, the use of money as liquid capital. Associated with these changes (both as cause and resultant) is an elaborate division of labor and its organization by multiple social forms: kin groups, guilds, governmental offices, and merchant enterprises. In these systems, productivity is comparatively high.

Industrial societies extend and develop the technological innovations of agrarian societies, and to these innovations they add a new one: the use of more sophisticated sources of inanimate energy, coupled to machines, in production. Capital is greatly expanded in this way, and as the capital base of an economy grows, the labor force becomes increasingly diverse, evidencing an extensive division of labor organized into a wide variety of shops, factories, bureaucracies, unions, and professional organizations which are, to varying degrees, coordinated by the state. And as a result, productivity is usually very high, especially in comparison with agrarian systems.

These brief descriptions of the productive processes in different societies are sufficient for my purpose, which is to illustrate the respective levels of productivity in different types of societies. Thus, if productivity were the only variable in equation (5.1), the concentration of material wealth would be greatest in industrial societies, next greatest in agrarian systems, followed, respectively, by advanced horticultural, simple horticultural, and hunting/gathering societies. But as Lenski discovered in his analysis of these same types of societies, inequality decreases somewhat with industrialization. This fact signals the importance of other forces operating to influence C_{MW}.

One of these other forces is the number of organizational subunits in a society. The existence and maintenance of any discrete organizational form requires resources; and the more organizational units in a society, the more resources must be dispersed to maintain these units. In table 5.2, I have tried to enumerate the organizational subunits that can be discerned in hunting and gathering, simple and advanced horticultural, agrarian, and industrial societies. I have listed types of subunits under general organizational dimensions: economic, political, religious, kinship, and educational institutions; community structures; voluntary associations; and geographical units. And at the far right of the table, I have made a rough estimate of the total number of organizational subunits.

As can be observed by reading across the rows of table 5.2, the number of organizational subunits in societies increases from hunting and gathering to horticultural, from horticultural to agrarian, and from agrarian to industrial. Hunting and gathering societies are small and exist in loosely defined territories, with the major axes of organization being nuclear kin units and the band. In comparison, even simple horticultural societies evidence more bases of organization. Kinship becomes organized around extended units composed of several nuclear families which are linked to other units in lineages and often in clans and moieties. One can also observe various political subunits: headman, council of elders, and military orders. With regard to religion, worship becomes more organized with a clearly defined shaman and various cults devoted to engaging in religious rituals. Because simple horticulturalists are relatively stable, villages become major organizational subunits. And with the growth in size and organizational diversity of simple horticultural populations comes an increased variety of voluntary groups: secret societies, social clubs, and friendship cliques.

Advanced horticultural societies extend this organizational base. Kinship is still the major organizational axis, but other structures be-

Table 5.2 Number of Organizational Subunits (*NO*) in Different Types of Societies

| | Spheres of Organization | | | |
	Economic	Political	Religious	Kinship
Hunting and gathering societies	individuals; nuclear groups; friendship groups	virtually none	ritual subgroups	nuclear units
Simple horticultural societies	kin groups	headman's kinship unit; council of elders; military orders	shamanic cults	nuclear units; extended units; lineages; clans; moieties
Advanced horticultural societies	kin groups; merchants; quasicorporate units	kings; local chiefs; beginning of state bureaucracy; army; courts; tax collectors	religious priests; religious cults; religious bureaucracy	nuclear units; extended units; lineages; clans; moieties
Agrarian societies	kin groups; merchants; guilds; corporate units	monarchy; bureaucratic state; army and military bureaucracy; courts; tax collectors; substates	church bureaucracy; many religious cults	nuclear and extended units; lineages, clans; moieties less evident
Industrial societies	diverse agencies of the state; diverse corporations; diverse unions; diverse professional associations	the state bureaucracy, national, regional, and local; courts; military bureaucracy; political parties and interests	dominant church bureaucracy; various denominations and cults	nuclear

come more pronounced. In the economic realm, one can observe merchant groups and clusters of kin who are organized, much like a corporation, to engage in various economic specialties, such as trade, transport, weaponry, milling, and jewelry. The political system is much more complex, with a king and his court, various headmen and local chiefs, an army, court officials, and tax collectors. Religion is now highly organized and elaborate with priests and their quasi-staff as well as organized worshipers. One can also observe the beginnings of educational organizations, as apprenticeship in some crafts and

Educational	Community	Voluntary Associations	Geographical	Total NO
ɔne	band	friendship cliques	50–100 people in loosely defined territory	few
ɔne	multiple villages	secret societies; friendship cliques	100–1,000 people in clearly defined and defended territories	few–some
ɔprenticeships some crafts ⁊d religious po-tions	villages, capital towns	social clubs; secret societies, friendship cliques	thousands of people; subregions of annexed and conquered peoples	some–many
ivate schools r elites; appren-ceship to crafts; rmal and ap- entice educa- ɔn of religious actitioners	villages, towns, cities, capital city	social, religious, economic, political clubs	thousands into many millions of people in large territories of conquered and annexed peoples; ethnic populations, substates	many
tensive public ⁊d private edu- ational system	towns; cities of many different sizes; metropolis; urban regions	extensive social, recreational, economic, political, religious, educational, community voluntary associations	stable boundaries; ethnic subpopulations; substates	very many

religious instruction for future priests sometimes occur. Community structure is now more diverse, with villages varying in size and perhaps in economic and political functions. Social clubs and secret societies becomes even more pronounced. And because advanced horticultural societies are typically imperialistic, they become very large and embrace substates of conquered and annexed peoples.

Agrarian societies extend these trends, but with some important modifications. Kinship, while still important, becomes less dominant as the organizational axis of the society as alternative structures proliferate and expand. In the economic realm, kin groups, merchant groups, guilds of workers, and incipient corporations that are distinct from kin groups are evident. In the political arena, a clear monarchy usually exists, with a bureaucratically organized staff of officers performing administrative duties. Furthermore, the military, the courts, and the tax-collecting bureaucracies all expand. Religion also becomes bureaucratized with diverse levels of religious officials and the formal organization of worship in the general population. Community structures become very diverse, ranging from small villages and moderate-sized towns to large cities. They also become somewhat differentiated in terms of whether economic (trade, commerce, agriculture, etc.), political, or religious functions dominate. In the educational realm, school structures for the monarchy and its court, plus officials in the state bureaucracy, army, judiciary, and religious bureaucracy, become clearly evident. In addition, control of apprenticeship by guilds and corporate units creates quasi school structures to impart necessary skills. Voluntary associations increase as a highly differentiated population seeks friends and contacts in a variety of economic, political, religious, and social associations. And because agrarian populations are almost always engaged in war and conquest, they often embrace large territories, creating substates with their own patterns of governance as well as regional variations in ethnicity of the population, economic organization, and religious practices.

With industrialization, extended kinship and unilineal descent patterns are no longer a major basis of organization. Almost all activity becomes bureaucratized, even voluntary associations (save for close friendship networks). In the economic realm, the state, private and public corporations, diverse unions, a wide variety of trade associations, and different professional associations organize economic activities. In politics, the bureaucratic state and its clear organization into national, regional, and local levels, plus the bureaucratic organization of police, courts, and social welfare, replace monarchal political forms. Moreover, political parties and diverse interest groups come into prominence as industrial systems move toward a democratic profile (although the degree of democracy varies enormously, as can be best illustrated by comparing the Soviet Union and the

United States). Religion becomes highly bureaucratized, with several denominational structures dominating and organizing worship among the population. The educational system is now vast and extensive, consisting of many organizational levels and units. Community structure involves more than towns, villages, and cities, but also new forms such as the metropolis and the urban region. Moreover, communities vary in their organizational form, ranging from agricultural service centers to residential communities, and from industrial cities to high-technology production/servicing centers. And with the growth and diversity of the population as well as with the increased leisure that comes with high-technology production, the number of voluntary organizations and associations inevitably increases in order to consume the leisure time of a large and diverse populace. Finally, industrial nation-states evidence clear boundaries which often embrace, either through conquest or through migration patterns, diverse ethnic groupings and their attendant organizations.

Thus, as productivity (P) increases in societies, so does the number of organizational subunits (NO). Indeed, as I will comment upon shortly, there is an obvious interaction effect between these two variables. The increase in organizational units mitigates against the increased inequalities in material wealth (C_{MW}) associated with high levels of productivity. But as equation (5.1a) indicates, NO is given considerably less weight than P. Moreover, just how much NO will influence C_{MW} is the result of the pattern of linkage among organizational subunits. If there is a hierarchical ordering, and there are few hierarchies, then there will be considerably more inequality than if there is little hierarchical ordering or if there are many hierarchies. This force is conceptualized in equation (5.1a) as NH, or the number of hierarchies that link organizational subunits in relations of power. Table 5.3 presents illustrative data on NH for different types of societies.

In the hunting and gathering societies, there are no hierarchies because individuals cannot mobilize power. At best, some individuals exert influence because of their expertise in important activities, such as religious ceremonies and hunting. Moreover, since hunting and gathering societies reveal few organizational subunits, there is little

Table 5.3 Number of Hierarchies (*NH*) in Different Types of Societies

	Economic	Political	Religious	Kinship	Educational	Community
			Types of Social Hierarchies			
Hunting and gathering societies	none	headman who influences	shaman	male head	none	none
Simple horticultural societies		political power of headman/chief	authority of shaman	kinship hierarchy: lineages, clans, moieties	none	dominant villages
Advanced horticultural societies		clear political hierarchy of king and lesser rulers	religious hierarchy of priests	kinship hierarchy: lineages, clans, moieties	none	capital towns
Agrarian societies	dominant guilds, merchants, crafts	monarchy, hierarchically orders all political leaders; sometimes feudal, other times state form	religious hierarchy of priests	kinship hierarchy less prominent	elite private schools	capital cities; dominant regions
Industrial societies	monopolies; oligopolies; dominant unions and professions; dominant manufacturing centers; the	hierarchical state bureaucracy, mitigated by political parties, interests, and local govern-	religious tolerance; multiple denominations	none	hierarchy of primary, secondary, college level schools	capital cities; dominant states/ regions

to pattern hierarchically. These facts are evident in the top row in table 5.3. In contrast, simple horticultural societies develop clear patterns of hierarchical organization in a number of structural spheres. Kinship tends to be hierarchical in terms of descent rules which link extended family units to lineages, clans, and moieties. Associated with such kinship hierarchies—indeed, coextensive with them in many cases—is a political hierarchy, culminating with a headman who can exercise control of other units. Moreover, the headman typically lives in a village which dominates other villages in the society. In addition, with the clear demarcation of shaman and his right to perform rituals, the beginnings of a religious hierarchy are evident. Thus, while there are relatively few organizational subunits in simple horticultural societies, they are organized in a hierarchical pattern. And often these political, kin, religious, and community structures overlap to such an extent that in essence there is only one hierarchy; and hence, in such systems, there will be even greater inequality in the level of material wealth than would be the case if any or all of these hierarchies were dissociated.[16]

Advanced horticultural societies reveal very clear hierarchies. There is a king who resides in a capital town (or village) and whose kinship group is typically dominant. There is also a religious hierarchy which is sometimes linked to the political hierarchy and at other times in a state of tension with political leaders. But whichever pattern dominates, advanced horticultural systems are structured in terms of clear hierarchies. Agrarian societies also reveal a clear hierarchical organization. The most extreme form is a strong feudal[17] system where virtually all relations are defined in hierarchical terms. Yet, whether a feudal or state system, almost all agrarian societies have a monarchy which controls other social units and extracts a high proportion of the total material wealth. Such a monarchy is hereditary and is often associated with traditionally dominant lineages, clans, or moieties, but the existence of a state bureaucracy—tax collectors, accountants, army, etc.—marks the decline of kinship hierarchies and their replacement by an alternative form of hierarchical organization. This political hierarchy is associated with a dominant city and/or religion. The only significant challenge to the political hierarchy comes from religious leaders; and in fact, the existence of these two centers of power assures considerable tension and conflict in agrarian systems. Other hierarchies exist in agrarian societies, but they are recessive and typically incorporated into the political hierarchy. Yet, the independent power of guild and merchant hierarchies increasingly poses a challenge to the traditional monarchy as well as to religious centers in agrarian systems.

Industrial societies are hierarchically organized, even in their capitalist form. Yet, there are multiple hierarchies which are often in conflict with each other. Religion and kinship lose most of their power to structure organizational units, but new organizational forms in the economy, polity, educational realm, and community system all reveal some degree of hierarchy. Monopolies and oligopolies in the manufacturing sphere are evident; dominant union and the confederation of smaller unions into a hierarchy are clear patterns; and the organization of professionals into associations which develop sanctioning power is typical. In the political arena, the centralization of power is typical. In the political arena, the centralization of power is a clear trend, as the national state takes power away from regional and local governments while extending its sphere of control over other units. And hierarchies in public and private schools as well as in cities and regions also appear in industrial systems, although these are more ambiguous and subject to change and alteration. Thus, industrial systems are hierarchical; some such as those in the West reveal multiple hierarchies, while those in the East will possess fewer hierarchies.

In table 5.4, I have summarized in rough form the data presented for equation (5.1a). Since productivity is given the greatest weight, inequality should increase with escalating productivity. Yet, as Lenski[18] observed, this relationship holds only through agrarian societies. The reason for the decrease in C_{MW} in industrial systems is, I argue, the result of the higher values of NO and NH. That is, the number of organizational subunits and hierarchies increases with industrialization. Up to industrialization, the increases in productivity and the subsumption of organizational subunits under one or a very few hierarchies work together to create high C_{MW}, while counteracting the effects of increasing NO. But once the values for NH and NO increase, they more than compensate for increased productivity, thereby creating a drop in C_{MW} in industrial systems. At times the

Table 5.4 Evolutionary Variations in the Concentration Material Wealth (C_{MW})

	C_{MW}	P (Productivity)	NO (Number of Organizations)	NH (Number of Hierarchies)
Hunting and gathering societies	virtual equality	very low	very few	none
Simple horticultural societies	some concentration	low	a few	a few
Advanced horticultural societies	much concentration	moderate	some	a few
Agrarian societies	very highly concentrated	high	many	one or two
Industrial societies	highly concentrated	very high	very many	numerous

relationship among these variables reveals interesting patterns. For example, it might be wondered why inequality is greater in the United States than in the Soviet Union when, clearly, there are fewer organizations and hierarchies in the Russian than in the American system. The answer to this seeming contradiction is that the weights of P are much lower in Russia than in the United States. And it can be recalled from equation (5.1a) that P is the most weighted term. Thus, equation (5.1a) predicts that as Russian productivity increases, inequality will increase dramatically and will surpass that in the United States as the values for P match those in the U.S. This prediction is based upon the assumption that in the USSR there will be fewer truly independent hierarchies than in the U.S.

Thus, the salient point in this example is that the variables in equation (5.1a) are *weighted* and must be analyzed in *relationship* to each other. Figure 5.3 stresses this point by stating the relationship between C_{MW} and each of the variables in equation (5.1a); and in figure 5.4, I have expressed the same ideas again by plotting the *general pattern* of relationship among the three variables across the evolutionary sequence implied in the comparison of hunting and gathering, horticultural, agrarian, and industrial social systems.

Figure 5.4 emphasizes that as societies move from a hunting and gathering to an industrial profile, P and NO exponentially increase, while NH reveals a more curvilinear pattern. Hunters and gatherers evidence little hierarchy; thus, they represent the maximum value for NH, since every social encounter, as it develops (and changes), is potentially a hierarchy as each individual vies for control of the relationship. The number of hierarchies steadily decreases until an agrarian stage of development (with the exemplar being a strong feudal monarchy), and then, as industrialization begins, the number of hierarchies increases. I suspect, also, that the value for NH levels off in accordance with the processes depicted in figure 5.2, although this point of leveling can vary for different empirical systems (compare, for example, the U.S. and USSR). In comparing particular empirical cases, then, it is necessary (a) to determine a society's general structural type (hunters-gatherers, horticulturalists, agrarian, industrial) and (b) to ascertain the degree of convergence or divergence of the slopes in figure 5.4 for each society.

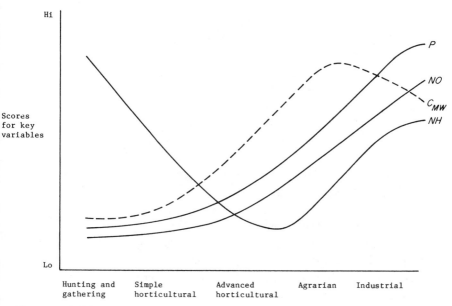

Figure 5.4 Relationships Among Critical Variables for C_{MW} During Societal Evolution

Implications for a More General View of Social Organization

As was argued in chapter 2, sociological theorizing has been too concerned with causality per se. That is, we have too often, I feel, begun theorizing with the intent of constructing a causal model; and as a result, we have tended to lower the level of abstraction in our theories and to let correlation coefficients cloud conceptual thinking. Yet, casuality is an important concern, and it is implicit in equation (5.1a). In stating the conditions under which C_{MW} varies, I have indeed made a causal argument. But that is not where I began; it is where I will end the chapter. And while this may seem to be a trivial point, it is not. Constructing causal models should come, I believe, *after* we have followed Auguste Comte's advice and (a) developed statements of affinity among generic properties of the universe and (b) stated the processes accounting for this affinity. Accordingly, now that the proper time has arrived, figure 5.5 presents the ideas in equation (5.1a) in a causal format.

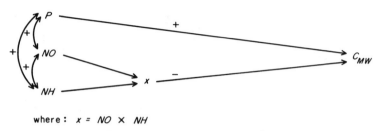

where : $x = NO \times NH$

Figure 5.5 A Causal Model of C_{MW}

By translating equation (5.1a) into a causal model, we raise several issues. First, a causal model allows us to readily visualize the effects of P, NO, and NH on each other—a matter that would make equations more cumbersome. That is, there are direct and indirect relationships among the three variables. The model allows us to visualize this fact and to ask: what is the strength and nature of these relationships? Second, a model like that in figure 5.5 leads us to ask: what causes variation in P, in NO, and in NH? As I indicated in chapter 2, a more general set of principles on human organization would include separate equations for these three properties of the social universe. The causal model in figure 5.5 simply highlights this point in my strategy by suggesting the need for arrows on the left side of the model.

Both of these considerations take us beyond the scope of this book into more general processes of social organization. I would like to close this, and subsequent, chapters by briefly addressing these issues, while recognizing that a more extensive analysis is for the future. In this way, it will be possible to set the stage for subsequent works in the larger theoretical project.

Causal Effects Among the Explanatory Variables

Turning first to the issue of the causal effects among P, NO, and NH, this is a more complicated question than portrayed in figure 5.5. The relations among the variables are all positive, but not equally so. Moreover, the effects of the variables are in some cases very strong, and in other cases, rather weak. Correlational analysis does not, therefore, allow us to visualize very well the specific processes connecting these properties of the social universe. My goal here is to enumerate them.

Productivity (P) and the number of organizations (NO) are interconnected in that, without increasing levels of P, NO cannot increase. Productivity sets limits on how many organizational subunits can be proliferated in a social system. Conversely, NO is certainly one of the conditions influencing P. Productivity will be limited, to some degree, by the number of organizational units that can engage in gathering resources, converting them into commodities, and distributing these goods to system members. Those forces that inhibit the development of organizational units will thus place a limit on productivity.

One of these is the number of hierarchies. A decrease in the number of hierarchies places a check on the number of organizational units that can be developed. Hierarchies can be maintained only with direct control of subunits; and as the number of subunits increases, the more likely is the hierarchy to break down. Thus, to the extent that expanding productivity increases the number of subunits in a system, pressure is exerted to increase the number of hierarchies. But, if a hierarchy is strong, it can operate to limit organizational growth, and indirectly, expansion of productivity.

In addition to these indirect effects between P and NH, there are more direct effects. Highly centralized control of P will slow down increases of productivity, since many of the surplus resources stemming from increased P will be used to maintain the hierarchy rather than reinvested into expanded productivity. Such hierarchical organization of P will, of course, allow for greater control and direction of P in accordance with system goals, but it will slow its expansion. Agrarian feudal systems often remain stable and static for just this reason: P and NH stand in equilibrium, with a given level of P being sufficient to maintain the hierarchy and with the usurpation of excess P for consumption by elites stagnating P at a particular level. More recently, one of the ironies of "state capitalism" in the USSR and elsewhere is that the effort to manage the economy directly in ways encouraging an expanded GNP are, to some extent, counterproductive. More recent "experiments" in free markets and private ownership in order to boost productivity are testimony to the Soviet leaders' recognition of this irony.

In terms of the relative strength of these relationships, I suspect that since P is the most heavily weighted variable, it operates to increase NO and NH directly and indirectly to a greater extent than they affect P. NO is increased directly by the proliferation of economic units, and indirectly by the effects of P in breaking down rigid hierarchies. Of course, initial increases in P have allowed for the creation of such hierarchies in the first place, as is most dramatically the case in horticultural and agrarian systems. But as P increases (by intent of political leaders or other forces beyond their control), NO will increase. Such pressures on NO operate indirectly as pressures on NH. Equally significant, expanding P will begin to create new hierarchies that begin to usurp resources and power away from political elites. Such pressures from P on NH are an indirect effect on $NO;$ increases in NH allow for growth in NO because the pressure to maintain control of, and a limit on, organizational units is now relaxed. The history of capitalism and the emergence of the bourgeoisie documents the extent to which increasing P can destroy political hierarchies and create systems with many diverse organizational units and multiple political, economic, and religious hierarchies. Thus, the direct and indirect effects of P on NO and NH should be viewed as the strongest, whereas the feedback effects of NH and NO and P and each other can be seen as less powerful.

Variations in the Explanatory Variables

If we were to construct separate equations for P, NO, and NH, it is evident from the above discussion that these variables would be prominent in each equation. That is, NO and NH would be terms in an equation for P, P and NO for NH, and P and NH for NO. But how heavily weighted would they be? My sense is that P would be heavily weighted for both NO and $NH;$ NO would be moderately weighted for P and $NH;$ and NH would be weakly to moderately weighted for P and NO.

The reason for this relative weighting is that P is, in my view (and hopefully one does not have to be a "Marxist" to hold this view), the prime mover in a social system. Social structural elaboration—its scale, scope, and form—is dependent upon the level of *P*. *NO* is also a critical force, as Weber recognized, in that it exerts a great influence on the nature of *P* and *NH*. *NH* is a force to be considered, but is likely to be influenced by changes in *P* and *NO* more than the reverse. These considerations lead us to ask: what other forces operate to effect the weights of these three variables? Such a question takes us into a much broader topic: the generic properties of societal organization. At this point, I can only mention some of these properties.

PRODUCTIVITY AND SOCIAL ORGANIZATION. Any set of principles on social organization will have to state the conditions under which productivity varies. That is, *P* will become the left-hand term in an equation. What, then, would the right-hand terms be? As I have already indicated, *NO* and *NH* would be two. Another would be population size (*N*); another would be access to natural resources (*NR*); yet another would denote the level of technology (*TE*); and there may be others. An initial statement, on the pattern of equation (5.1), would be:

$$P = h(N) \circ i(NO) \circ j(NH) \circ k(NR) \circ l(TE) \qquad (5.2)$$

The next step (a project for the future) would then be to weight the variables and develop a more precise equation, as was done in translating equation (5.1) into (5.1a).

NUMBER OF ORGANIZATIONS. One term affecting the level of *NO* is, of course, *P;* another is *NH*. Consequently, the more hierarchies and the greater the level of productivity, the greater the number of organizational subunits. What other conditions increase, or decrease, the number of organizations? Again, population size (*N*) is critical, since as size increases, more subunits are necessary to organize activities. Another important condition, I suspect, is the differentiation (*DF*) of market systems (*MS*) that employ money (*MY*), or $DF_{MS,MY}$. As Weber[19] recognized, without the capacity to use money in a market to hire and sell labor, services, and goods, there is a limit to how many organizational units can be generated. Thus, as we begin to think about developing an elementary principle on *NO,* the following equation will guide inquiry.

$$NO = h(P) \circ i(NH) \circ j(N) \circ k(DF_{MS,MY}) \qquad (5.3)$$

NUMBER OF HIERARCHIES.   The number of hierarchies is limited by *P* and *NO.* There cannot be many hierarchies if there are few organizational subunits and insufficient productive surpluses to support them. But as the data presented earlier in this chapter highlight, the relationships among *NH, P,* and *NO* may be curvilinear. *P* and *NO* must increase to some minimal level in order to create any hierarchy, since there has to be something to organize hierarchically as well as resources to support the hierarchy. It is only after the values for *P* and *NO* become comparatively high that the number of hierarchies in a system begins to increase. What other conditions affect the values for *NH?* I would imagine that the differentiation of market systems employing money ($DF_{MS,MY}$) would be critical, because until there is an alternative to power and authority as a basis for distribution of goods and services, the number of hierarchies will be limited. Again, population size (*N*) is critical, as is its degree of geographical dispersion, (absolute distances as well as travel time from point to point in a system), or as I prefer to phrase it, dispersion (*DS*) in space (*S*), or DS_S. Thus, large and geographically dispersed populations are less readily organized hierarchically than are smaller, more proximate populations. Thus, an inquiry into the conditions influencing *NH* will begin with the following equation:

$$NH = h(P) \circ i(NO) \circ j(N) \circ k(DF_{MS,MY}) \circ l(DS_S) \qquad (5.4)$$

Concluding Comment

Now that the development of one elementary principle (equation 5.1a) is complete, I should highlight again the basic thrust of the theoretical strategy being proposed. First, I begin with the question: at the most abstract level, ignoring many of the empirical particulars involved, what are the most generic properties of the social universe influencing a particular property of interest (in this case, C_{MW}). Second, how can these properties be seen as related to each other in their effects on the property of interest (in other words, what are their relative weights, form of relation to the property of interest, and interrelations as they effect this property?). Third, what are the underlying processes that connect properties of the universe that have been isolated in an elementary principle? Fourth, what are the more general implications for social organization of an elementary principle?

In approaching each property of societal stratification systems in this way—that is, C_{MW}, C_{PO}, C_{PR}, DF_{HO}, and RA_{HO}—a more concise set of elementary principles on societal stratification can be developed. Subsequent chapters will resemble the present one as I seek to develop elementary principles of societal stratification, and at the same time, comment upon their implications for an expanded set of principles on patterns of human social organization.

Chapter Six THE UNEQUAL DISTRIBUTION OF POWER

The Concentration of Power

The term "concentration" may initially appear somewhat ambiguous. In using this term, I am referring to the fact that in all societal social systems, the capacity of social units to control each other's activities[1] is unequally distributed. That is, some units have more of this capacity than others, and hence, the question of concentration addresses the issue of what proportion of social units control what proportion of power in a system?

While it is useful to view power in terms of a Gini coefficient, as was done in figure 4.1, there remain profoundly troublesome conceptual problems. First, power is not finite, in that the total amount of power in a system can increase or decrease. Second, and this point is related to the one above, power is dialectical, in that the existence of concentrations of power tends to create resistance to such power, often resulting in the mobilization of counterpower which not only increases the overall level of power in a system but which can also decrease its degree of concentration, at least for a time. Third, power is very hard to measure, since the ways that "control of social units" is exercised are complex, often subtle, and frequently difficult to observe among units at the behavioral and interactive level.

These and other problems[2] in conceptualizing power must be accepted, since to abandon efforts to theorize about this property of the universe would be to ignore one of the key dynamics of social systems. Thus, while the conceptualization of power (*PO*) in terms of its degree of concentration (C), or C_{PO}, may seem not only ambiguous but also naive, we must begin somewhere to visualize this phenomenon at the systemic level. I have chosen, for better or worse, the concept of C_{PO}, which is, in reality, another way of stating formulations that emphasize the "centralization" and "consolidation" of power. For in my effort in the pages to follow, centralization and consolidation are processes that influence the overall degree of concentration of power in a social system. Hence, these terms will be used throughout this chapter to understand the dynamics influencing the level of C_{PO}. It should be mentioned again that this is the second of three chapters on the unequal distribution (I) of valued resources which was conceptualized in chapter 4 as:

$$I = W_1(C_{MW}) + W_2(C_{PO}) + W_3(C_{PR})$$

where:

$$W_1 > W_2 > W_3$$

Our theoretical task is to understand at the most abstract level those generic conditions associated with the degree of C_{PO} in societal social systems.

An Elementary Principle on the Concentration of Power

Below, equation (6.1) states at the most abstract level those properties of the universe associated with the concentration of power, or C_{PO}:

$$C_{PO} = f(P) \circ g(IC) \circ h(IT) \circ i(ET) \qquad (6.1)$$

where:

    P = the level of economic productivity in a society (defined as in chapter 5)

    IC = the total level of internal conflict among subunits of a society

    IT = the total volume of internal transactions among the subunits of a society

    ET = the level of perceived threat from sources external to a society

and where:

$$i(ET) > f(P) > g(IC) > h(IT)$$

Equation (6.1) states that the degree of concentration of power (C_{PO}) in a society is an unspecified function of the level of productivity (P), the level of internal conflict (IC), the volume of internal transactions (IT), and the level of external threat (ET). The weightings reveal that external threat is the most important force, followed, respectively, by productivity, internal conflict, and internal transactions. As will be recalled from chapter 3, this proposition borrows much from Herbert Spencer, who in his discussion of "militant" and "industrial" societies[3] isolated certain generic properties connected to the centralization of power. I summarized Spencer's argument in chapter 3 in the following way:

$$\text{(Spencer) } C_{PO} = W_1[\log(ET)] + W_2(IC^{\exp}) + [W_3(IT^{\exp}) \times W_4(P^{\exp})]$$
where:
$$W_1 > W_2 > W_3 > W_4$$

In this proposition, Spencer visualizes the concentration of power (C_{PO}) in a society as a logarithmic function of the level of external threat (ET) and an exponential function of the degree of internal conflict (IC), the volume of internal transactions (IT), and the level of productivity (P).

My rationale for developing equation (6.1) borrows from Spencer's analysis,[4] and then extends it in ways that take into account more recent formulations.[5] As the weightings in equation (6.1) underscore, the perception of threat to a society from external sources (ET) is the most critical variable. As Spencer[6] emphasized, societies engaged in war become politically centralized, exercising great control over the mobilization and allocation of resources. Georg Simmel[7] made the same point in his recognition that conflict increases the level of despotism and intolerance of deviance among those who are parties to a conflict. Figure 6.1 seeks to portray the causal dynamics of this process.

Perceptions of threat on the part of political decision-makers usually set in motion processes for the concentration of political power. Such perceptions by the general population may take somewhat longer, but will eventually move decision-makers, or if these do not exist, will result in their creation or emergence. It should be emphasized

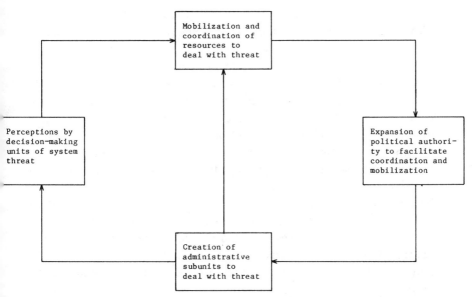

Figure 6.1 The Relationship Between External Threat (*ET*) and the Concentration of Power (*C~PO~*)

that the "threat" need not have a strong objective basis; it is only the perception of threat that counts. Such perceptions cause social units to mobilize and to coordinate their efforts for dealing with the threat. And the greater the perceived threat, the more intense these actions. Yet, mobilization of human and material resources as well as their coordination is difficult without a centralized political authority to make decisions. Systems without such authority typically develop it when mobilizing to deal with a threat, whereas systems with a well-developed and centralized subsystem of political authority usually expand its prerogatives, resulting in an increase in C_{PO}. As I emphasized in the last chapter, increasing political control involves extending chains of hierarchical command and proliferating new administrative units (see figure 5.2). Such administrative expansion increases the capacity of a system to mobilize and coordinate resources; and as is implied by the arrows in figure 6.1, there is a positive feedback process involved. As hierarchically organized administrative units expand, they attempt ever greater levels of mobilization, creating pressures for the expansion of political authority, which, in turn, requires extension of the administrative hierarchy. A decrease in the threat, or the processes outlined in figure 5.2 in the last chapter, can operate to break this cycle. Yet, as Spencer[8] worried and as more commentators on the "military-industrial complex" in the United States have pondered,[9] once political centralization revolves around dealing with a threat, efforts are often made by administrative units to perpetuate a condition of threat, as is emphasized by the arrows at the bottom of figure 6.1. In this way, another cycle increasing mobilization, expansion of political authority, and extension of administrative control is initiated again. This positive feedback cycle can be arrested by the processes outlined in figure 5.2 or by cessation of the threat, as typically occurs when a war is won, or lost.[10] Thus, the more pervasive, ill-defined, and difficult to terminate is an external threat (e.g., a "cold war," economic competition in a world system, and the like), the more likely are the positive feedback cycles in figure 6.1 to increase the degree of concentration of power, or C_{PO}.

In figure 6.2, I have outlined the critical processes underlying the relationship between P and C_{PO}. As productivity increases, problems in the distribution of goods and services, the creation of fixed and liquid capital, the management of resources, the need to stabilize labor-management relations, and the development of technologies all escalate. The net result of efforts to resolve the many small (and few major) "crises" that emerge with respect to each of these general problems is to expand political authority to deal with them. Typically, new administrative and regulatory units are created in response to each crisis. In some systems, these may be arranged hierarchically, and in other systems, they constitute a confederation of agencies. But in both cases, they increase the concentration of power. Further, as the cycle at the bottom of the figure 6.2 documents, the expansion of regulatory agencies allows for increased P which, in turn, escalates further the major problems listed in figure 6.2, thereby initiating a new wave of political expansion and administrative growth.[11]

The other cycle in the middle of figure 6.2 denotes the fact that as regulatory agencies proliferate, their very number, especially when they exist as a loose confederation of agencies with overlapping re-

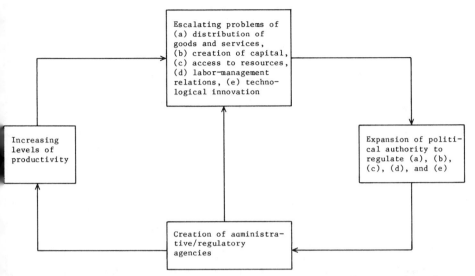

Figure 6.2 The Relationship Between Productivity (*P*) and the Concentration of Power (*C_{PO}*)

sponsibilities (as is the case in the United States), escalates the problems they are created to resolve. The irony of this situation is that the typical response is to extend political authority by (1) developing superagencies or umbrella agencies to consolidate administrative functions and/or (2) creating a clearer hierarchical ordering of such agencies. These cyclical processes are broken, as both Spencer and Vilfredo Pareto recognized,[12] when productivity begins to stagnate from overregulation and when capital is lost through the tax revenues used to sustain the governmental bureaucracy. Under these conditions, productive units mobilize counterpower and employ this power to force cutbacks, or as is more typically the case, to slow the rate of increase in political regulation.[13]

Figure 6.3 delineates the key processes underlying the relationship between internal conflict (*IC*) and *C_{PO}*. Conflict results from incompatible goals among subunits in a system; that is, subunits come to perceive that their members' interests and goals cannot be achieved because the interests and goals of other units stand in the way. This perceived incompatibility is not always accurate, nor does it neces-

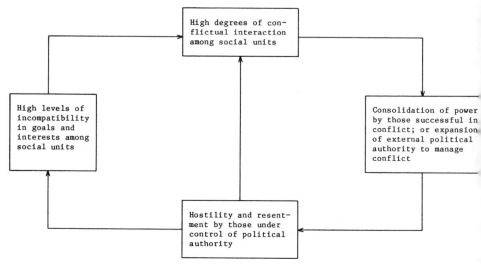

Figure 6.3 The Relationship Between Rates of Internal Conflict (*IC*) and the Concentration of Power (C_{PO})

sarily cause conflict.[14] But it is likely to increase conflictual interaction among social units as each acts to inhibit the other's attainment of its goals. At times, such conflictual interaction can erupt into violence, but more typically, milder forms of internal conflict prevail. To pursue conflict often involves the mobilization of power by parties to a conflict; and thus, increases in conflict can initially operate to decrease C_{PO}. But over time, conflict tends to increase C_{PO} by either of two routes: (1) one party to a conflict prevails over its adversaries and simply imposes its will over its vanquished opponents, or (2) internal conflicts create pressures for existing centers of political authority to expand their power in order to regularize, repress, or mitigate conflicts among units. In both cases C_{PO} increases. Yet, increases in C_{PO} reveal a dialectical quality, in that as power becomes concentrated, resentments and hostilities of subordinates escalate. The existence and persistence of such hostility operate to increase the very process that generates them—increasing C_{PO}. As political elites perceive their goals and interests to be incompatible with those of subordinates and begin to experience (or at least fear) conflictual interaction with subordinates, they are likely to engage in actions to increase C_{PO}. These actions may actually increase the likelihood of conflict; and should open conflict occur between politically organized subordinates and superordinates, C_{PO} will, for the duration of the conflict, decrease. But in the end, it will increase again as the party which prevails seeks to consolidate its advantage.[15] Thus, while the relationship between IC and C_{PO} is complex and often dialectical in form, there is, nevertheless, an association between high rates of IC and increases in C_{PO} in societal social systems.

Figure 6.4 outlines the relationship between the volume of internal transactions (IT) in a system and the degree of C_{PO}. As the volume of transactions increases, problems of coordination among, and control of, social units escalate, with the result that pressures for increased C_{PO} mount. Typically, administrative and regulatory agencies expand (legal codes, courts, regulatory agencies, administrative offices) in order to facilitate an increased volume of internal transactions.[16] Of course, the proliferation of too many such administrative/regulatory units can, in itself, create problems of coordination and control, but as I noted for figure 6.2, these are usually resolved by further increasing C_{PO} and consolidating courts, legal codes, agencies, and offices into a more hierarchical pattern.

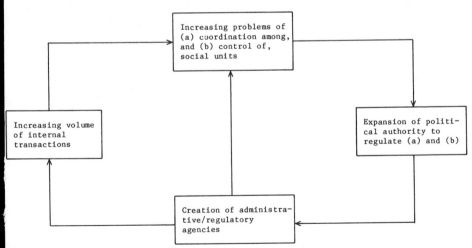

Figure 6.4 The Relationship Between the Volume of Internal Transactions (IT) and the Concentration of Power (C_{PO})

Figures 6.1 through 6.4 and the discussion surrounding them outline my views on the processes connecting *ET, P, IC,* and *IT* to C_{PO}. A rough understanding of these processes offers some guidelines for developing a more precise elementary principle. Equation (6:1a) represents an initial effort along these lines.

$$C_{PO} = W_1\left[\log(ET)\right] + \left[W_2(P^{\exp}) \times W_3(IC^{\exp}) \times W_4(IT^{\exp})\right] \quad (6.1a)$$

where:

$$W_1 > W_2 > W_3 > W_4$$

In equation (6.1a), the concentration of power (C_{PO}) is viewed as a logarithmic function of external threat (*ET*) and an exponential function of productivity (*P*), internal conflict (*IC*), and internal transactions (*IT*). As in equation (6.1), *ET* is weighted most heavily, followed respectively by *P, IC,* and *IT*. The relation between C_{PO} and *ET* is seen as logarithmic because initial increases in perceived threat lead to more concentration of power than subsequent ones. The relations between C_{PO}, on the one hand, and *P, IC,* and *IT*, on the other, are considered to be exponential because initial increases in the weights for *P, IC,* and *IT* do not increase C_{PO} dramatically. It is only after the weights for *P, IC,* and *IT* reach moderate levels that they result in large increases in C_{PO}. Productivity, internal conflict, and internal transactions are seen as multiplicatively related in that an increase in one will increase the effects of the others on C_{PO}. And the product of *P, IC,* and *IT* is additively related to *ET* in its effect on C_{PO}.

In figure 6.5, the relationship between each explanatory variable and C_{PO} is plotted.[17] The exact degree of C_{PO} is a particular empirical case will be determined by the slopes for these variables. Yet, with equation (6.1a) and figures 6.1–6.5, we have a general vision of those properties and processes that influence the unequal distribution of power in societal social systems.

The Elementary Principle Illustrated

Table 6.1 presents the data on hunting and gathering, simple and advanced horticultural, agrarian, and industrial societies with respect to the variables presented in equations (6.1) and (6.1a).[18] Obviously,

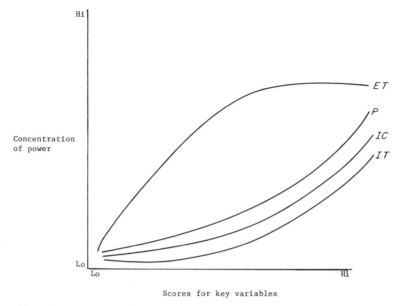

Figure 6.5 The Relationship Between C_{PO} and Each Explanatory Variable

a composite table such as this does not capture the uniqueness of a given society, but that is not my intent. My goal is to represent the modal case, with deviations being accounted for by unique environmental circumstances.

The concentration of power is low in hunting and gathering societies because the weights for productivity, internal conflict, internal transactions, and external threat are all low. Since hunters and gatherers have only simple tools and must carry all their material possessions as they move about a territory, production is low. Internal conflict is not high, and when it does occur, the nuclear families of the individuals involved in the dispute simply part company and form new bands. There is rarely an effort to compel individuals or families to stay in the band. The volume of internal transactions is low because there is little to trade, especially since individuals consume plants or animals on the spot or bring them back to the band for communal sharing. Moreover, adult individuals can all make any of the necessary implements of living for themselves, thereby making trade and exchange less critical.

Table 6.1 The Concentration of Power (C_{PO}) in Different Types of Societies

	C_{PO} (Concentration of Power)	P (Level of Productivity)
Hunting and gathering societies	*None:* informal headman and shaman exert influence but no one is compelled to comply	*Low:* hunting and gathering technology, using simple tools, organized in small bands
Simple horticultural societies	*Moderate to High:* chief with a staff and army. Can coerce conformity and has the right to extract surplus and labor of others, although there is usually a redistributive requirement on chief	*Low to Moderate:* gardening, hunting, domestication of animals are basic technologies. Simple tools used by members organized around extended kinship groupings
Advanced horticultural societies	*High:* king with enormous power to extract material surplus, labor, and property of others. Well-developed taxation formula. Well-developed army and system of bureaucratic administration among king and subheads of villages and broader territories. Yet, there is a strong redistributive ethic	*Moderate:* intensive planting, herding, domestication, and some hunting technologies used; labor organized by kinship and community, with craft specialization becoming visible
Agrarian societies	*Very High:* monarchy with power to extract material surplus, labor, and property of others. Well-developed taxation formula. Extensive army and system of bureaucratic administration from centralized city and region to other cities and regions. No redistributive ethic. Feudal organization more likely when transportation is difficult	*Moderate to High:* intensive planting, herding, and domestication. Use of metal tools and animal power. Sail and water power also employed. Extensive division of labor of individuals organized by extended families, communities, and manors
Industrial societies	*Moderate to High:* multiple or single party democracy; organized parties and interests; some legislative decision-making; strong executive branch and extensive system of bureaucratic administration of regions and cities; progressive taxation system. Extensive army and police	*Very High:* elaborate agricultural, herding and manufacturing technology. Extensive division of labor organized by factories and bureaucracies. Inanimate sources of power coupled to machines

IC (Level of Internal Conflict)	IT (Volume of Internal Transactions)	ET (Degree of Perceived External Threat)
Little: conflict leads to fission of the band, with conflict parties separating and forming a new band	**Few:** individuals' consumption and communal sharing. Little trade or exchange of goods and services	**Little:** prolonged conflict with other bands is unusual; environmental disaster (famine, drought) increases influence of informal headman and shaman
Moderate to High: personal feuds; tension among and within generations of descent groups; tension and competition among lineages, clans, and moieties; tension among villages	**Moderate:** individual exchange; redistribution of extracted surplus by chief; exchange among descent groups and villages	**High;** warfare among societies is very common; environmental problems frequent
High: personal feuds; tension among and within generations of lineages; competition among communities and kin groups; tension between king and subjects; tension among conquered and conquering peoples	**Moderate to High:** volume of trade is positive function of degree of craft specialization; system of taxation; organized markets; system for redistribution of some extracted surplus; merchandizing becomes a trade specialization; money is sometimes used. Much individual, kin, and community trade and barter	**Very High:** engaged in constant war and conquest. Empire building, defense, and exploitation are constant activities
High: personal conflicts; conflict at every level of state bureaucracy; conflict between monarchy and church; conflict between members of the nobility, especially at time of secession; tension and open conflict among regions, especially when organized in a feudal manner; conflict between conquered and conquerors; conflict among tradesmen and guilds; conflict among cities, especially between trade centers and capital	**High:** well-developed system of markets and transport systems to distribute goods and services; extensive system of taxation, tolls, duties; money extensively used; banking and merchandising become clear specialties	**High:** war is frequent. Conquest and empire building, defense and exploitation are constant activities. Revolt is frequent
Low to Moderate: conflict related to internal diversity and size of population. Tension between state and populace. Tension among levels of government. Open conflict among diverse interests and ethnic groupings	**Very High:** extensive markets and transport systems to distribute goods and services. Extensive taxation and social welfare systems. Extensive governmental subsidy system. Money and credit extensively used. Banking and merchandising become as prominent as manufacturing	**Moderate to High:** warfare is episodic. Tension among nations is persistent. Economic and ideological competition is often high. Confrontation often occurs indirectly through limited conflicts among indigenous populations of less-developed nations

Simple horticultural societies have considerably more concentration of power than hunters and gatherers. They possess a chief with a staff of elders, high-ranking kinsmen, and proficient warriors. They can use their warriors to coerce conformity; they possess the right to extract surplus food and labor of others; and they often assign plots of lands to individuals and families for cultivation. Yet, much of the food surplus that is extracted must be redistributed back to individuals, primarily because it will spoil if not eaten. But the right to extract surplus and to coerce, if necessary, represents a dramatic increase in the level of C_{PO} over what exists among hunters and gatherers.

The increase in C_{PO} is the result of higher weights for the variables in equation (6.1a). Productivity allows for a surplus of food which frees some from full-time gardening, with the result that war and crafts can be pursued. In fact, horticulturalists are almost constantly at war with their neighbors, with the result that adult males spend much time making weapons and defending their villages or attacking those of others. Thus, increased weights for P and ET would be sufficient to generate higher levels of C_{PO}, but also, there are at least moderate weights for IC and IT in simple horticultural societies. There are many personal feuds over land, mates, weapons, and honor; and if these are not to rip the society apart (a disastrous consequence for people who settle on the land), there must be political authority to adjudicate the dispute. Moreover, there is considerable tension between political elites and nonelites, since C_{PO} always generates resentment. In addition, there is always competition, jealousy, and resentment among descent groups (lineages, clans, and moieties) and among rival villages. All these sources of tension and potential for conflict force the concentration of power to control and resolve disruptive disputes. Internal exchange of food, jewelry, weapons, and wives forces some degree of C_{PO} in order to assure that exchange commitments are honored. Thus, as the levels of P, IC, IT, and ET increase, especially P and ET, so does the level of C_{PO} in simple horticultural societies.

Advanced horticultural societies reveal higher weights for all the variables in equation (6.1). Productivity is much greater, internal conflicts increase as the king extracts more surplus and as conquered peoples resent and resist their conquerors. Internal trade increases as the number of craft specialists increases, often necessitating markets and the use of money. And as the king seeks to expand, hold, or defend the empire, external threat is always high as war, conquest, and defense become predominant activities. The high weights for these variables assure a high level of C_{PO}. Advanced horticulturalists evidence highly concentrated power with a king who has considerable power to extract the material surplus, to conscript the labor of others for civil projects or war, and to resolve disputes among individuals, kin groups, or villages. The concentration of power often assumes a quasibureaucratic character as the king (or paramount chief) stands above local headmen, each with control over warriors and administrators. Yet, as with chiefs in simple horticultural societies, what is extracted, especially that which can spoil, is redistributed back to the people. But the king and his court still retain much that is valued, especially weapons and jewelry.

Agrarian societies simply elaborate the structural base created by advanced horticulturalists. C_{PO} becomes highly concentrated in a monarchal form of governance, where taxation of material surplus, conscription of labor, and mobilization for war are conducted without great obligations for redistribution. Even when the monarchal system is feudal, with centers of counterpower to the monarch, such as local lords and religious institutions, there is a centralized bureaucracy for taxation and war. Nobility are required to meet taxation quotas set by the monarch, administered by his bureaucrats, and enforced by his army. Such concentration of power reflects the high weights for all the variables in equation (6.1a). Productivity is high, with more efficient agriculture, herding, and domestication and with the use of animal, wind, and water power. There is a large surplus to extract, thereby freeing labor to pursue war and other specialties such as crafts, metallurgy, merchandising, transport, weaving, milling, and other productive areas of specialization. Internal conflict is incessant as the monarch seeks to exercise his prerogatives against resistance and as lords, towns, merchants, guilds, and other subunits compete and conflict. The volume of internal transactions escalates dramatically as the number of specialists increases and as the regions of the society become somewhat specialized in the productive activities. Money and markets become clearly differentiated; and roads traveled with carts or waterways used by boats greatly facilitate the volume and distance of trade. And as is the case with horticulturalists, war is frequent as the monarch seeks to expand territories to control restive peasants or nobility in various regions. Thus, the level of C_{PO} is probably greatest in agrarian societies, since there is a high level of P and ET, coupled with high levels for IT and IC.

Industrial societies reveal considerable variability in their level of C_{PO}. Some are full political democracies, whereas others are, at best, only partial democracies. Yet, in all industrial systems, there is a complete monopoly by the state on the capacity for coercion and there is a large central bureaucracy that regulates and controls virtually all activities. The existence of political parties, career bureaucrats, interest lobbies, elected legislative bodies, regional and local governments, and a national supreme court decentralizes power somewhat, but there is still a high level of concentration of power in industrial systems. The reasons for this concentration reside primarily in the desire to control and regulate high levels of productivity, to coordinate the very high volume of internal transactions, and to periodically go to war and/or maintain a state of military readiness. Internal conflict is sporadic and typically institutionalized by a well-developed court system. While riots and strikes (as well as terrorism) are prominent, they are less critical to C_{PO} in industrial systems than the very high levels of P and IT and the periodic mobilization for war (ET) or the long-term maintenance of military readiness (ET).

Thus, as is the case with C_{MW}, it would seem that C_{PO} also reveals a curvilinear pattern. C_{PO} increases as one moves from hunting and gathering to simple horticultural systems, from simple to advanced horticultural, and from horticultural to agrarian, but it decreases somewhat in the transition to an industrial form of economic organization. But this decrease is far from unambiguous. In the Western democracies, especially those in Europe, there is a clear decrease. In Eastern countries, the creation of the state may concentrate power even more than was the case in agrarian predecessors, especially if the agrarian stage was a decentralized and warring feudal system. In China, for example, the state clearly concentrated power as it consolidated the old feudal empire. In the United States, the trend appears to be toward the concentration of power over its agrarian and early industrial phase. Thus, by looking closer, we can see that C_{PO} probably varies more than C_{MW} in industrial systems; and the explanation for this variability resides in the varying weights for the variables in equation (6.1). In particular, industrial systems that must deal with high levels of IC and ET are the most likely to evidence high C_{PO}. In figure 6.6, I offer a comparison of the evolutionary trends in C_{MW} and C_{PO}.

As is evident from figure 6.6, C_{PO} is dependent upon C_{MW}, primarily because an increase in P is necessary for higher levels of both C_{MW} and C_{PO}. Consolidation of power requires larger material surpluses to maintain and use political power. But as the relative weights for the critical variables in equation (6.1a) vary over evolutionary history, it is clear that P is not the only driving force behind C_{PO}. This fact is illustrated in figure 6.7, where I offer some guesses, based on the data in table 6.1, as to the relative slopes of P, IT, IC, and ET during societal evolution.

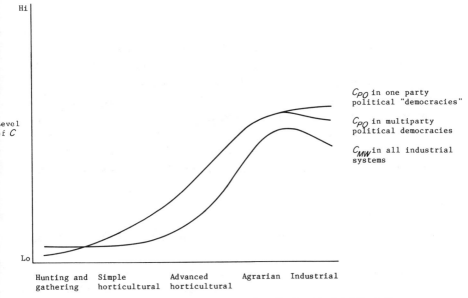

Figure 6.6 Relative Degrees of C_{PO} and C_{MW} During Societal Evolution

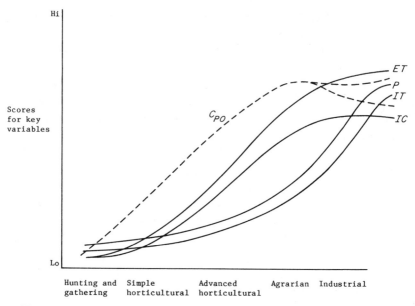

Figure 6.7 Relative Slopes for *ET, IT, IC,* and *P* During Societal Evolution

As is diagrammatically argued in figure 6.7, the dramatic increase in *ET* and *IC,* coupled with rising *P.* accounts for the early increase in C_{PO} in horticultural and agrarian systems. During the transition to industrial systems, *ET* and *IC* remain high but level off, which helps account for the drop in C_{PO} in multiparty political democracies. But C_{PO} is still high because *ET* and *IC* persist and *P* and *IT* increase dramatically (see figures 6.2 and 6.4). Thus, because the values for all the variables in equation (6.1a) are high in industrial systems, C_{PO} will reveal high levels, despite pressures for democratization.

Implications for a More General View of Social Organization

Equation (6.1a) only addresses the relations of *P, IC, IT,* and *ET* to each other they affect the level of C_{PO}. But obviously, these variables reveal direct and indirect effects on each other. Moreover,

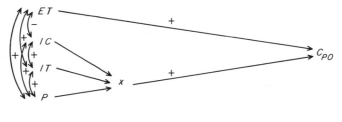

where : $x = (IC) \times (IT) \times (P)$

Figure 6.8 A Causal Model of C_{PO}

once we have isolated these variables, questions arise as to what other social forces influence the weights of these variables. As was done in chapter 5 on C_{MW}, we can construct a causal model to highlight these issues.

A simple model like that in figure 6.8 underscores the causal connections among the variables in equation (6.1a). However, equation (6.1a) allows only certain relations to be examined—that is, relations between ET, P, IT, and IC, on the one hand, and C_{PO} on the other. My purpose here is to liberate the analysis from consideration of the effects of these variables on C_{PO} and begin to explore in more detail the effects of these variables on each other. Moreover, we can also address, if only briefly, the question of what additional variables would be necessary to develop a separate equation, or elementary principle, for ET, P, IT, and IC.

Causal Effects Among the Explanatory Variables

External threat (ET) has important effects on productivity (P), the nature and volume of internal transactions (IT), and levels of internal conflict (IC). Systems under external threat alter productive processes in ways designed to deal with the threat. Typically, efforts are made to escalate as well as to circumscribe the spheres of production. A war mobilization is perhaps the prototypical case as P is increased and channeled toward the war effort.

Such processes have direct and indirect effects on the nature and form of internal transactions (IT). Increases in ET escalate political control of internal transactions (*IT*), as is the case when nations at war institute such measures as wage and price freezes, rationing, suspension of normal contract procedures, and the like. Also, as productivity becomes increasingly chaneled, the kinds of internal transactions are restricted; and this channeling may even cut down on their total volume, since certain types of transactions may be subject to government controls or outright nationalization.

Similarly, as Simmel noted,[19] nations at war restrict deviance and repress internal conflict (*IC*). Thus, *ET* operates to mobilize political authority in order to restrict the levels of *IC*, through force if necessary. However, if *ET* is not sufficiently high, political repression generates resentments, and in fact, it may even increase *IC* through the processes diagramed in figure 5.2. The conflict and turmoil in the United States over the Vietnam War illustrates this fact, because it is clear that the American public and a significant minority of decision-makers did not perceive sufficient *ET* to justify political efforts to stifle dissent. Only to the extent, then, that *ET* is perceived to be great does it operate to decrease the level of *IC* in a societal system.

There is also a feedback effect of *IC, IT,* and *P* on *ET*. As systems organize *P* to deal with *ET*, it becomes increasingly difficult to alter *P* back toward its original profile before the existence of the threat. As capital investments are made in productive activities designed to deal with threats, a series of vested interests arise to resist alteration of *P*. Similarly, for the same reasons, as internal transactions (*IT*) become skewed to deal with *ET*, they too resist a complete return to their former state. Herbert Spencer[20] worried about this process in England as threats from the crumbling British Empire skewed *P* and *IC* in ways that Spencer found reprehensible (in terms of his laissez-faire ideology). More recently, the military-industrial complex in the United States, and the alterations in government-private industry contracting procedures, resist dismantling to peacetime levels and forms. In fact, once *P* and *IT* are developed around a type of external threat, those who have interests in the maintenance of the threat often act to perpetuate a state of *ET* and the high levels and patterns of *P* and *IT* that revolve around their interests. Hence, it is not surprising that societies with large military establishments usually find a way to go to war, or at least mobilize to deal with escalated threats by "enemies." Thus, *ET* can be maintained and even escalated by those whose interests reside in *P* and *IT* that deals with a particular state of *ET*.

A similar feedback process can operate with respect to *IC*. Political leaders in systems with considerable internal conflict often create external threats in an effort to justify political repression in the name of "national unity" in the face of an *ET*. The problem with such a strategy is convincing the general population that an *ET* is real and sufficient to legitimate repression of *IC*. For if an *ET* is not perceived as sufficient, *IC* will increase. Often the personal charismatic qualities of leaders, such as was the case with Hitler, are critical in convincing a population with high levels of *IC* that an *ET* is real and sufficient.

As the second most weighted term in equation (6.1a), and as the most important force behind virtually all social processes, productivity (*P*) has both direct and indirect effects on *IT, IC,* and *ET.* As *P* increases, so does *IT,* since there is a greater volume of commodities and services to distribute. Moreover, as *P* and *IT* escalate, there are more potential areas of conflict (*IC*). Expansion of *P* requires structural differentiation of productive roles (*DF$_P$*) thereby increasing the potential for conflict among differentiated units. And as *IT* increases, there are more transactions that can become arenas for dispute and conflict. Yet, if procedures can be developed for mediating the conflict-producing effects of increased *DF$_P$* and *IT,* as is the case with the consolidation of power in courts and regulatory agencies, then there is a positive feedback loop to *P,* since the system's capacity to deal with one level of *DF$_P$* and *IT* allows for increases in these processes. But, in systems which, for a variety of reasons that usually revolve around problems in creating legitimate and efficient political bureaucracies, cannot resolve the conflicts inherent in *DF$_P$* and *IT,* *IC* operates a negative feedback on *P* and suppresses its further expansion.[21]

ET is also influenced directly and indirectly by *P.* To a great extent, systems with low *P* cannot afford the "luxury" of perceiving threats; they simply must ignore them, accept their consequences (if real), or rely on other institutional responses such as mobilization of religious activity to alleviate anxieties. Moreover, in societies where efforts to mobilize P to deal with an ET have not been successful, there is often a concerted effort by decision-makers to seek other means for dealing with the threat, including capitulation, creation of alliances, redefinition of system goals, or mobilization of religion. Conversely, the definition of whether P has successfully, or unsuccessfully, dealt with an ET greatly influences the course of P. Systems where P has been unsuccessful in dealing with increased ET are less likely than those which have enjoyed success to escalate P or channel it in directions dictated by ET, *unless* the failure to deal with an ET becomes the basis for the emergence of a belief system and political movement that revolves around the ET (as was the case, for example, with Hitler in Germany in the post–World War I era). And in systems where P has been seen as successful in dealing with an ET, then this success encourages further development of P in this direction. For example, most political empires are the result of mobilizing P to pursue conquest to the point when (a) productivity proves inadequate, (b) problems of political administration escalate, (c) revolutionary or succession movements tax both (a) and (b) above, or (d) another empire invades and usurps territory.

In sum, then, there are complex causal effects among the forces denoted by the terms in equation (6.1a). As is also evident, if we sought to develop separate equations for ET, P, IT, IC, these causal effects would require us to include some of these terms in each equation. Yet, there are other forces operating to influence the level of ET, P, IT, and IC; and I would be remiss in considering the general organizational implications of equation (6.1a) if I did not mention some of these, if only in a cursory manner.

Variations in the Explanatory Variables

PRODUCTIVITY.   Since the general conditions influencing the level of P were examined in the last chapter, there is little need to do so again here. The reader is referred to equation (5.2).

INTERNAL TRANSACTIONS.   Productivity is certainly one critical condition influencing the IT. Indeed, one might be tempted to argue

$IT = (P^{\exp})$. Yet, there are some other conditions which, while also related to P, have independent effects on IT. One of these is population size (N); another is number of organizations (NO). The larger is the population and the more subunits into which it is organized, the greater is the level of IT. Yet another condition is the differentiation of a market system (DF_{MS}), especially one using money $(DF_{MS,MY})$. A final condition influencing IT is C_{PO}, since without some degree of concentrated power, the regulation of high volumes of internal transactions becomes problematic. For without some centralized regulation, there is an upper limit for IT which can only be surpassed with increases in coordination by centralized political authority. This relationship is, no doubt, curvilinear in that a very high degree of C_{PO} can also limit the volume of IT for a system of a given size and level of productivity. Thus, in approaching the theoretical problem of isolating the most generic conditions influencing the volume of internal transactions in social systems, we can begin with the following equation:

$$IT = h(P) \circ i(N) \circ (NO) \circ (DF_{MS,MY}) \circ (C_{PO}) \qquad (6.2)$$

While this equation will, no doubt, require reformulation, it represents a starting point for using the theoretical principle on C_{PO} as a wedge into broader issues.

INTERNAL CONFLICT.   This is one of the most problematic concepts in social theory, primarily because sociology does not have an agreed-upon definition of "conflict."[22] Some have argued for encompassing definitions that include such states as "antagonism," "tension," and "conflict of interest," whereas others feel a more delimited behavioral view is conceptually appropriate. And depending upon the type of conflict involved—say, for example, "class conflict" vs. "economic competition"—different conditions will be seen as critical. There is no easy resolution to this dilemma, but I opt for a more delimited view of conflict as a form of *overt* interaction among subunits in a system where the actions of one unit to achieve its goals inhibit those of others from realizing their goals. The level of internal conflict (IC) denotes the number of such conflicts and their average level of intensity.

Armed with this definition, which, I acknowledge, is still vague and in need of refinement, we can begin to visualize those generic conditions increasing IC. I suspect that IT is one condition, as I suggested earlier. Another is the level of differentiation (DF) of a population (N), or DF_N. The more differentiated in terms of identifiable attributes is a population, the more likely is conflict. A critical force which increases the intensity of conflict is concentration of material wealth especially if there is a high correlation between C_{MW} and DF_N. Increasing this correlation are relatively low levels of vertical social mobility (MO). Thus, as we begin to consider the more general conditions in social systems under which conflict varies, equation (6.3) provides at least a starting point:

$$IC = h(IT) \circ (DF_N) \circ (C_{MW}) \circ (MO) \qquad (6.3)$$

EXTERNAL THREAT. To a great extent, the level of perceived threat depends upon the particulars of the social/political/economic/geographical/ecological environment of a society. Yet there are certain generic conditions beyond contextual circumstance that will increase the likelihood that external threats will be perceived or created by both the members and the decision-makers in a society.

One of these is declining productivity (P), especially when coupled with high levels of concentration of power (C_{PO}). Thus, politically centralized systems that are experiencing a decline in productivity will often seek to attribute such problems to external sources (e.g., environmental vicissitudes, geopolitical forces, economic competition from other societies). Systems where political leaders have only a tenuous hold on power are most likely to see their leaders attempt to "create" threats as a way of deflecting attention of the populace away from failings in their leadership. Thus, we can propose the following equation as a point of departure:

$$ET = h(P) \circ i(C_{PO}) \qquad (6.4)$$

In sum, then, it is with the ideas expressed in equations (5.2), (6.2), (6.3), and (6.4) that we can begin to use equation (6.1a) as a wedge to address more general patterns of social organization. Obviously, these ideas are in only a rough stage of development and will require more thought and reflection. The salient point at this stage is to begin thinking about the more general implications of the elementary principles, and at the same time, not let the complexities of this larger task interfere with and inhibit the pursuit of the more limited goals of the present. Thus, while interesting to consider, these general organizational implications are secondary to the major purpose of this chapter: to develop an elementary principle on C_{PO}. It is also necessary to keep this more delimited task in mind as we approach the analysis of the concentration of prestige, or C_{PR}, in the next chapter.

Chapter 7 THE UNEQUAL DISTRIBUTION OF PRESTIGE

Prestige as a Valued Resource

In general terms, prestige denotes the process of bestowing honor and esteem. As such, prestige has both attitudinal and behavioral dimensions. People in a society carry with them cognitions about what positions in the society should be given esteem and honor. And people behave in terms of these cognitions when they confront each other and engage in deference and demeanor rituals.[1] Most sociological accounts of prestige have focused on the attitudinal dimension of prestige,[2] whereas anthropological accounts of traditional populations have been more likely to stress the behavioral dimension.

The fact that prestige is both an attitudinal and behavioral process presents conceptual difficulties, especially in trying to visualize it as a basic system resource. Are we to define prestige in terms of its attitudinal or behavioral properties, for example? Moreover, this conceptual (and I might add, measurement) problem is compounded by the fact that prestige is not finite or inelastic. Since prestige is an attitude, it can be rather easily increased or decreased as people engage in cognitive manipulations. And since it is also a behavior, its level can be altered by changes in the deference and demeanor rituals among individuals. Thus, it becomes difficult to visualize prestige at the aggregate level, as something that is divided up among people in a society.

While there are conceptual problems in defining and measuring wealth and power, I do not think that they are so great as in defining prestige. Prestige is a different kind of resource; it is more illusive than power or wealth. Yet, we cannot ignore it in analyzing social systems, since it is *the* major stratifying resource in small groups and collectivities (see figure 4.2). Moreover, it is often used as compensation to those denied power and wealth; and yet, at the same time, it is given to those with power and wealth. Thus, while its analysis presents problems, the bestowing of prestige is an important dynamic in human social systems.

My goal in this chapter is to visualize prestige as a resource that is unequally distributed to the members of societal social systems. But even when my discussion is limited in this way, conceptual problems persist. One revolves around the issue of *how much* prestige must be given for a person or social position to be considered "prestigious"? In other words what is the threshold between high and low prestige? A related problem concerns the question of *how many* people must be willing to bestow high levels of prestige to a person or position for it to be considered "prestigious"? Is a simple majority enough, or must a larger number be willing to give honor? A similar problem is what *degree of consensus* must exist among people in terms of how much and on whom prestige is bestowed? Must there be high or only moderate consensus? Yet another problematic issue concerns whether persons or positions are to be the referent of honor or prestige. Still another is whether people's behaviors or attitudes, or some combination of these, are to be the index of "bestowing" and "giving" prestige.

These and other issues confound the study of prestige; and I cannot resolve them here, despite having given considerable thought to the matter. The emphasis in this book on the concentration (C) of prestige (PR), or C_{PR}, does not obviate these problems. For in asking what proportion of people in a society receive what proportion of its prestige, all the problematic issues mentioned above can be invoked. For example, do I want to focus on the attitudes or behaviors of individuals? How much esteem must be given for it to count as a valued and scarce resource? How many people with what degree of consensus must give esteem for it to count as prestige at the societal level?

These kinds of problems have led some to suggest that prestige be abandoned as a topic of stratification. My view is that while we presently do not understand precisely what prestige is, it is nevertheless something that humans take very seriously. It affects how we feel about ourselves and how we think about, and act in, the social world. Hence, despite the problems with viewing prestige as a systemic resource, we must continue to examine it as an important property of human social systems.

In my effort to examine C_{PR}, I will, in effect, ignore the problems that have been listed above. The result will be a less precise analysis than I would ordinarily like to present. The alternative, however, is less appealing: not to address what is an important social dynamic. Perhaps some of the problems in theorizing about the distribution of prestige can be resolved if we "work with" the concept of prestige in its current ill-defined form. By successively trying to specify the conditions under which esteem is bestowed, we can over time refine the concept in ways that will be more satisfactory. This is my hope and rationale for going ahead, despite my inability to resolve the problematic nature of the concept.

An Elementary Principle on the Concentration of Prestige

As can be recalled from chapter 3, Kingsley Davis and Wilbert Moore developed an elementary principle on inequality which stated:[3]

$$\text{(Davis-Moore hypothesis) } I = W_1\left[-\log\left(\frac{FI}{N}\right)\right] + W_2\left[-\log\left(\frac{AP}{N}\right)\right]$$

where:
  FI = the number of positions in a social system that are defined by the members of that population as functionally important
  AP = the number of personnel available to fill positions defined as functionally important
  N = the size of the population in a social system
and where:

$$W_1 > W_2$$

More recently, Bernard Barber[4] has recognized that this principle is, in reality, a hypothesis about the distribution of prestige, primarily occupational prestige in more differentiated systems. My proposal is to build upon both the Davis-Moore hypothesis and Barber's "theory" of occupational prestige in an effort to state the general conditions under which C_{PR} increases, or decreases.

In equation (7.1), I have tried to specify some of the conditions influencing the concentration of prestige, or C_{PR}:

$$C_{PR} = f(N) \circ g(Po) \circ h(SK) \circ i(FI) \circ j(Mw) \qquad (7.1)$$

where:

N = the number of people in a society

Po = the number of people in status positions which are *perceived* by members of the society to carry high levels of power

SK = the number of people in status positions which are perceived by members of a society to carry high levels of skill

FI = the number of people in status positions which are perceived by members of a society to carry a high degree of functional importance

Mw = the number of people in status positions which are perceived by members of a society to bring a high level of material wealth

and where:

$$f(N) \gtrless g(Po) > h(SK) > i(FI) > j(Mw)$$

Propositions on the distribution of prestige must state why people give honor and esteem to some and not others. What properties must positions or persons possess in order to be perceived and acted upon as deserving prestige? My view, as expressed in equation (7.1) above, is that those positions in societal social systems that are perceived to carry power (Po), skill (SK), functional importance (FI), and material wealth (Mw) will be given prestige. As I say this, several points of clarification and qualification must immediately be emphasized. First, people's perceptions of power, wealth, functional importance, or skill need not be accurate; indeed, they are often inaccurate (and that is why Po and Mw are not given the same notation as in the last two chapters). Second, in order for prestige to be given to a position or a person, the position or person must possess high levels of $Po, SK, FI,$ or Mw. Third, for a person or position to be prestigious, there must be a large majority who agree in both their perception (however accurate or inaccurate) and their willingness to give honor and esteem. Fourth, for a person or position to be given high prestige, it must be perceived as possessing more than one attribute; that is, *Po, Mw, FI,* and *SK* alone do not result in high prestige. A person or position must have at least some combination of two of these attributes; and the more of these that a position or person is perceived to have, the greater its prestige. For example, if a position is seen as having high levels of *Po, Mw, SK,* and *FI,* it will have more prestige than one that has only three of these attributes. Fifth, as the weightings indicate, some of these attributes are more likely to produce prestige than others. People bestow the most prestige on those positions perceived to possess power (*Po*), followed, respectively, by positions perceived to involve skill (*SK*), functional importance (*FI*), or material wealth (*Mw*).

There are a number of interesting implications to the points above. First, people tend to think in terms of syndromes of attributes and are not willing to give high prestige to a position or person who has only one attribute. For example, holding material wealth in itself[5] will not bring high prestige; such *Mw* must be associated with *Po, SK,* or *FI.* Indeed, humans seek to determine "what else" is associated with any one attribute before developing the attitude or behavioral tendency to give esteem. Second, as I will explore at the end of the chapter, there are causal effects among these attributes. I suspect that since wealth is used to buy power, and vice versa, these two represent a distinct cluster of attributes. Similarly, since perceptions of skill are often associated with people's capacity to do difficult tasks that are also seen as functionally important, *SK* and *FI* constitute another perceptual cluster that individuals use for assigning prestige.

These considerations must be further qualified by introducing the last term in equation (7.1), *N* or the total number of people in a society. An emphasis on C_{PR} requires a concern with the total number of persons or positions receiving high prestige as a *proportion* of the total persons or positions. Thus, by introducing the term *N,* I am skewing the analysis to persons more than positions. This is done not so much for conceptual reasons as for convenience, since it is easier to visualize and measure population size than the total number of system positions. At any rate, questions revolving around C_{PR} pertain to the proportion of total persons in a society who receive prestige;

and the smaller the proportion, the greater the level of C_{PR}. With this last element from equation (7.1) in place, we can now attempt to develop a more precise statement, as is done in equation (7.1a):

$$C_{PR} = \left\{ W_1 \left[-\log\left(\frac{Po}{N}\right) \right] \times W_4 \left[\left(\frac{Mw}{N}\right)^{-\exp} \right] \right\}$$
$$+ \left\{ W_2 \left[\left(\frac{SK}{N}\right)^{-\exp} \right] \times W_3 \left[\left(\frac{FI}{N}\right)^{-\exp} \right] \right\} \quad (7.1a)$$

where:

$$W_1 > W_2 > W_3 > W_4$$

Equation (7.1a) states that the degree of concentration of prestige (C_{PR}) is a negative logarithmic function of the number of persons in positions as a proportion of all persons (N) who are perceived to possess power (Po), or Po/N, and a negative exponential function of the number of persons in positions as a proportion of all persons (N) who are perceived to possess skill (SK), functional importance (FI), and material wealth (Mw), or SK/N, FI/N, and Mw/N. Po/N and

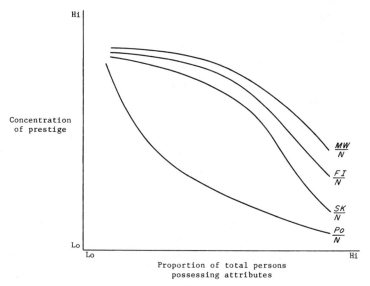

Figure 7.1 The Relationship Between C_{PR} and Each Explanatory Variable

Mw/N are seen as multiplicatively related in terms of their effects on C_{PR} for the reasons outlined above. Similarly, SK/N and FI/N are also multiplicatively related in the effects on C_{PR}. And the products of these two clusters are additively related in their effects on C_{PR}. In figure 7.1 the relationship of each variable to C_{PR} is delineated. Naturally figure 7.1 does not specify the relationships among the variables, but only the general nature of the relationship between each variable and C_{PR}. The exact slope for a particular empirical system will, of course, vary depending upon empirical circumstances, but I hypothesize that the form of the slopes will remain invariant.

The Elementary Principle Illustrated

In table 7.1 the data on the concentration of prestige in hunting and gathering, horticultural, agrarian, and industrial societies are summarized, albeit in an impressionistic way.[6] I have indicated the positions given prestige in terms of perceived power, skill, functional importance, and material wealth (again, whether these perceptions are accurate is not important). As I discuss each of these, I will give some indication of the number of people in these positions and the level of prestige given to persons in these positions.

By reading across the top row of table 7.1, the moderate concentration of prestige for hunters and gatherers can be understood. Prestige is given to skilled hunters and those believed to be capable of making contact with supernatural forces; and while this is the only real source of inequality in these societies, the intensity of the honor bestowed, and the deference behavior associated with prestige, is only moderate. In contrast, simple horticulturalists give considerable honor to their chief, kinship heads, shaman, and successful warriors; and they bestow moderate levels of prestige on certain craft specialists. Thus, the number of positions, and people in them, that receive prestige and deference increases, but so does the size of the population—thereby increasing concentration over what is typically the case among hunters and gatherers. Several positions are seen to have power: the chief, leaders of kin groups, and the leaders of warriors. In addition to these positions, the shaman and craft specialists will also be accorded prestige because of their skill. While all adults are typically viewed as functionally important, the chief, skilled warriors, and shaman will be accorded additional prestige because they are seen as more functionally important than others. The chief, shaman, and perhaps leaders of warriors and kin groups will possess wealth, but the chief is the most likely to hoard material wealth. Yet, he must give much of it away to those from whom it was extracted in order to gain prestige. Thus, simple horticulturalists bestow prestige on more positions and on considerably more people who occupy these positions than do hunters and gatherers; and they bestow greater levels of esteem, particularly for those who possess power and skill, although in some systems there is a strong redistributive ritual involving the giving away of material wealth to gain prestige.

Advanced horticulturalists bestow high levels of prestige on the king, his court, local headmen, and leaders in the military, religious hierarchy, and administrative system. While merchants/traders, some crafts, and the emerging engineering specialists receive some prestige, they do not enjoy so much as the above-mentioned positions. The king receives the most prestige because of his power; local headmen and high-ranking warriors receive prestige because they hold power by virtue of executing the king's orders. Moderate levels of prestige are given to administrative, craft, engineering, and military roles in terms of their skills; whereas religious leaders receive high prestige (and at times power and wealth) because of their imputed skills. Many positions are seen as functionally important, and hence the prestige accorded them is somewhat diluted. Yet, the king, his administrative staff, the military, heads of kin groups and/or local headmen, religious practitioners, craft specialists, merchants/traders, and engineers are all seen as particularly important. While the normal economic tasks of the society—planting, herding, domestication—are obviously seen as important, the fact that most societal members can perform them, or at least many can, mitigates against people's perception of their importance. In terms of material wealth, the king as well as his court of kin, wives, advisers, orators, and the like enjoy considerable material privilege and prestige *if* they are "generous" and give at least some of their wealth away. Religious leaders and military leaders, as well as local headmen and successful merchants,

Table 7.1 The Concentration of Prestige (C_{PR}) in Different Types of Societies

	C_{PR}	Po	SK	FI	Mw
Hunting and gathering societies	*Moderate:* informal headmen and shaman are given prestige in societies ranging in size from 30 to 100	no positions are perceived to possess power	exceptional hunters, shaman, headman	all adult roles are perceived to be functionally important	no positions are seen to command wealth
Simple horticultural societies	*Moderate to High:* chief, shaman, great warriors, kin-group heads, and certain craft specialists possess prestige in societies ranging in size from 200 to 2,000	chief, kin-group heads, leaders of warriors	chief, shaman, some warriors, craft specialists	all adult roles are perceived as functionally important, but chief, warriors, and shaman seen as more important than others	chief, shaman, successful warriors, kinship heads have wealth, but must give it away to gain prestige
Advanced horticultural societies	*High:* king, his court and family; religious, military, and administrative leaders; and local headmen in a population ranging from 500 to 100,000	king, local headmen, high-ranking military and administrators	some administrative, religious, and military positions; some crafts; some engineers	king; the king's staff of administrators, warriors, engineers; religious practitioners; some crafts; kin-group heads; some merchants/traders; local headmen	king and his court; high-ranking military and religious leaders; local headmen; successful merchants/traders; yet, those with wealth must be "generous" and give away some of the wealth to receive high prestige

Agrarian societies	*Very High:* monarch and his court, royal family; high-level administrative, military, and religious leaders; local lords; city mayors and town headmen; and affluent merchants/traders in societies ranging in size from 100,000 to many millions	monarch; high-ranking military, religious, and administrative officers; court officials; local lords; important merchants/traders	craft specialists; merchants; engineers; religious priests; some warriors/soldiers; some civil administrators; court judges	religious priests, military personnel, engineers, literate administrators of the monarch; the monarch; local lords; some craft personnel; some merchants; judges in courts	monarch and his court and royal family; high-ranking priests, military, and administrators; local lords and mayors; successful merchants; high-ranking judiciary
Industrial societies	*Moderate to High:* high-level governmental, religious, corporate, union, professional association, and military personnel; high-skill professions; and successful businessmen/women in societies ranging from 1 million to many millions	chief executive, regional and local executives; legislators; court officials; high-level military and administrative leaders; leaders of large corporations, unions, and associations	virtually all of the many professions and apprentice crafts seen as skilled	most professions and apprentice crafts seen as functionally important; key political and religious positions seen as functionally important	some positions in most professions; some small businesses; executives in large corporations, unions, and associations; some speculators and brokers; and varieties of "public figures"

also enjoy prestige associated with their wealth; and although they are also required to be "generous," they perceive less of a redistributive obligation than the king. Thus, while more positions and individuals in these positions receive prestige in advanced than in simple horticultural societies, the population base is much larger in advanced systems, with the result that prestige is usually much more concentrated.

Agrarian societies reveal even greater concentrations of prestige than advanced horticulturalists. The monarch and his court of advisers as well as the royal family enjoy enormous prestige; and high-level administrators, judicial officers of the courts, religious officials, and military officers receive almost as much prestige as the king. Local lords, city mayors, and affluent merchants/traders also enjoy considerable prestige. The monarch, religious leaders, high-ranking military, top administrators, and high judicial officials have much power, and hence much of their prestige comes from their perceived power. Similarly, but to a lesser degree, local lords and successful merchants/traders receive prestige because of their powers. A large number of individuals—craft personnel, merchants, engineers, church and military officers, bureaucrats, and court personnel receive prestige as a result of special skills. In fact, it is in agrarian societies that one can observe what becomes a paramount feature of industrial systems: the bestowing of prestige on a wide variety of skilled specialists. In terms of perceived functional importance, the same positions and individuals in these positions as in advanced horticultural systems receive prestige, although some new positions, such as officers of the judiciary and local lords, emerge in agrarian societies and are also accorded prestige because of their perceived importance. In agrarian systems, the hoarding of great material wealth by the monarch, his court, and high-ranking administrative and military officers is not always a source of prestige, as resentments against conspicuous materialistic displays without a compensating redistributive ethic begin to build. Other wealthy individuals—priests, merchants/traders, local lords and mayors—similarly become targets of resentment. Thus, in agrarian societies, the concentration of wealth becomes a potential source of tension, unless it is defined by the population as emanating from special skills and/or functional importance. Those who enjoy wealth and whose positions are seen by the population as highly skilled and functionally important can achieve some increase in prestige by virtue of their wealth, but if there is the perception that the wealthy are not skilled or functionally important, their wealth aggravates the existing tensions in the society. In sum, then, agrarian societies evidence very high concentrations of prestige, especially since the population base of the society is so great. But these societies also evidence severe tensions between, on the one hand, the masses, most of whom receive no prestige whatsoever and some of whom are stigmatized (beggars, the crippled, poor, etc.), and the more affluent and powerful sectors of the society on the other hand. In these societies, there may be public deference to elites but it often stems from fear rather than from the bestowal of esteem. And as esteem is withdrawn, one of the forces making power and privilege seem legitimate is destroyed, often setting the stage for societal revolution.

Industrial systems reveal less concentration of prestige, primarily because a more democratic system creates multiple centers of power and because an industrial economy generates a highly differentiated and skilled work force. Moreover, many more positions than in agrarian systems reveal high levels of interdependence and are seen as functionally important. And because an industrial economy extends the level of affluence to more people, or at least the perception of affluence, many more individuals can enjoy prestige because of their consumption patterns and the perceived material wealth that consumption is assumed to mark. The result is that many individuals can lay claim to prestige, since they are defined as powerful, skilled, functionally important, or wealthy.

In fact, the dispersion of prestige represents, in many ways, a compensation for the inequalities in wealth and power that exist in industrial systems. In contrast, agrarian systems tend to concentrate all valued resources—power, prestige, and wealth—and it is for this reason that they evidence considerable revolutionary conflict. Horticultural systems concentrate prestige, but much of this concentration is generated by a redistribution of some of the material wealth—thereby diffusing, somewhat, potential tensions.

In figure 7.2, I have sought to portray the relative relationships among Po/N, SK/N, FI/N, and Mw/N on C_{PR} during societal evolu-

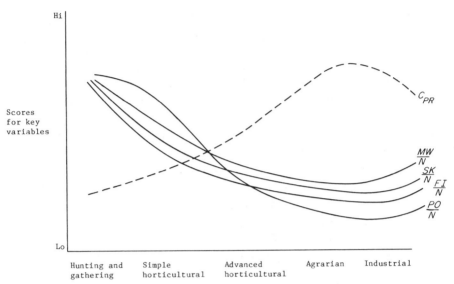

Figure 7.2 Relationships Among Critical Variables for C_{PR} During Societal Evolution

tion. This figure is more complicated than its predecessors in the previous chapters, because it deals with proportions of persons/positions perceived to possess *Po, Mw, SK, FI*. Thus, as the proportion of persons decreases, C_{PR} increases. In interpreting figure 7.2, it is important to remember that while the absolute number of persons/positions perceived as having *Po, SK, FI,* or *Mw* increases during initial societal evolution, their proportion of the ever-increasing size of the population (*N*) often decreases. Hence, C_{PR} increases up to and through an agrarian stage of evolution, and then with industrialization there appears to be a decrease in C_{PR} as the proportion of positions with perceived *Po, Mw, SK,* and *FI* increases somewhat under the impact of occupational specialization.

Implications for a More General View of Social Organization

As I stated earlier, prestige is a different kind of resource from material wealth or power. In having an important attitudinal component and in being the result of people's perceptions about *Po, SK, FI,* and *Mw,* it is less embedded in social structural arrangements than power and material wealth. I am not arguing that power and wealth do not have an attitudinal and perceptual base; indeed, what is defined as wealth or power is intimately related to people's attitudes and perceptions. Yet, even having said this, I would still argue that the distribution of prestige is more of a social psychological process than is the distribution of wealth or power.

Causal Effects Among the Explanatory Variables

These considerations pose analytical problems in discussing the more general organizational implications of prestige. This is especially true when analyzing the causal effects among the variables in equation (7.1a), as is evident in the causal model presented in figure 7.3.

There is clearly a causal effect, as I argued earlier, between *Po* and *Mw* in that people tend to perceive these as occurring together. People who are perceived to have wealth are likely to be viewed, and for good reasons (see figure 5.1), as having power, and vice versa. Similarly, *SK* and *FI* interact, in that perceived skill is partially de-

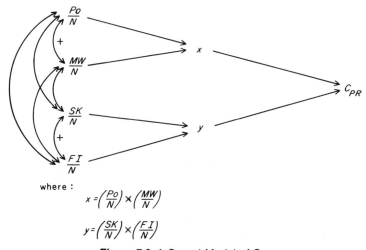

where :

$$x = \left(\frac{Po}{N}\right) \times \left(\frac{MW}{N}\right)$$

$$y = \left(\frac{SK}{N}\right) \times \left(\frac{FI}{N}\right)$$

Figure 7.3 A Causal Model of C_{PR}

fined in terms of perceptions of how functionally important a position is, and vice versa. Yet, for the other relations among variables presented in figure 7.3, it is not clear just what causal effects, if any, prevail. The causal model alerts us to potential effects, but I cannot specify what these are and how they operate. Thus, the model presents us with areas for further analytical and empirical work.

Variations in the Explanatory Variables

Turning to the question of what forces are related to variations in each of the explanatory variables in equation (7.1a) and the causal model, there is at least some possibility of beginning to anchor these variables in social structural processes. For in asking, what conditions are related to variations in Po/N, SK/N, FI/N, and Mw/N, we can begin to develop equations that have structural variables.

PERCEPTIONS OF POWER AND SOCIAL ORGANIZATION. People's perceptions on the existence of power are typically realistic, primarily because their daily routines are affected by those with power. The exact locus of power may be somewhat misperceived, as will the persons or positions with the most power; but people's general sense about the existence of control is rarely inaccurate. Sociologists have, I think, believed too readily rhetoric about "false consciousness" and have assumed people to be more naive than they actually are. Thus, in asking what forces affect the proportion of positions/persons perceived to have power, we can develop an equation like the one below:

$$\frac{Po}{N} = h(C_{Po}) \tag{7.2}$$

The perception of power is related to the actual existence of power; and the proportion of positions perceived to have power will be an inverse function of the degree of concentration of power. At least this is one place to begin theorizing about the conditions producing Po/N.

PERCEPTIONS OF MATERIAL WEALTH AND SOCIAL ORGANIZATION. Perceptions of material wealth, like those of power, are related to the concentration of wealth. In systems with highly concentrated wealth, people's perceptions of wealth persons will be more accurate than in systems where wealth is sufficiently dispersed so that people can purchase symbols of wealth. Thus, in a general way, the proportion of positions/persons who are perceived to have wealth is related to the actual concentration of wealth. That is,

$$\frac{Mw}{N} = h(C_{MW}) \tag{7.3}$$

Mw/N is an inverse function of the level of C_{MW}. The more concentrated the wealth, the smaller the proportion of people/positions perceived to possess wealth. In beginning with this equation, we might want to add the effects of C_{PO} or its Marxian variant C_{IM},[8] but for the present, I sense that an emphasis on C_{MW} is probably the best place to begin theoretical activity.

PERCEPTIONS OF SKILL AND SOCIAL ORGANIZATION. The possession of qualities defined as "skillful" is an important resource in all social systems. In systems where a labor market exists, skills can be translated into material wealth (this might represent one process connecting SK and Mw in the model presented in figure 7.3).Equally important, the perception of skill brings its holder prestige, which can often be used as compensation for a lack of power or wealth. Just what forces affect the proportion of people/positions seen to possess skill is difficult to determine, however. In equation (7.4), I offer a few tentative ideas:

$$\frac{SK}{N} = h(NO \circ i(DF_P) \circ (P) \tag{7.4}$$

In equation (7.4), I argued that the proportion of people perceived to have skill is a function of the number of organizational subunits (NO), the degree of differentiation of productive roles (DF_P), and the overall level of productivity (P). That is, the more organizational subunits in a society, the more differentiated production; the greater the level of production, the more specialized people's roles, the greater the levels of training required for some roles, and hence the more opportunities to be perceived as possessing skill. I suspect that, in addition to the obvious causal effects among these variables, the relations between SK/N, on the one hand, and NO, DF_P, and P, on the other, are exponential, because it is only with a large number of organizations, high degrees of differentiation, and high levels of productivity that the creation of new roles defined as skilled exceeds the corresponding increases in population size (N). Thus, while the absolute number of persons/positions seen as skilled increases during societal evolution, this increase does not begin to exceed the corresponding increase in the population base until the industrial stage of development begins.

PERCEPTIONS OF FUNCTIONAL IMPORTANCE AND SOCIAL ORGANIZATION. The perception that one is functionally important, like the perception of skill, is inherently rewarding. But it is also rewarding because it brings prestige. The proportion of people who are defined as functionally important may reveal a curvilinear pattern during societal evolution. In systems with little specialization, most persons and roles are defined as important; but as systems become increasingly differentiated, only some roles are defined as functionally important, with the large "masses" seen as expendable and interchangeable. The result is that FI/N decreases. Yet, as differentiation continues, there is more functional interdependence among a greater number of specialized roles, with the result that more positions and persons will be defined as functionally important. Hence, FI/N increases. Thus, it seems reasonable to initiate theoretical activity in the following way:

$$\frac{FI}{N} = h(DF_P) \tag{7.5}$$

In looking back on the model in figure 7.3 and on equations (7.2) through (7.5), I must admit to a certain dissatisfaction. As I stressed earlier, it is in "working with" a concept like prestige that we can develop a better understanding of its properties and dynamics. The model and equations provide some theoretical leads, but I am not sure just how important they are. My guess is that those presented in the previous two chapters are more significant in understanding general organizational processes in societies.

Inequality: An Overview of the Concentration of Material Wealth, the Concentration of Power, the Concentration of Prestige

In the last three chapters, distributive processes have been examined. These have been viewed as the unequal distribution of valued resources, or inequality (I). More specifically, I have conceptualized inequality (I) as the sum of the degree of concentration (C) in material wealth (MW), power (PO), and prestige (PR); that is, $I = W_1(C_{MW}) + W_2(C_{PO}) + W_3(C_{PR})$, where $W_1 > W_2 > W_3$. As was argued in chapter 4, these weightings of the resources are generally correct for societal social systems, but the weighting of prestige presents a contradiction in that it is a more important resource in very small social systems where material wealth and power are not evident. Thus, prestige will be more critical in hunting and gathering societies than either power or material wealth, if only by default (since wealth and power do not exist in great quantities).

This fact raises another interesting question: with the exception of the above, are there patterns in the *relative* importance of C_{MW},

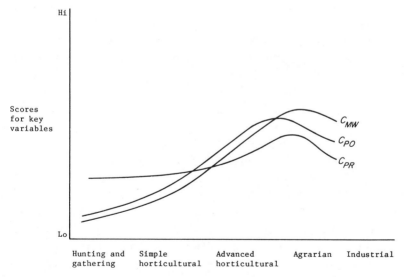

Figure 7.4 Patterns in the Relative Concentration of Wealth, Power, and Prestige

C_{PO}, and C_{PR} during societal evolution? Assuming the relative weightings to be correct, is there variation in divergence or convergence of these resources in hunting and gathering societies, simple and advanced horticultural systems, agrarian societies, and industrial systems? Figure 7.4 represents an effort to estimate the patterning in the relative concentration of wealth, power, and prestige.

The general shape of these curves conforms to the pattern found by Lenski[9] in his survey on inequality in hunting and gathering, simple and advanced horticultural, agrarian, and industrial societies. But unlike Lenski, I have plotted the concentration of not only material wealth, but also prestige and power. In this way we can see the *relative* degree of concentration in each. Of course such a figure tells us little about the correlation among *MW, PO,* and *PR,* since we do not know from figure 7.4 if the same positions and persons hoard *MW,* wield *PO,* and receive *PR.* Moreover, it does not assess the weights of these resources in terms of their impact on the dynamics of a society. Yet, figure 7.4 does have interesting implications. The concentration of material wealth and power increases in a parallel manner until an agrarian stage of development is evident; then, as a society industrializes, the respective concentrations decrease, with power decreasing more than wealth in democratic societies. Compared to material wealth and power, prestige is more highly concentrated in hunting and gathering and perhaps very simple horticultural systems. This is so in hunting and gathering societies because material wealth and power hardly exist, with prestige being the only resource that can be unequally distributed. In horticultural systems, much material wealth is redistributed by those who have the power to extract it, bringing them great prestige. But with an agrarian system, we can observe the use of concentrated power to hoard wealth, and as I observed earlier, the resentments that this generates often lowers the prestige of those who use their power to retain wealth. With industrialization, power becomes more pluralistic with democratization, whereas prestige becomes more diffuse because power, skill, and the illusion of functional importance and wealth are spread across more occupations and organizations. Wealth also declines in concentration, but not so dramatically as power and prestige (although the illusion of less concentrated wealth exists because people can use expanded credit systems to buy many material symbols of wealth). Thus, while the general pattern in the distribution of *MW, PO,* and *PR* is the same, their relative concentrations vary in different types of societies. Many of the internal dynamics of a society will be greatly influenced by the relative concentrations of these resources, and hence, an analysis of C_{MW}, C_{PO}, and C_{PR} in any society must attempt to examine this relative concentration. At this juncture, I will not conduct such an analysis, but merely indicate its potential for furthering our understanding of distributive processes in societies.

Chapter Eight THE FORMATION
OF
SUBPOPULATIONS

What Is Social Class?

One of the most ambiguous sets of concepts in sociological theory includes the labels "class" and "social class," "stratum,"
"rank," and similar designations. The general metaphor of such terms
is sufficiently clear; that is, one can conceptualize most societies as
composed of subgroups and subpopulations that can be rank-ordered
in terms of their resources and that, as a result, differ from each other
in terms of such matters as values, beliefs, behaviors, and overall
life-style. As far as this formulation goes, there is little disagreement.
Yet, the following comments by Randall Collins[1] suggest that even
on these matters, there are dissenting voices:

> Our prominent images of stratification share the propensity to cloud our
> eyes with reifications. Stratification is seen as a ladder of success, as a
> hierarchy of geological layers, as a pyramid . . . but this is not what
> a human society *looks like*. What it looks like . . . is nothing more
> than people in houses, buildings, automobiles, streets—some of whom
> give orders, get deference, hold material property, talk about particular
> subjects, and so on.

Yet, Collins is certainly in the minority. For most sociologists societies can be visualized, for some purposes of analysis, as composed
as hierarchical layers. But as soon as other issues are introduced to
discussions, then some of sociology's most acrimonious debates
emerge. Below, I have listed some of these additional issues:

Is "class" a multidimensional property so that one can observe different class systems for various dimensions of inequality, such as power, wealth, and prestige?

Is "class" an economic force, determined solely by people's relationship to the means of production? (or some other major property of the world— e.g., values, power, etc.).

How many "classes" are there in _____ (fill in a general type, or a specific society?

Are "class boundaries" clear in _____ (fill in a general type, or a specific) society?

Is a "classless" society possible? (Desirable?)

Are "classes" inherently antagonistic?

Is there a "power elite" in all societies that controls the activities of most people?

Such a list could consume several pages. My point is to emphasize that the concept of "class" (or alternatively, "social class," "rank," "stratum") is filled with conceptual ambiguities and ideological overtones. It is a subject for debate, moral preachings, concept-mongering, and a host of less worthy intellectual activities. Yet, despite its ambiguity, it is a central idea in theorizing about stratification processes.

As I stated in chapter 4, the notions of class and stratum denote a number of discrete processes; and one of the reasons behind the conceptual and empirical debates over these ideas is that different theorists emphasize, sometimes only implicitly, varying social processes. For example, some stress the "causes of" classes; others address the life-style of already formed classes; still others stress the degree of inequality among classes; and some will emphasize the size, diversity, boundedness, scope, or one particular property of classes.

In this and the next chapter, I will draw upon the many insights that have emerged from diverse efforts to understand social class processes. But I will seek to reconceptualize the concept of "class." This will not be a dramatic reconceptualization but it will, I hope, redirect our thinking about this property of societal social systems. As I discussed earlier in chapter 4, "social class" is not a unitary phenomenon. It is a label that sociologists give to a number of discrete processes, two of which are the formation of differentiated and relatively homogeneous subpopulations (DF_{HO}) and the linear rank-ordering of these subpopulations (RA_{HO}). These two processes are viewed as variables in that any empirical system will evidence different degrees of DF_{HO} and RA_{HO}.

Redefining Social Class

I prefer not to use the term "social class," since it now carries so many diverse connotations. Realistically, however, the concept is so well engrained in the sociological imagination that it is wise to be explicit in terms of how I will use the concept of social class. Thus, despite my misgivings, I offer the following definition of social class (SC):

$$SC = W_1(DF_{HO}) + W_2(RA_{HO})$$

where:

$$W_1 > W_2$$

If the concept of social class is to have any meaning, it must denote the existence of subpopulations. For those who prefer an "economic" definition of class, reference to the equations that will be developed later clearly reveals the importance of economic forces in the differentiation of subpopulations. Social class also has a ranking dimension which, I feel, allows for the introduction of "cultural" variables, most notably values. Thus, to the extent some conceptualization of "class" is preferred, I visualize "social class" as a term that sociologists employ to describe the multiplicative and interactive effects of differentiation of homogeneous subpopulations and the ranking of these subpopulations. This definition probably does not please many; but since I am forced by sociological convention to employ the concept, the above definition is what I mean by "class," "social class," "stratum," "rank," and similar terms that denote the intersection of RA and DF processes.

In this chapter, an analysis of the differentiation of homogeneous subpopulations (DF_{HO}) will be undertaken. In the next chapter, the ranking of these subpopulations (RA_{HO}) will be examined. As can be recalled from chapter 4, the differentiation of homogeneous sub-populations, or DF_{HO}, is defined in the following way:

> DF_{HO} = the degree and extent to which subsets of members in a society reveal common behavioral tendencies and similar attitudes so that they can be distinguished from other subsets of members in a society

This definition still reveals a number of ambiguities which, at the very least, should be mentioned. First, it does not address very clearly the issue of how many subsets of members need to be differentiated to have high degrees of DF_{HO}. Second, it does not specify which behaviors and what attitudes are critical to the conceptualization of homogeneity. In many ways, these are empirical issues that are re-solved by examining specific societal systems. Yet, it can also be argued that they are conceptual questions, and that is why I mention them here. For example, would a society with three homogeneous subpopulations highly differentiated from each other reveal a higher degree of DF_{HO} than one with two equally homogeneous subpopula-tions? Since one would expect the dynamics of these two systems to be different, the answer to this hypothetical question must be affir-mative. The conceptual problems come in assessing systems that re-veal different numbers of subpopulations and varying degrees of homogeneity within these subpopulations. For instance, one hypo-thetical society has six clearly differentiated subpopulations that re-veal somewhat less homogeneity than the four subpopulations of an-other society. Which of these hypothetical societies evidences more DF_{HO}? My answer is the latter, which indicates that homogeneity of subpopulations will be given more weight in this analysis than the number of subpopulations. This weighting does not completely re-move the ambiguities in the definition of DF_{HO}, but it does help sig-nal the general thrust of my analysis.

Armed with the above definition, we may begin the theoretical task of trying to specify at an abstract level those generic properties of the universe that are related to DF_{HO}. And as was the case in previous chapters, we need to specify, as best we can, some of the underlying causal processes that connect these generic properties to DF_{HO}.

An Elementary Principle on the Differentiation of Homogeneous Subpopulations

In equation (8.1), an initial formulation of those forces related to DF_{HO} is provided:

$$DF_{HO} = f(N) \circ g(I) \circ h(D) \circ i(DF_P) \circ j(MO) \qquad (8.1)$$

where:

N = the total number of people in a society

I = the degree of inequality in the distribution of rewards

D = the rate and intensity of discriminatory actions in a society against selected minority populations

DF_P = the degree of differentiation of productive positions in a society

MO = the movement of individuals or collectivities from one subpopulation to another (see chapter 10)

and where:

$$f(N) \gtrapprox g(I) > h(D) > i(DF_P) > (MO)$$

As Spencer[2] and Durkheim[3] argued a century ago, there is a basic relationship between social differentiation (DF) and population size (N). Part of this relationship is purely mathematical, in that a small population cannot be divided into as many subunits as a large one. But there are also substantive lines of argument: (1) differentiation of productive and political activities is necessary to sustain and control larger populations; (2) differentiation of larger populations will result from the increasing difficulty of sustaining high rates of face-to-face interaction as the number of interacting parties increases; (3) differentiation of larger populations will ensue from the increasing difficulty of maintaining physical proximity of individuals as their numbers increase. Thus, certainly one of the driving forces behind differentiation is population size.

In figure 8.1, I have attempted to portray the causal processes underlying the relationship between DF and N. While this diagram

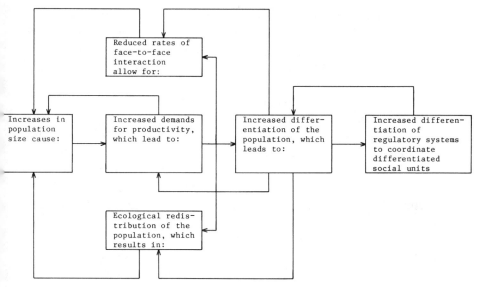

Figure 8.1 Population Size (*N*) and Differentiation (*DF*)

appears complicated, it denotes only the most general direct, indirect, and feedback relationships among properties of the social universe. Increases in population size decrease the rates of face-to-face interaction, escalate demands for productivity, and force ecological redistribution which, in turn, cause differentiation of the population in terms of interaction styles, productive activities, and living space. Increased differentiation creates severe problems of coordination and control which lead to the development of regulatory systems (and hence, C_{PO}). There is a series of feedback processes involved in these causal relations. Once rates of face-to-face interaction are reduced, a source of resistance to population growth (that is, people's desire to maintain "communitas") is weakened. As productivity increases, a larger population can be supported. And as people become willing to be mobile and to relocate, they also become able and willing to accommodate increases in their numbers through further relocation. Increased differentiation of the population also operates as positive feedback on these processes and on the capacity for a population to grow. For once the population is differentiated by productive activity, location, and interaction patterns, there is greater capacity to organize a larger population, especially if this differentiated population can be controlled and coordinated by well-developed regulatory systems.

Although population size may increase the degree of social differentiation (DF), it does not account for the degree of homogeneity (HO) of differentiated social units. For our concern is not just with differentiation but also with those forces related to the creation of homogeneous subpopulations. This point of emphasis requires isolating those forces that are related to increasing not just differentiation but also homogeneity of differentiated subpopulations. Inequality (I) is certainly one such force, since when people possess varying levels of resources their perceptions and actions will differ. For depending on the level and configuration of people's resources, they are able to do some things and not others.[4] And those with similar levels of resources are likely to act in convergent ways. Hence, a high degree of inequality in the distribution of resources assures that there will be differences in people's shares of resources; and those with similar shares are, in general, likely to be similar in their attitudes and modal behaviors.

Another condition fostering homogeneity in subpopulations is discrimination, for when selected members of a society are consistently subject to discrimination (D), they are likely to be excluded from certain positions and forced into a relatively narrow range of productive roles, thereby differentiating them from others while at the same time forcing a convergence of attitudes and behaviors. Moreover, victims of discrimination are likely to band together as a way of insulating themselves from the abuses of discrimination, with the result that as their rates of interaction increase they become more alike in outlook and behavior, which, in turn, makes them easier targets of discrimination. In addition, discrimination usually limits people's access to resources; and this tendency reinforces those processes by which inequality operates to increase homogeneity. Thus, a society in which there are high levels of discrimination against identifiable targets will evidence homogeneity in the attitudes and behaviors of those subject to such discrimination. These processes are outlined in more detail in figure 8.2.

In figure 8.2, I have summarized some of the direct, indirect,

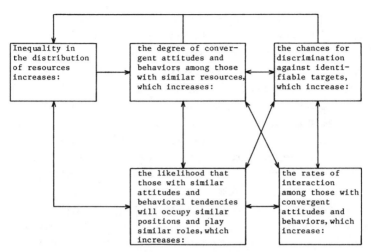

Figure 8.2 The Relationship Between Inequality (*I*), Discrimination (*D*), and Subpopulation Homogeneity (*DF*$_{HO}$)

and feedback relations among DF_{HO}, *I,* and D. Inequality creates pressures for convergent attitudes and behaviors among those with similar resources; in turn, such convergence increases the likelihood that those with similar resources will occupy similar positions and interact frequently, which, as a result, feeds back and furthers their convergence in attitudes and behaviors. Discrimination simply intensifies and accelerates these processes by increasing rates of interaction, incumbency in similar positions, and convergence of attitudes and behaviors, all of which make selected subpopulations easier targets of discrimination. These homogenizing processes operate to increase inequalities by stratifying the distribution of attributes and resources necessary to gain power, wealth, and prestige.

Differentiation of productive positions (DF_P) is another force creating homogeneity. When individuals' basic roles are distinctive, they are likely to develop common outlooks, because (a) their experiences are similar, (b) their rates of interaction are high, and (c) their shares of resources converge. Moreover, if these roles are separated in time and space, there are further pressures for the convergence of attitudes and behaviors. For when people are separated from other groups in time and region, especially when performing their major income-producing roles, they are likely to develop a common perspective and to engage in modal behaviors that distinguish them from others. These processes can be seen as a special case of those forces diagramed in the middle portions of figure 8.1 and the lower portions of figure 8.2, but in the interests of clarity I have also presented them in figure 8.3. Once people are differentiated in their productive roles, they are likely to: (a) be separated in time and space, (b) reveal high rates of interaction, and (c) be targets of discrimination. In turn, (a), (b), and (c) are mutually reinforcing on each other and on DF_P.

The rate of mobility in a society greatly influences the degree of homogeneity within a differentiated subpopulation. As people move from one subpopulation to another, they increase their rates of interaction with diverse peoples. They carry with them old attitudes and behavioral styles, but they also adopt those of the new subpopulations that they join. The result of these "mixing processes" is for homogeneity to decline when rates of mobility are high. These processes are delineated in figure 8.4. Especially interesting, as will be explored in chapter 10, are the feedback effects of decreasing homogeneity on mobility. For as homogeneity declines, subgroups present less hostile barriers and are less likely to dscriminate against those who would enter. And once this positive cycle is initiated, mobility

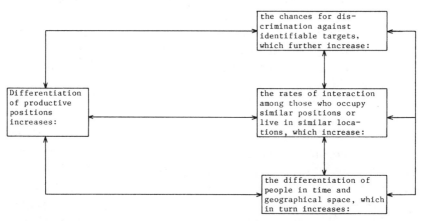

Figure 8.3 The Relationship Between Differentiation of Productive (DF_P) Positions and Subpopulation Homogeneity (DF_{HO})

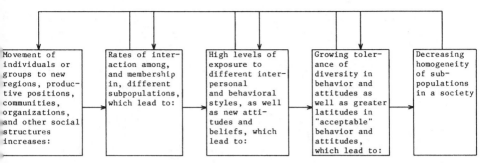

Movement of individuals or groups to new regions, productive positions, communities, organizations, and other social structures increases:	Rates of interaction among, and membership in, different subpopulations, which lead to:	High levels of exposure to different interpersonal and behavioral styles, as well as new attitudes and beliefs, which lead to:	Growing tolerance of diversity in behavior and attitudes as well as greater latitudes in "acceptable" behavior and attitudes, which lead to:	Decreasing homogeneity of subpopulations in a society

Figure 8.4 Social Mobility (*MO*) and Subpopulation Formation (*DF_{HO}*)

operates to decrease homogeneity of subpopulations, while decreases in homogeneity encourage greater mobility.

The weightings of the variables in equation (8.1) follow from my comments above. Population size (*N*) is an important *initial* force, in that population must become sufficiently large to be differentiated. But after a certain size is reached, inequality (*I*) becomes equally important, since differentiated subpopulations will develop internal homogeneity only as their shares of resources converge. Discrimination (*D*) is next most critical, since it forces a convergence of productive activities and resources of its victims and escalates their rates of interaction. Differentiation of productive activities in a society (*DF_P*) is also a critical force generating homogeneity, but less so than discrimination (although it increases opportunities for discrimination). The separation of work activities divides a population in terms of experiences, access to resources, and opportunities for interaction; but, at the same time, it creates for those in similar positions common experiences, similar levels of access to resources, and increased opportunities for interaction. As a result, those in similar productive positions are likely to converge in their attitudes and behaviors. These tendencies are reinforced if productive activities are also differentiated in time and space. However, these processes of occupational endogamy can be counteracted to the extent that a population can be mobile from region to region, group to group, occupation to occupation, and community to community.

These considerations, then, led to my initial formulation of the processes involved in the differentiation of subpopulations in a society. The next step, in accordance with the theory-building strategy outlined in chapter 2, is to specify more clearly the relations among these properties as well as their relations to the central variable, DF_{HO}. Equation (8.1a) provides this additional specification:

$$DF_{HO} = \left\{ W_1\left[\log(N)\right] \times W_4(DF_P{}^{\exp}) \times W_5(MO^{-\exp}) \right\}$$
$$+ \left\{ W_2(I^{\exp}) \times W_3\left[\log(D)\right] \right\} \qquad (8.1a)$$

where:

$$W_1 \gtrless W_2 > W_3 > W_4 > W_5$$

In this equation, I have indicated some of the relationships between DF_{HO}, on the one hand, and N, I, D, DF_P and MO, on the other, as well as some of the relations among N, I, D, DF_P, and MO as they affect DF_{HO}. The weightings in equation (8.1a) indicate that the size of the population (N) is a most critical initial influence on DF_{HO}, equaled subsequently by inequality (I). Discrimination (D), the differentiation of productive roles (DF_P), and rates of mobility (MO) follow, respectively, the influence of N and I. Each variable will, by itself, promote an increase in DF_{HO}, but the weightings stress which will be most critical. The relationship between DF_{HO} and N is logarithmic, in that initial increases in population size have more influence on the differentiation of homogeneous populations than later increases in N. The relationship between I and DF_{HO} is exponential because initial increases in inequality have less influence on DF_{HO} than additional increases in I. The connection between D and DF_{HO} is logarithmic because initial levels of discrimination immediately force separation and isolation of victims; subsequent discriminatory actions institutionalize this initial differentiation, but less so than the initial acts of discrimination. The relation between DF_P and DF_{HO} is exponential in that early differentiation of productive roles leads to less differentiation of whole subpopulations than do subsequent increases in differentiation. The relationship between MO and DF_{HO} is negatively exponential in that initial increases in mobility rates have less impact in breaking down homogeneity than do subsequent increases. The relationships between DF_{HO} and each explanatory variable are portrayed in figure 8.5.

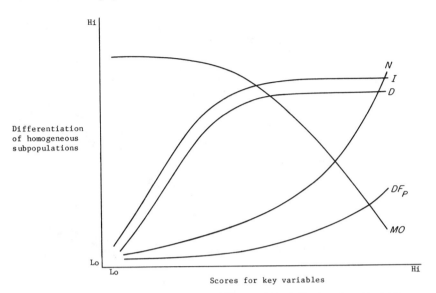

Figure 8.5 The Relationship Between DF_{HO} and Each Explanatory Variable

There are multiplicative relations between population size (N) and differentiation of productive roles (DF_P) in their effects on DF_{HO}. As is implicit in figures 8.1, 8.2, and 8.3, population size requires increased productivity that, along with other forces, is achieved by the differentiation of productive roles which, as production escalates, encourages the differentiation of homogeneous populations. There is also a multiplicative relation between N and DF_P, on the one hand, and MO on the other, in terms of their effects on DF_{HO}. Growing size and productivity often force movements of people that increase rates of interaction of diverse people, and hence, decrease DF_{HO}. Obviously, there are not just multiplicative but also mutually causal effects among these variables, but such effects will be discussed later. These multiplicative effects of N, DF_P, and MO on DF_{HO} stand, as a whole, in an additive relationship to I and D in their effects on DF_{HO}. In turn, inequality (I) and discrimination (D) are multiplicatively related in that increases in one will escalate the level of the other in its effect on DF_{HO}.

In sum, then, equation (8.1a) specifies some of the generic conditions that increase or decrease the degree of DF_{HO}. Figures 8.1 through 8.4 outline some of the crucial direct, indirect, and feedback causal processes that underlie the relationships presented in equation (8.1a). My goal has not been to review the subtlety of these processes but only to signal the general way that they are implicated in DF_{HO}. It is consideration of the general processes specified in figures 8.1 to 8.4 that led to my translation of equation (8.1) into (8.1a). My interpretation of these processes may, of course, be flawed; and if so, I invite others to rewrite the equations and causal models in ways that they feel better conform to the operative processes of the social universe.

The Elementary Principle Illustrated

As was done for the equations on inequality in the last three chapters, data on hunting and gathering, simple and advanced horticultural, agrarian, and industrial societies are arranged with respect to the critical variables in equation (8.1a).[5] Hunting and gathering societies evidence little homogeneity of subpopulations, primarily because they are too small to generate subpopulations that are distinct from kin groups or friendship cliques. Moreover, there is insufficient economic specialization of productive roles, inequality, and discrimination to encourage the differentiation of homogeneous subpopulations, even if the size of these societies is larger. High rates of territorial movement and the occasional mobility of families from band to band work to prevent subpopulation homogeneity within bands. Simple horticultural societies develop subpopulations that are coextensive with descent groupings (lineages, clans, moieties), villages, and regions. But aside from a sense of self-identity among kindred, village residents, and those in different regions, it is hard to visualize their homogeneity as distinguishing these subpopulations from each other. They behave in similar ways and hold convergent (if not the same) attitudes, primarily because differentiation of productive positions is not elaborate. And even distinct specialties, such as shaman or craftsman, are part time and thus do not separate individuals from their kin and village units. While political leaders, the council of elders and advisers, successful warriors, and shamans enjoy prestige, power, and some material wealth, they are not dramatically elevated above others. Moreover, since their numbers are small and they must also engage in many of the same productive activities as nonelites, they do not constitute a well-defined or homogeneous subpopulation. Only captured outsiders who are subject to discrimination can be viewed as a distinctive subpopulation, but their homogeneity is not necessarily high, since they may come from different areas and vary in terms of age, sex, and culture.

In advanced horticultural societies, increases in population size and the division of labor allow some degree of differentiation and homogeneity to emerge among groups of political and religious leaders. Some occupational specialties, especially if they are tied to a distinct region or village, can encourage the development of a distinct and homogeneous subpopulation, especially when mobility rates are low. For example, herding or fishing specialists might come to be quite homogeneous, although their distinctiveness can be mitigated by their integration into more inclusive descent groupings or by movement of individuals to and from these specialties. But slaves, by virtue of their increased numbers and their degraded status, become a clearly differentiated, and increasingly homogeneous, subpopulation.

In agrarian systems, distinct subpopulations with considerable internal homogeneity emerge. The political, religious, administrative, and military elite are clearly differentiated from the rest of the population, and to a great extent, from each other. Economic specialists—traders, merchants, and craft specialists—also become differentiated and homogeneous, especially when they discourage mobility by restricting access (through ascriptive guilds) into their specialties. Peasants and slaves are also distinctive; and if the society is sufficiently large in territory, or feudal in structure, considerable differentiation by region can occur, particularly if mobility is not encouraged. And if descent remains strong and organizes people's activities into clans or moieties (and thereby limits mobility), then the larger descent groups become differentiated into homogeneous subpopulations, especially if they exist in different regions or engage in specialized productive roles.

Table 8.1 The Degree of Subpopulation Homogeneity (DF_{HO}) in Different Types of Societies

	DF_{HO}	N	DF_P
Hunting and gathering societies	none	35 to 100	little: division by age/sex
Simple horticultural societies	homogeneity among descent groups, villages, and regions	200 to 2,000	little: division by age/sex. Some occupational specialties
Advanced horticultural societies	homogeneity among political and religious elite, as well as among villages, descent groups, and regions. Some homogeneity of economic specialties. Much homogeneity of slaves and conquered peoples, if they come from same culture/society	500 to 100,000	extensive: division by age/sex. Elaborate occupational specialization
Agrarian societies	unambiguous distinctions and homogeneity among political elites, religious elites, bureaucratic officials, traders/merchants, craft specialists, slaves, and peasants. Some homogeneity by region, town/village, and descent group, especially if system is feudal	100,000 to many million	extensive: division by age/sex. Vocations. Numerous specialized productive roles
Industrial societies	unambiguous distinctions among and convergence of behaviors and attitudes among nonmanual, manual, poverty, and ethnic/religious/nationality/racial subpopulations; clear but somewhat ambiguous distinctions among and convergence of behaviors and attitudes of political/economic elites, skilled professionals, routine nonmanual workers, craft manual, noncraft manual. Homogeneity by region and size of city	1 million to several hundred million	elaborate: division by age/sex, professions, vocations. Very extensive and elaborate division of specialized roles

I	D	MO
ery little; some inequalities in prestige	none	considerable; there are no ranks and subgroups to move in and out but populations move about a region and often divide and re-form
much inequality in terms of power and prestige; some inequality in material wealth, but often counteracted by a redistributive ethic	proto-slavery, discrimination by descent group, village	little; ascription by descent group and village
much inequality in terms of power, prestige, and material wealth. Some redistribution of material wealth	slavery, discrimination by descent group, village, region	little; ascription by descent group and village. Some opportunities for mobility in trades and religious specialties
enormous inequality of power, prestige, and material wealth	slavery, ethnicity, religion, and race are basis for discrimination. Some discrimination by guilds, occupational groups, descent groups, political rank, and regions	little to some; ascription by descent group, village, region, religious affiliation, and ethnicity; some opportunities in new productive specialties, the military, and the administrative bureaucracy of the emerging state
much inequality in material wealth. Somewhat less inequality in power and prestige	ethnicity, religion, and race basis for discrimination. Some discrimination between manual and nonmanual occupations. Some discrimination by family background, geographical region, and sector of economy	some to considerable; ascription by ethnicity/race and family background, but emphasis on educational credentials as the criterion for assuming specialized occupational roles greatly increases mobility

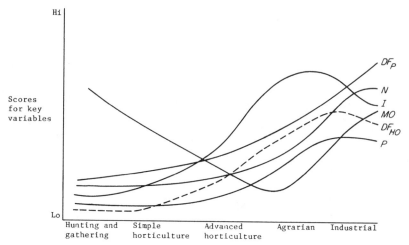

Figure 8.6 Relationships Among Critical Variables for DF_{HO} During Societal Evolution

Industrial systems develop large subpopulations among agricultural, unskilled manual, skilled manual, unskilled nonmanual, skilled nonmanual, elites, and the poverty sector. They also evidence racial/ethnic, sexual, and regional discrimination that creates some homogeneity in terms of these dimensions. The reasons for the development of these lines of differentiation reside in the large size of the population, coupled with high levels of differentiation of productive roles in time and space as well as with high levels of inequality and discrimination. But rates of mobility do increase as a result of the opportunities provided by DF_P, and as a result, homogeneity of most subpopulations decreases in comparison wth subpopulations in an agrarian system. These relationships among the key variables as they effect DF_{HO} during societal evolution are presented in figure 8.6.

Implications for a More General View
of Social Organization

As I have sought to do in the previous chapters, it is now appropriate to consider some of the more general organizational implications of equations (8.1) and (8.1a). As before, this will be done by examining some of the causal effects among the variables in the equations, and then exploring some of those generic conditions influencing the level for each of the variables in the equations.

Causal Effects Among the Explanatory Variables

In figure 8.7, a causal model stating the relations among the variables in equation (8.1a) is presented. Inequality is, as we saw in equation (5.1a), related to productivity, and hence, to DF_P. Increasing levels of I promote DF_P, and vice versa. For as societies become differentiated into diverse positions, the allocation of material wealth, power, and prestige also becomes differentiated in the pattern presented in the previous chapters. Population size (N) is strongly related to both DF_P and I, for without a comparatively large population its differentiation becomes problematic, in terms of either productive po-

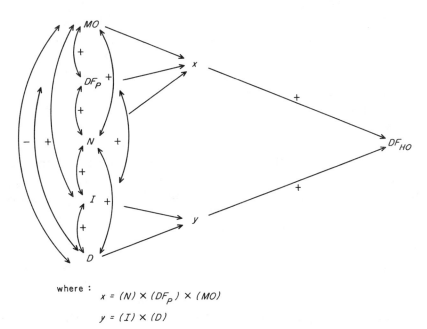

where :

$$x = (N) \times (DF_p) \times (MO)$$

$$y = (I) \times (D)$$

Figure 8.7 A Causal Model of DF_{HO}

sitions or shares of resources. But as is indicated in figure 8.1, such differentiation is often caused by growing N, since as populations expand, their support and organization become problematic and result in escalation and differentiation of productive activities (DF_P) which, in turn, cause greater degrees of I. Conversely, increased differentiation allows a population to grow even further.

Mobility (MO) and DF_P are positively related because new productive positions encourage mobility; and mobile people often create new positions. Mobility and population size (N) present an ambiguous picture. Growing populations often force mobility of members, who by necessity must seek new opportunities elsewhere. But in many societies, high rates of mobility often decrease family size, and over time, operate to decrease N. Mobility is negatively related to inequality, since mobility usually increases people's access to new resources, whereas inequality often operates as a barrier to mobility. Yet, at times, this negative relationship does not hold, as is best illustrated by urban "shanty towns" in much of the Third World where rural impoverishment has forced peasants to migrate to slums outside large cities. In general, mobility (MO) and discrimination (D) are negatively related, in that the movement of people will eventually make less visible or less salient those features used to discriminate. Yet, this pattern is far from ambiguous, since initial movements of distinctive individuals create intense discrimination by those receiving the mobile population. The resulting DF_{HO} of the mobile population is only broken down over a prolonged period of subsequent residential and occupational mobility.

Discrimination (D) also evidences complex direct and indirect relations with DF_P, I, and N. Once a population is sufficiently large to reveal DF_P and I, the variations in life-style (attitudes and behavioral tendencies) of people in different productive roles and with varying levels of resources become a basis for discriminatory actions. That is, before people can be the victims of discrimination, they must be identifiable targets. Biological characteristics are probably the most critical factors (e.g., sex, skin color, bodily configurations) in making individuals identifiable targets of discrimination, but cultural factors are also crucial; and ethnic differences tend to reflect patterns of differentiation in productive positions and shares of resources. Conversely, once target populations become victims of discrimination, they are confined to certain productive roles and are denied access to at least some scarce resources. And as a result, D operates to maintain or increase levels of DF_P and I.

Variations in the Explanatory Variables

As is immediately evident in considering the conditions influencing the levels of DF_P, I, N, D, and MO we have already discussed some of these conditions. Equations (5.1), (6.1), and (7.1) have presented the conditions under which I varies. Equation (5.2) has presented those forces related to P, and since P is highly correlated with DF_P, there is little new that we can say about DF_P, at least in the general terms that have guided the analysis in previous chapters. (More precise weightings and statements on the conditions influencing P can, of course, allow us to understand how these conditions increase or decrease DF_P, but that level of precision is beyond the scope of this book.) In contrast to DF_P and I, the other variables in equation (8.1) have not been discussed extensively.

Population size (N) is, to a great extent, the result of idiosyncratic empirical circumstances and not always an appropriate topic of theoretical analysis. Yet, we will consider below some of the general conditions related to population size (N). Discrimination (D) is a variable that has been the subject of a large amount of empirical and conceptual work, with the result that we are in a position to develop a preliminary theoretical principle. Similarly, mobility (MO) has been the subject of a large research literature, especially in the context of stratification. And in fact, the size of this literature and the tendency of sociologists to study mobility as a distinctive stratification process force us to analyze mobility separately in chapter 10. Before seeking to develop preliminary propositions on these variables, however, I should emphasize again the following point.

As we will see shortly and even more clearly in chapter 10, the same variables are beginning to reappear to set conditions for each other's operation. As will be recalled from chapter 2, this fact is explicitly incorporated into the strategy being proposed in this volume. There is a limited number of generic properties in the social universe; and thus, as we proceed to "wedge" our way further into more general organizational processes, it is not surprising that the number of principles that remain to be developed will progressively decrease.

POPULATION SIZE AND SOCIAL ORGANIZATION. As has been evident in this and the preceding chapters, population size (N) is a crucial social force, one which Herbert Spencer and Georg Simmel[6] originally emphasized and which only recently has reemerged in theoretical work.[7] It is important, then, to consider those generic conditions that effect the level of N. At the same time, however, it is also important to recognize the limitations in such an effort, for as I mentioned above, N is greatly influenced by the unique empirical and historical circumstances of a society and cannot always be a topic of theoretical inquiry.

Population size is, I suspect, positively related to productivity (P) and social differentiation (DF). The causal arrow in this relationship runs, as we have already observed, both ways. Increased levels of P are often necessary as N increases; but the reverse is also true. Escalating productivity enables populations to grow, whether by allowing people to support more offspring, by encouraging migration into a prosperous system, or by facilitating political and economic conquest of new territories.

Similarly, growing N causes increased differentiation DF, but the reverse relationship is also important to examine. Systems that increase their level of differentiation can support larger populations than when less differentiated. Thus, as systems differentiate into regions, subclans, strata, types of communities, and diverse organizational spheres, they create a "social skeleton," to use Spencer's analogy, that can support a larger "mass of tissues."

There are constraints on such expansion of a population. One is P, since there must exist the capacity to support a larger N. Another is C_{PO}, since without the capacity to control large masses and coordinate differentiated units, the system collapses and breaks down into smaller, autonomous population units. Yet another constraint is ecological space (ES), although this is not a powerful constraint in that the use of technologies (*TE*) to enhance *P* can allow large populations to support themselves in relatively small areas. A final important consideration is the value standards (*VS*) of a population, for systems vary in the extent to which these encourage population growth (VS_N) or discourage it (VS_{-N}).

Thus, if we are to consider those generic forces (as opposed to historically and empirically specific factors) that affect the size of a population, we could begin with the following proposition:

$$N = h(P) \circ i(DF) \circ j(ES) \circ k(VS_N) \tag{8.2}$$

DISCRIMINATION AND SOCIAL ORGANIZATION. While the specific "theories of" race and ethnic relations all differ somewhat in their details, focus, and points of emphasis, they all see the process of "discrimination" as a key force; and they all view discrimination against subpopulations as likely to increase under certain generic conditions. That is, discrimination is likely when: (1) the minority subpopulation can be a visible target for discriminatory acts by a majority or a minority with power; (2) the minority subject to discrimination is perceived as a threat (economic, political, social) to the well-being of the majority or powerful minority; and (3) the minority subpopulation can be made the victims of prejudicial attitudes, negative stereotypes, and stigmatizing beliefs.

With these insights, it is possible to develop an initial proposition on *D*. Discrimination cannot occur without differentiation (*DF*) of a subpopulation in terms of identifiable attributes. Thus, *DF,* particularly differentiation of people biologically or culturally, is a critical condition of *D*. Another critical force is the perception of threat (*PT*) by the majority population, or its powerful minority segments. And finally, the control and concentration of the capacity for ideological manipulation (C_{IM}) is essential for the creation and maintenance of prejudicial beliefs and stereotypes.

Thus, in beginning to consider at the most abstract level those conditions influencing the level of *D,* we can extract the following proposition from the existing literature:

$$D = h(DF) \circ i(PT) \circ j(C_{IM}) \tag{8.3}$$

MOBILITY AND SOCIAL ORGANIZATION. The rate of movement of individuals is a critical property of any social system. As we have seen, it greatly influences the weights of the other variables in equation (8.1a) and the causal model presented in figure 8.7. The generic properties of the social world that influence MO will be explored in detail in chapter 10. In many ways, chapter 10 will represent an illustration of how I propose to analyze the other variables included not just in equation (8.1) but also in the other equations presented in earlier chapters. We will need to develop more precise equations, as well as models of the underlying processes connecting the variables in the equations, if we are to use an analysis of stratification to understand more general processes of social organization.

Concluding Comment

This chapter opened by addressing the ambiguity in, and controversy surrounding, the notion of "social class." This is the first of two chapters on social class which I view as a term denoting two distinct processes: the differentiation of homogeneous subpopulations and the linear ranking of these subpopulations. I am not arguing that these are the only class processes; but I am asserting that these are two of the most important. It is time to recognize that "class" or "class system" is not a unitary thing but only a label given to a number of discrete social processes. Hence, we cannot have *a* theory of social class. Instead, our theoretical principles will pertain to processes which, when viewed together, can be described by the term "social class."

Chapter Nine # THE RANKING OF SUBPOPULATIONS

Evaluation and Ranking as Basic Social Processes

In all social contexts, people evaluate others and rank them. The underlying psychological dynamic for this process can probably be found in the "social comparison" process that was initially given expression by Leon Festinger.[1] But unlike Festinger, I emphasize that people not only compare and evaluate their behaviors and cognitions to relevant others, they also do just the reverse: they compare and evaluate others in terms of their established opinions and typical ways of doing things. This basic cognitive process underlies the dynamics of ranking.

Our concern is not with individual acts of evaluation but with patterns of ranking for entire societies. Societies vary in the extent to which their members agree on the relative rank of individuals and subpopulations. In some, there appears to be a high degree of consensus, so that individuals and subpopulations can be seen as a lineal rank-ordering in terms of imputed "worthiness." In others, there is constant tension as individuals and groups attempt to assert their standards of worthiness in the evaluation of each other. Most societies, of course, fall somewhere in between these two extreme states.

To a great extent, stratification involves the dynamics of evaluation and ranking. For in most metaphorical portrayals of stratification, there is an image of people who can be placed in ascending "layers of perceived worth"; and as I argued earlier, this is not a sociologist's reification, but rather an image of the social world that people create, maintain, and use in dealing with each other. And these hierarchical layers are not just people's dim or explicit awareness of statistical distributions of extrinsic objects like money; on the contrary, they represent cognitive evaluations of the attributes of others. Sometimes there is a high correlation between an extrinsic object like money and people's imputation of worth, but this only signals that in such societies money is an attribute which is highly valued. There are, however, many other traits that are used as sources of evaluation, and these reflect the particular moral standards that a population possesses.

In general, we can say that a consensus of evaluation and a linear rank-ordering of worthiness among members of a population occur when two conditions can be met:

(1) there is a high degree of differentiation of actors—whether individuals or collectivities—in terms of identifiable attributes
(2) there is a high degree of consensus among members of a population over their moral standards of evaluation

More formally, we can say that ranking (*RA*) is a joint and positive function of the degree of differentiation (*DF*) among actors (*A*) and the level of consensus (*CN*) over their standards of evaluation (*S*). That is,

$$RA = f(CN_S) \circ g(DF_A)$$

In the context of stratification, we will need to make simple deductions from this principle. For our concern is not just with the ranking process per se but with the ranking of homogeneous subpopulations, or RA_{HO}. As was done in chapter 4, we can define RA_{HO} as follows:

RA_{HO} = the degree to which homogeneous subsets of members in a society are differentially evaluated and lineally rank-ordered

Thus, we are concerned with a particular type of ranking, RA_{HO}. As can be expected, this form of ranking is explicable in terms of simple derivations of the right-hand terms in the equation above. These derivations involve specifying system-level properties of CN_S and DF_A.

An Elementary Principle on the Ranking of Homogeneous Subpopulations

Using the general formula above, we can make the following derivation:

$$RA_{HO} = f(CN_{VS}) \circ g(DF_{HO}) \tag{9.1}$$

where:

CN_{VS} = the degree of consensus among members of a population over value standards

DF_{HO} = the degree and extent to which subsets of members in a society reveal common behavioral tendencies and similar attitudes so that they can be distinguished from other subsets of members in a society

and where

$$f(CN_{VS}) > g(DF_{HO})$$

This equation borrows much from Talcott Parsons' functional theory of stratification.[2] But as equation (9.1) underscores, Parsons' theory is, in reality, a principle of ranking rather than a more general "analytic model" for stratification. Just as the Davis-Moore hypotheses[3] turned out to be more concerned with inequality of prestige (C_{PR}) than with general stratification processes, so the Parsonian framework can be viewed in more delimited terms as a principle of ranking. In simply recalling the Parsonian principle from chapter 3, my debt to his ideas should be evident:

$$(\text{Parsons}) \ I = \left[\log(CN_{VS})\right] + (DF_A{}^{\text{exp}})$$

Following Parsons' lead, equation (9.1) indicates that the ranking of homogeneous subpopulations is an unspecified function of the degree of consensus in a population over value standards and the degree of homogeneity in differentiated subpopulations. Ranking cannot occur unless people agree on standards of evaluation; and without differentiation of subpopulations, there is little to which these standards can be applied. What I am arguing, then, is that at the societal level of organization, consensus over value standards is critical if a clear and relatively linear rank-ordering is to occur. While differentiation per se probably leads to efforts at ranking, the resulting rank-orderings will be ambiguous, or the subject of controversy, without some degree of consensus over values. Conversely, consensus over values will lead to efforts at ranking of virtually any differences among members of a population, but these rankings have more meaning for stratification at the societal level when they pertain to subpopulations that are readily identifiable by their distinctive attributes.

Figure 9.1 attempts to represent the processes connecting the variables in equation (9.1). The differentiation of homogeneous subpopulations is likely to heighten perceptions by members of a society to those attributes that make a subpopulation distinctive. Thus, the more clearly differentiated and homogeneous a subpopulation, the more likely are members and nonmembers alike to become attuned to its members' most noticeable traits. These traits, in turn, become a basis for evaluation and ranking as people in a society make comparisons among the traits of different subpopulations. Conversely, as the feedback arrows at the bottom of figure 9.1 show, once some degree of evaluation and ranking has occurred, people's perceptions of a subpopulation's distinctive features become increasingly heightened, which, in turn, increases a subpopulation homogeneity as members who are treated similarly by the general population tend to act and think in convergent ways. Hence, the more evaluation and ranking that occurs, the more perceptions and actions of the majority are likely to converge and influence their responses in ways that escalate homogeneity. To a limited extent, then, RA_{HO} increases DF_{HO}, although not to the same degree as the forces outlined in the last chapter. The reason for not including RA_{HO} in the equations and models of the last chapter is my sense that high levels of DF_{HO} *must already exist* (as a result of the forces presented in equation [8.1a]) for the relations specified in figure 9.1 to operate in ways that increase DF_{HO}.

Consensus over value standards (CN_{VS}) greatly accelerates the processes just described. When members of a society reveal relatively high levels of consensus over their abstract moral standards of what is good, right, correct, and appropriate (that is, their values), then

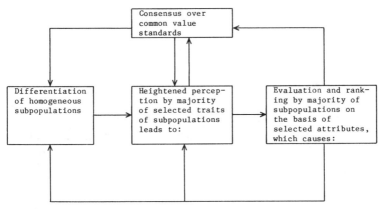

Figure 9.1 The Process of Evaluation and Ranking of Subpopulations (RA_{HO})

perceptions, evaluations, and rankings are guided by common criteria. Moreover, even if differentiation of distinctive traits is not high, the existence of common moral standards leads people, I believe, to seek out what is distinctive, or to make explicit those traits that are initially implicit, and evaluate these traits. Thus, the more consensus over values and the stronger are such values, the more likely are people to fine-tune their perceptions in ways that allow them to differentiate, evaluate, and rank members of subpopulations. And once this process is initiated, it increasingly affects people's attitudes and responses toward members of subpopulations in ways that increase DF_{HO}, thereby initiating and sustaining perceptions, evaluations, rankings, and, I should emphasize, value standards.

It is in the direct, indirect, and feedback processes outlined in figure 9.1 that we can visualize why rank-orderings are so difficult to change, once they are established. Perceptions of traits that are subject to moral evaluation are difficult to change because of selective perceptions guided by moral overtones; and to the extent that reinforcement of value standards is the result of people's perceptions and evaluations of particular traits, the relative rank-ordering of individuals with these traits becomes that much more difficult to change.

With these considerations in mind, we can now begin to make equation 9.1 more specific. This is done in equation (9.1a):

$$RA_{HO} = W_1 \left[\log(CN_{VS}) \right] \times W_2(DF_{HO}{}^{exp}) \tag{9.1a}$$

where:

$$W_1 > W_2$$

In equation (9.1a), I suggest that the relationship between ranking and consensus over value standards is logarithmic in that initial degrees of consensus immediately set into motion tendencies among members of a population to rank-order. In contrast, the relationship between ranking and differentiation of homogeneous subpopulations is exponential in that a considerable degree of differentiation of a number of subpopulations must occur before ranking processes are initiated. As the weights indicate, consensus over values is more important than differentiation, for I suspect that as soon as people agree over values, they seize upon virtually any difference among individuals or subgroupings as a basis for ranking, whereas a considerable amount of differentiation can occur without ranking, especially if there is little consensus over values. The two variables are seen as multiplicatively related in their effects on RA_{HO}, with CN_{VS} given more weight than DF_{HO}. The relationship between each variable and RA_{HO} is represented in figure 9.2.

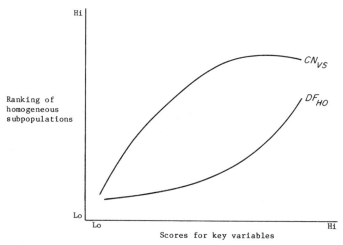

Figure 9.2 The Relationship Between RA_{HO} and Each Explanatory Variable

The Elementary Principle Illustrated

In table 9.1, data on the variables in equation (9.1a) for hunting and gathering, simple and advanced horticultural, agrarian, and industrial societies are summarized. Hunting and gathering societies do not rank subpopulations, since they are not sufficiently large to generate high DF_{HO}. But because they reveal high CN_{VS}, they do rank-order individuals in terms of their economic and religious skills. Simple horticultural systems evidence some rank-ordering, since they reveal high levels of value consensus and some degree of differentiation of homogeneous subpopulations. But the comparatively low levels of DF_{HO} prevent such systems from developing a clear and linear system of ranked subpopulations. Advanced horticultural systems typically manifest high levels of value consensus and sufficient differentiation to generate ranked subpopulations, at least with respect to religious/political elites, some economic specialties, and slave populations. Yet, since the weights for DF_{HO} are still somewhat low, ranking is often in terms of individual skills and attributes as much as it is for subgroup attributes.

Agrarian systems reveal moderate to high value consensus and clear differentiation of homogeneous subpopulations, with the result that they will typically have higher levels of RA_{HO}. And if there is high value consensus, then such systems will evidence a linear ranking of political and religious elites, high-level administrators/warriors, craft specialists, peasants, and slaves (and often clear rank-orderings within each of these ranks). Industrial systems possess moderate to high consensus over abstract values, but there is much contradiction and dissension in the application of these values. Also, dissent groups are always present and offer challenges to prevailing values. The differentiation of subpopulations is less pronounced in industrial than in agrarian systems, except where discriminatory forces are at work. There are distinctions among occupational positions in terms of perceived skill/education/income, but except for distinctions between high skill/high education/high income professional and low skill/low education/low income jobs, homogeneity is relatively low (though still present, especially for the manual/nonmanual division in occupations). The result of these weightings for CN_{VS} and DF_{HO} in

Table 9.1 The Ranking of Homogeneous Subpopulations (RA_{HO}) in Different Types of Societies

	RA_{HO}	CN_{VS}	DF_{HO}
Hunting and gathering societies	*None*, since there are no homogeneous subpopulations. But there is clear ranking of individuals in terms of their personal attributes	*High* consensus over values	*None*, since populations are too small to be extensively differentiated into sub-populations. See table 6.1.
Simple horticultural societies	*Some*, since there is often a rank order among descent groups, villages, and regions. Rank-ordering of individuals, particularly headman, shaman, kin leaders, and successful warriors	*High* consensus over values	*Some* homogeneity among differentiated descent groups, villages and regions. See table 6.1.
Advanced horticultural societies	*Considerable* rank-ordering of political and religious elites, of various kinds of economic specialties, and of kin groups, villages, and regions. Also, slaves and conquered peoples are assigned lower ranks	*High* consensus over values, although there may be dissident subpopulations of slaves and captives in war	*Considerable* homogeneity among political and religious elites as well as among villages, kin-groups, religions, and slaves/conquered peoples (if they come from same society/culture). See table 6.1.
Agrarian societies	*Clear* rank-ordering of population into levels, with political and religious elites at the top, followed by military and administrative leaders, bureaucratic personnel, economic specialties (which have their own rank-ordering), peasants, and slaves. Also, some ranking by kin group, town, and region	*Moderate* to *High* consensus over values. Some dissidents who challenge existing economic, political, and religious arrangements by attacking value standards	*Considerable* homogeneity among political, religious, military, and administrative elites, various economic specialists, peasants, and slaves. Also, in larger systems, homogeneity by town/village, descent group, and region, especially if the system if feudal.
Industrial societies	*Considerable* rank-ordering among elites, nonmanual professionals, nonmanual routine and manual skilled, manual unskilled; rank-ordering by poverty, race/ethnicity is clear. *Ambiguity* among rank-ordering of unskilled nonmanual and skilled manual.	*Moderate* to *High* consensus over general and abstract value premises. Considerable variation in application of values among subgroups. Dissident groups prominent	*Considerable* homogeneity by occupation/education, race/ethnicity, region, and size of city. See table 6.1

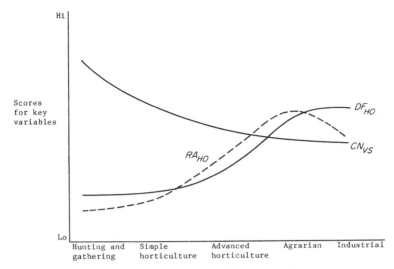

Figure 9.3 Relative Slopes for DF_{HO} and CN_{VS} During Societal Evolution

industrial systems is a considerable degree of RA_{HO}, but this rank-ordering is far from linear among those subpopulations that fall between the very high-ranking and very low-ranking subpopulations.

In figure 9.3, the relative slopes for differentiation of homogeneous subpopulations (DF_{HO}) and consensus over value standards (CN_{VS}) are plotted during societal evolution. As is evident, consensus over value standards declines during evolution, primarily under the impact of increasing size and differentiation of the population. The differentiation of homogeneous subpopulations increases, but levels off after initial industrialization as the effect on DF_{HO} of a growing number of subpopulations in industrial systems is mitigated by a decline in their average level of homogenity. The point where these two curves intersect (the transition from advanced horticultural to an agrarian system) is probably the stage where linearity of rankings of multiple subpopulations is explicit; and it is for this reason that "social class" is typically viewed as most pronounced in such systems.

Implications for a More General View of
Social Organization

Causal Effects Between CN_{VS} and DF_{HO}

As I have implied in several places in this and the last chapter, consensus over value standards (CN_{VS}) and the differentiation of homogeneous subpopulations (DF_{HO}) are interrelated not just in their effects on RA_{HO} but also in the effects on each other. This can be visualized in figure 9.4, where a causal model of the relationships among the variables in equation (9.1a) is presented. The multiplicative relation between CN_{VS} and DF_{HO} affects RA_{HO} in the manner delineated in figure 9.1.

As is also evident in figure 9.1, consensus over value standards heightens people's perceptions and evaluations of differences in actors' traits, with the result that social relations will be circumscribed by those traits which have been selected for evaluation. As traits are differentially evaluated, people are treated differently in the course of interaction; and as a consequence, subpopulations can often emerge on the basis of their differential treatment. Thus, as consensus over values increases, it becomes ever more likely that variations in the attributes of individuals will become a basis for evaluation, interaction, and subpopulation formation, since once some degree of differentiation of a subpopulation has occurred as a result of selective in-

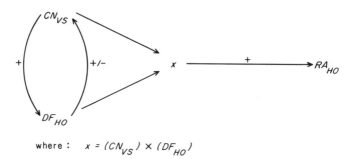

where : $x = (CN_{VS}) \times (DF_{HO})$

Figure 9.4 A Causal Model of RA_{HO}

teraction, members of the subpopulation will often seek each other's company and increase their rates of interaction. This process is especially likely to be initiated if individuals are subjected to negative evaluations and discrimination (see analysis in the last chapter, especially figure 8.2). And as rates of interaction increase, people's modal behaviors and attitudes converge, thereby increasing DF_{HO}.

As is evident from figure 9.4, the relationship between CN_{VS} and DF_{HO} is also reciprocal. Consensus over value standards (CN_{VS}) is either increased or decreased by DF_{HO}, depending upon varying conditions. The existence of DF_{HO} often creates a divergence of value standards, as individuals pursue different activities and interact more with each other than others outside their subgroups. This problem was, of course, given forceful expression by Émile Durkheim,[4] but at the same time, he proposed a "solution" to the dilemma of how differentiating social systems can maintain some degree of moral consensus. If values can become "generalized"—that is, they can become more abstract—then they can provide a common set of moral standards for diversely located groups and subpopulations.[5] Durkheim, and Talcott Parsons after him,[6] assume that such "value generalization" is inevitable, but my view is that it is a process that occurs only under some conditions which need to be specified. For our present purposes, however, it is only necessary to recognize consensus over value standards can actually increase under those conditions that facilitate their generalization. In fact, if such generalization does occur, DF_{HO} can further increase CN_{VS} by providing an array of traits that enables individuals to affirm their common value standards as they differentially evaluate these traits. For as people use value standards to evaluate differences, the standards themselves take on greater clarity; and as their use reinforces the boundaries of existing subpopulations, people come to "accept their place" and hence the value standards. Of course, such is not always the case; people often recoil and rebel against their plight in the evaluational dynamics of a society. Just what conditions produce acceptance or rejection of evaluations have yet to be fully articulated at a theoretical level, although many of the propositions of conflict theory are relevant to the issue.[7] Thus, the ways that DF_{HO} increases or decreases the level of value consensus have yet to be fully worked out. We can, I think, begin to deal with this theoretical issue by examining more directly those conditions that are related to variations in CN_{VS}.

Variations in the Explanatory Variables

We can return to Durkheim's analysis of social solidarity for further understanding of those conditions under which consensus over value standards emerges.[8] In Durkheim's analysis, consensus over value standards decreases under those conditions causing the transition from mechanical to organic solidarity, or to a state of increase of social differentiation (DF). These conditions include increasing population size (N) and concentration in ecological space (ES). Increases in N and decreases in ES escalate "moral density" and "dynamic density," and hence social competition which, in turn, forces increased social differentiation. Expanding transportation systems, increased migration, and development of communications technologies all operate to increase the "density" that increases competition and DF. In Durkheim's analysis, then, we have some clues as to some generic conditions that are related to CN_{VS}. At the most abstract level, I see the most useful theoretical leads to inhere in the variables N, ES, and DF. That is, unlike Durkheim, who was concerned with the causal relations among these, I sense that CN_{VS} is a negative function of N, DF, and ES. The larger, more differentiated, and more geographically dispersed a population, the less the level of value consensus.

But as I noted earlier, Durkheim also presumed that the collective conscience becomes "generalized" or "abstracted."[9] My view is that this is true only some of the time, but for our present analysis, we need to recognize that the generality (GN) of value standards (VS), or GN_{VS}, is a critical variable in analyzing CN_{VS}. I hypothesize that CN_{VS} and GN_{VS} are positively related, counteracting somewhat the effects of N, DF, and ES on CN_{VS}. Thus, I would initiate inquiry with the following speculation:

$$CN_{VS} = h(N) \circ i(DF) \circ j(ES) \circ k(GN_{VS}) \tag{9.2}$$

We would, no doubt, want to add additional variables and perhaps reexamine those above. Moreover, we would want to specify the processes that underlie the assertion in the above equation that these properties of the social universe are interconnected. At any rate, we have a place to begin more extensive inquiry.

Concluding Comment

In this chapter, I have concluded my conceptualization of social class (SC) as a joint function of DF_{HO} and RA_{HO}. This conceptualization does not contradict existing formulations, but it is far less grandiose than many. If the concept of social class is to prove theoretically useful, we must stop using it as a vague metaphor and begin to recognize that in using terms like social class we are, in reality, addressing several distinctive processes, two of which are DF_{HO} and RA_{HO}. There may be more, but these are, in my view, the most critical.

I am not asserting that the conceptualization offered in these last two chapters is free of its own ambiguities. I have mentioned where I sense that there is imprecision and vagueness in the definition of DF_{HO} and RA_{HO}, but even with these points of vagueness, there is a concrete set of variables with which we can begin the process of conceptual refinement.

Chapter Ten MOBILITY PROCESSES

Social Mobility and Social Stratification

Social mobility is probably *the* most researched and analyzed topic in the literature on stratification, if not in general sociology. At the conceptual level, mobility is often viewed as the defining characteristic of "class" and "caste." Low rates of movement among individuals from one ranked subpopulation to another are typically conceptualized as indicative of "class" boundaries; and if the rates of movement are very low, then a "caste" system of stratification is said to exist. Conversely, high rates of mobility are seen to signal a "class" or "open class" system of stratification.

In light of its centrality to conceptualizing different types of stratification systems, it is not surprising that the vast majority of empirical studies on stratification revolves around mobility processes. I will have several points to emphasize about this research in a moment, but for the present, several conceptual issues need to be explored. As will be recalled from chapter 8, I included mobility (MO) as a term in equations (8.1) and (8.1a). This inclusion is in line with the use of mobility as one of the defining characteristics of social class. But as will also be recalled from chapter 8, I deferred speculation about the forces related to variation in MO because I wanted to explore MO in more detail. This special attention to mobility violates the theoretical strategy of this book. In terms of the strategy advocated in chapter 2, MO should receive no more attention than any of the other explanatory variables in equations (5.1) through (9.1). The reason for developing a separate principle on MO at this point is, to be honest, a matter of pragmatism: for most sociologists and anthropologists, the study of stratification is never complete without an extensive analysis of mobility. This emphasis, I feel, is misplaced, for *MO* should be viewed as only one of several forces involved in DF_{HO}—as I indicated in equations (8.1) and (8.1a). Nevertheless, I will bow to convention in the literature on stratification and provide a separate treatment of social mobility.

If any good can be salvaged from this inconsistency in my analysis, it is that I can close this analysis with an illustration of what needs to be done as a next step in the theortical strategy advocated in this book. For I am taking a term in equation (8.1a) and developing a statement on the conditions under which it varies. In so doing, I am using equation (8.1a) as a starting point for addressing more general organizational processes in human societies. Thus, this chapter can, if one prefers, be considered an adjunct to the analysis in chapters 5–9, or it can be seen as a way to pursue the theoretical strategy outlined in chapter 2.

Problems in Mobility Studies

In the context of stratification processes, mobility is typically conceptualized in terms of "vertical mobility" where concern is with the movements of individuals and collectivities up and down a system of rank-ordered positions.[1] As mentioned above, I cannot think of a social process that has been more extensively researched than vertical mobility. There is an enormous research literature on those conditions that increase, or decrease, people's chances for vertical mobility. Most of this research emphasizes upward mobility of individuals and focuses on the "status attainment" process.[2] The typical study in this genre goes something like the following: (1) develop a composite index of SES which is to be used as an indicator of individuals' original "class position";[3] (2) correlate some additional variables with this index; and (3) observe the effects of these variables on mobility variables, such as actual movement of people or the stated aspirations of individuals. Such research studies typically employ a causal model in which the SES variables are considered to "cause" certain variations in "intervening variables" such as family socialization practices; and then, the direct and indirect effects of the SES and the intervening variables on the dependent variables—whether actual mobility or mobility aspirations—are examined. I should note that the largest coefficient in such causal models is the arrow that descends from the top of the model—that is, the arrow denoting unexplained variance. Yet, despite this fact, American sociologists continue to study "status attainment" in the fond hope of explaining some additional variance with the incorporation of yet another intervening variable or with the use of another measuring instrument for the same old variables. Rarely do these researchers question the utility of the SES index, which typically is a composite of inequality processes (heavily loaded toward income and prestige) and ranking processes. Indeed, I believe that mobility research has become so ritualized that we are likely to learn little more than we already know from the current literature.

The inadequacies of mobility research, I feel, reflect more fundamental conceptual problems. The first problem is ideological. Conceptualization of mobility processes by American sociologists has focused on whether or not America is indeed "the land of opportunity" where people can "pull themselves up by their bootstraps." Emphasis has therefore been on individuals rather than collectivities, and it has isolated those variables that are presumed to affect opportunities for upward (as opposed to downward, and horizontal) mobility. This ideological bias is particularly evident when upward mobility is seen as more related to individuals' achievements, aspirations, drives, and motivations than to "structural factors" such as the changing occupational structure or demographic transformations. Indeed, in current practice there are two mobility processes: (1) those "stratus attainment" conditions where individuals acquire attributes or have access to opportunities that allow them to pull themselves up the social hierarchy and (2) those residual processes, typically termed "structural mobility," that allow for mobility even among individuals with flawed motivations and aspirations. The first mobility has received much more attention than the second, even though I suspect that the second explains much more of the variance. Until this conceptual bias, which is in reality an ideological bias, is overcome, theory and research on mobility will continue to be skewed and, quite frankly, theoretically rather uninteresting.

A second conceptual problem in the study of mobility is the functional emphasis of much theory and research. The process of mobility itself is rarely addressed. Rather, the "functions of," or the "consequences of" mobility (if the functionalism is to be more covert) are typically emphasized in theoretical efforts. That is, the functions of mobility are usually assessed in terms of whether or not mobility increases, or decreases, the integration of a social system. Some argue that low rates of mobility increase the incidence of class conflict;[4] others focus on the effects of low or high mobility on "class consciousness";[5] still others explore the functions of mobility for rates of social interaction and integration;[6] and some stress the effects of mobility for relative deprivation and social disintegration;[7] and so on. Even if the functionalism in this work is recessive, mobility is still considered an independent variable in most theorizing. It is rarely conceptualized as a process that itself requires an explanation.[8]

There are, however, some notable exceptions to my general point. For recently Bruce Mayhew and John Skvoretz[9] have argued that mobility—its rate and magnitude—is related to basic parameters of a social system, namely its size and volume of wealth. Sorokin's[10] original effort as well as these few recent theoretical studies are, I believe, much closer to what we need to be doing theoretically. In this chapter, I will present my preliminary ideas on those forces that are related to mobility as a generic social process.

I suspect that the elementary principle to be developed can help us understand not just vertical mobility but also horizontal mobility where movement up and down a system of ranks is not at issue. Yet, I will make explicit claims only on the rate of vertical mobility—that is, on the number of people, whether as individuals or as members of collectivities, that move from one position to another in a system of ranked positions. Below, I have phrased the formal definition to stress my more delimited emphasis:

MO = The movement of individuals or collectivities of individuals from one ranked subpopulation to another, with the degree of mobility being defined in terms of (a) the proportion of individuals in a society who are mobile and (b) the distance across rank-ordered subpopulations that those who are mobile travel

With this definition and the more general issues raised thus far, we are in a position to develop the elementary principle.

An Elementary Principle on Mobility

In equation (10.1) below, I present what I perceive to be the critical properties of the social universe that are related to mobility as defined above:

$$MO = f(DF_{HO}) \circ g(RA_{HO}) \circ h(NP) \circ i(CP) \circ j(C_{OR}) \circ k(C_{IR}) \quad (10.1)$$

where:

DF_{HO} = the degree of differentiation of homogeneous subpopulations (see chapter 8)

RA_{HO} = the degree of linear rank-ordering among differentiated subpopulations (see chapter 9)

NP = number of productive positions in a society

CP = rate of change in the types of productive positions in a social system

C_{OR} = the concentration (or conversely, the dispersion) of organizational resources in a society

C_{IR} = the concentration (or conversely, the dispersion) of individual resources in a society

In equation (10.1), the rate of vertical mobility (MO) is seen as an unspecified function of the degree of differentiation of homogeneous subpopulations (DF_{HO}), the degree of ranking of these subpopulations (RA_{HO}), the absolute number of productive positions in a system (NP), the rate of change in the composition and nature of these productive positions (CP), the concentration of organizational resources (C_{OR}), and the concentration of individual resources (C_{IR}).

As we saw when examining DF_{HO} in chapter 8, MO influences the degree of DF_{HO}. But this relationship is reciprocal, in that the existence of clearly differentiated and internally homogeneous subpopulations presents barriers to those who leave or enter them. At times, the problem of leaving a subpopulation is obviated when the resources of that population are used to raise the mobility of the entire subpopulation; and conversely, as subpopulations experience a loss of resources, they may become, as a whole, downwardly mobile. But if individuals seek to leave a subpopulation, they must abandon old supportive ties and enter into what are often stressful, if not hostile, relations with members of a new subpopulation. In figure 10.1, I have represented diagrammatically some of the crucial processes underlying the relationship between DF_{HO} and MO. This figure is somewhat similar to figure 8.4, but since we are now exploring the impact on DF_{HO} of MO, the processes outlined are somewhat different.

The initial existence of a subpopulation increases rates of interaction among its members relative to their interactions with members of other subpopulations. As rates of interaction increase, interpersonal styles of interaction and behavior converge, as do people's attitudes and beliefs. As a result of this convergence, socialization processes, modes of social control, and types of interpersonal rituals also develop a distinctive pattern. As is evident in figure 10.1, these processes are reciprocal and mutually reinforcing; and as a result, members of subpopulations become visible targets of discrimination/exclusion or embracement/inclusion by subpopulations whose members reveal different attributes. Sometimes this discrimination is

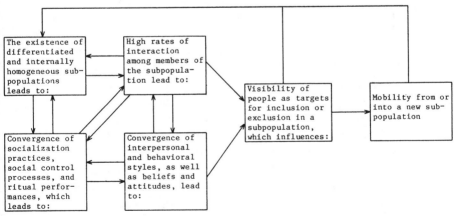

Figure 10.1 The Process of Group Endogamy and Mobility

overt and institutionalized, but more often it is subtly exercised in diverse contexts, such as in the schools and the workplace. The overall result is to decrease rates of mobility, which, as we saw in chapter 8, increases differentiation among, and homogeneity within, subpopulations (DF_{HO}). As I have conceptualized mobility, it must, by definition, be related to ranking, since without a rank-ordering of subpopulations, there is no hierarchy to move up or down. But more substantively important is the fact that ranking presents barriers to mobility. If there is a linear rank-ordering of populations, members of higher-ranking populations will guard their privileges from those in lower ranks, and they will expend considerable energy to maintain their place in the hierarchy in order to prevent downward movement. Figure 10.2 further conceptualizes the processes underlying the relationship between RA_{HO} and MO.

The existence of rank-orderings among populations serves as an incentive for both higher- and lower-ranked groupings to mobilize resources to either preserve or increase their rank. One of the ironies of this process is that mobilization by lower ranks threatens higher ranks, who fear loss of their relative position or at least its contamination and dilution, with the result that they escalate their mobilization, which, in turn, increases awareness of their common interests. As upper ranks mobilize, typically the resources of lower ranks are reduced, and hence also reduced is the latter's capacity to mobilize. A further irony is that as upper-ranked groupings mobilize their resources, they develop heightened awareness of those criteria that distinguish them from others and they use these criteria to exclude and/or discriminate against those who do not meet them. And as lower-ranked groupings mobilize, they come to accentuate those attributes that make them easier targets for discrimination, especially when upper ranks have better articulated those characteristics that distinguish them from lower-ranking groupings. The ironical result is decreased mobility, which, in turn, feeds back and makes less ambiguous RA_{HO}.

At periodic points in this set of processes, rankings become established and accepted with little overt effort to change them. But as alterations in productive roles occur, these processes are again initiated; and if these change-producing processes are sufficiently great, they can operate to counteract the effects of RA_{HO} and MO. The pro-

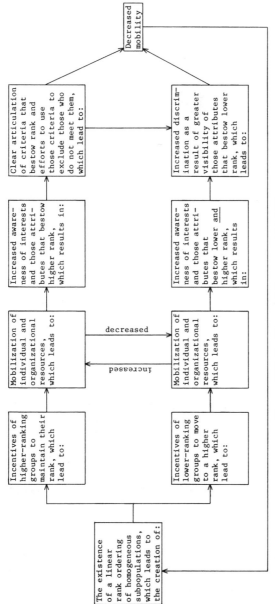

Figure 10.2 Ranking and Decreased Mobility

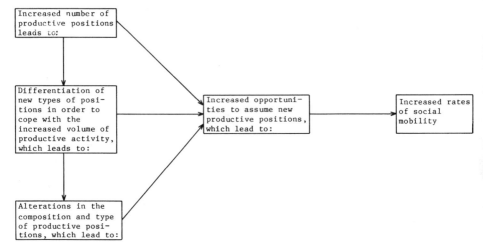

Figure 10.3 Productive Positions and Social Mobility

cesses by which *NP* and *CP* operate to increase *MO,* even in the face of RA_{HO}, are outlined in figure 10.3.

Mobility is related to the number of positions for the simple reason that if there are more positions, there are more places in the system to move to or from. And if the composition of positions is changing, then people will be forced out of some positions and have opportunities to enter into other positions. Thus, the number of productive positions and their rate of change are also critical forces behind the movements of individuals or collectives of individuals in social systems. Such "structural" considerations have been too often seen as residual to understanding mobility; on the contrary, I view them as central to understanding mobility, per se, whether horizontal or vertical.

As is indicated in equation (10.1), mobility is also a function of the organizational resources of individuals as well as to the unique qualities of individuals. If people belong to, and affiliate with, organizations, the resources of these organizations can be used to increase an individual's or a group's chances for mobility. And the more people in a society who have access to organizational resources, the less their concentration, and the greater the overall rate of mobility. These processes are delineated in more detail in figure 10.4.

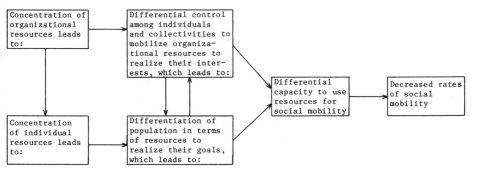

Figure 10.4 The Effects of Concentration of Individual and Organizational Resources on Social Mobility

As is evident in the figure, individuals' access to organizations, such as unions, professional associations, family groups, schools, church groups, community action groups, civic associations, and the like can increase people's resources and chances for mobility by allowing them to use the organization to achieve their goals and interests. Such access also affects the kinds of individual resources—interpersonal, financial, educational, skill-level, motivational, etc.—that people possess and can use to realize their goals. Conversely, possession of individual resources can influence people's access to organizations and the resources that organizations control (for example, the capacity of schools to give credentials to motivated and accomplished students). The result of these reciprocal processes is to decrease mobility rates by allowing those with resources to preserve their position and by preventing those without resources from being able to move up in social rank.

The processes outlined in figures 10.1 through 10.4 give us some guidance in specifying more precisely the relations among the variables in equation (10.1). Equation (10.1a) presents my best guess as to the relationship between DF_{HO}, RA_{HO}, NP, CP, C_{OR} and C_{IR}, on the one hand, and *MO* on the other.

$$MO = \left[W_1(DF_{HO}^{-\exp}) \times W_2(RA_{HO}^{-\exp}) \right] + \left\{ W_3(NP^{\exp}) \times W_4[\log(CP)] \right\}$$
$$+ \left[W_5(C_{OR}^{-\exp}) \times W_6(C_{IR}^{-\exp}) \right] \quad (10.1a)$$

where:

$$W_1 \gtrless W_2 \gtrless W_3 \gtrless W_4 > W_5 > W_6$$

In equation (7.1a), the rate of mobility is seen as a negative exponential function of the degree of differentiation of homogeneous subpopulations (DF_{HO}) and a negative exponential function of rank-ordering of these subpopulations (RA_{HO}). That is, with initial increases in the degree of DF_{HO} and RA_{HO}, the rate of mobility will initially decline at a slower rate than with subsequent increases in DF_{HO} and RA_{HO}. These two variables are viewed as multiplicatively related in their effects on MO. The product of DF_{HO} and RA_{HO} is then viewed as additively related to the product of the number of positions (NP) and the rate of change in the types of positions (CP). The number of positions is exponentially related to mobility, since the number of positions must increase considerably before it has a great impact on mobility. The rate of change in positions is logarithmically related to mobility, as initial changes in the types of productive positions immediately accelerate mobility and the effect then levels off. These two variables are considered to be multiplicatively related in their effects on MO. Increases in numbers are likely to involve the addition of new types of positions, while changes in the types of positions are usually related to increases in the number of positions (see figure 10.3), and as a result, mobility increases. The concentration of organizational resources (C_{OR}) in a system is seen as multiplicatively related to the concentration of individual resources (C_{IR}) in its effects on MO, because decreases in access to organizational resources also lessen the resources available to individuals, whereas decreases in the dispersion of individual resources usually decrease the distribution of skills that can be used to gain access to, or create, organizational resources. Each of these variables bears a negative exponential relationship to mobility, with their product being additively related to the products of other terms in equation (10.1a). As is indicated by the weightings, I cannot at this time ascertain the relative weights for DF_{HO}, RA_{HO}, NP, or CP, but I am sure that they should be given more weight than C_{OR} which, in turn, should be given more weight than C_{IR}. These relationships between each variable and MO are graphically represented in figure 10.5.

The rationale for the relationships specified in equation (10.1a) is summarized in figures 10.1 through 10.4. Let me summarize it more discursively. Rates of interaction within homogeneous subpop-

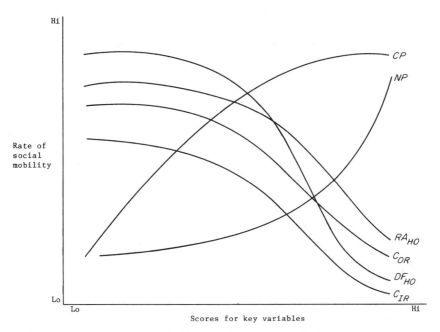

Figure 10.5 The Relationship Between *MO* and Each Explanatory Variable

ulations are greater than those outside the subpopulation, creating pressures for similarity in behaviors and attitudes. Such similarities present a barrier to those who would enter this subpopulation, since there is likely to be dissimilarity in the attitudes of subpopulation members and those who would seek to enter a population (or more correctly specific groupings of individuals in a subpopulation). Unless anticipatory socialization occurs, or individuals can acquire the necessary behavioral and attitudinal repertoire quickly upon entrance to a new subpopulation, considerable discrimination against would-be entrants into a subpopulation will ensue. Ranking of subpopulations accelerates these processes by giving members of a subpopulation something to lose if those below them can penetrate their groupings. For the more the persons who can occupy a given rank, the less will be its worth. Of course, high-ranked groupings become incentives for upwardly mobile individuals or groups of individuals, but, other things being equal, these pressures are more than compensated for by people's desire to preserve their position. Thus, as homogeneity and ranking of subpopulations increase, processes that inhibit mobility are increasingly operative; and hence, DF_{HO} and RA_{HO} are multiplicatively related in a negative exponential curve to MO.

The number of productive positions in a society is, I feel, an obvious but still very important force. If there are few positions, there are a limited number of chances for movement. But as the number of positions increases, changes of movement into new positions also increase. When such increases are associated with changes in the types of productive positions, then there are even more new opportunities for individuals or groups of individuals. Moreover, to an unknown extent, increasing numbers and types of productive positions break down pressures for DF_{HO} and RA_{HO}, since as the productive positions around which much subgroup formation is built change, so do the interaction patterns of people in various subpopulations. As patterns of interaction change, group boundaries and rank-orderings break down and/or are realigned; and during these changes, additional opportunities to be mobile are created.

Just whether individuals, or collectivities, can take advantage of opportunities created by such changes is influenced by their organizational and individual resources. Conversely, people's capacity to maintain their rank, and thus not lose out relative to others, in the face of changes in the number and nature of positions is also related to their level of access to resources. If organizational resources are highly concentrated, then those in higher positions can maintain their relative station in both static or changing systems. But if there is wide dispersion of resources, then pressures for change in people's positions can be generated. Moreover, once changes occur as a result of these pressures, or for other reasons, people have the organizational resources to take advantage of the opportunities created by such changes. Dispersion of individual resources accelerates these processes by allowing more people to use their skills to create effective organizations that generate pressures for new opportunities and by increasing the number of persons who can take advantage of whatever opportunities become available.

Thus, mobility is a pervasive process in societal social systems. But the degree of vertical mobility is a function of a number of generic forces. My conceptualization of these forces as DF_{HO}, RA_{HO}, NP, CP, C_{OR}, C_{IR} redirects the emphasis in the current literature away from IR and OR processes that, while important, are less critical than CP, NP, DF_{HO}, and RA_{HO} processes. This redirection of emphasis is, I feel, appropriate when examining different types of empirical systems.

The Elementary Principle Illustrated

Table 10.1 presents a summary of the data[11] on hunting and gathering, simple and advanced horticultural, agrarian, and industrial societies as they relate to the variables in equation (10.1a). As is evident, it is only in industrial systems that one finds comparatively high rates of mobility. Moreover, the forces behind the similar rates of mobility in nonindustrial societies vary for different types of societies. Among hunting and gathering populations, there can be little vertical mobility, since there are low weights for all the critical variables. In simple horticultural systems, much mobility is by collective units, such as descent groups or villages, that develop organizational resources and use them in ways that increase their rank. Among more advanced horticulturalists, these same patterns of group mobility are also evident, but some mobility occurs by virtue of increases in the number of productive roles, although the existence of more clearly ranked and homogeneous subpopulations counteracts this source of mobility. Moreover, because there is fairly high concentration of organizational and individual resources, mobility is further stymied for both individuals and collectivities of individuals.

Agrarian systems reveal high degrees of homogeneity and ranking of subpopulations which decrease opportunities and set into motion exclusionary, discriminatory, and ascriptive practices among members of subpopulations. Moreover, because of these ascriptive processes associated with a clear rank-ordering of subpopulations, organizational and individual resources are highly concentrated, thereby making mobility out of, and into, new subpopulations even more difficult. What mobility does occur is the result of the relatively large number of productive positions, and the slow changes in the types of

Table 10.1 Vertical Social Mobility (*MO*) in Different Types of Societies

	MO	*DF$_{HO}$*	*RA$_{HO}$*
Hunting and gathering societies	*Low;* except for some individuals assuming higher worth than others in terms of economic and religious skills	*None;* see table 6.1	*None;* see table 6.2
Simple horticultural societies	*Low;* individuals within descent groups, or entire descent groups, can improve their rank	*Some;* homogeneity among descent groups, villages, and regions. See table 6.1	*Some;* rank-ordering of descent groups, villages and regions. Much ranking of individuals. See table 6.2
Advanced horticultural societies	*Low to Moderate;* individuals and descent groups can improve their rank	*Considerable;* homogeneity among political and religious elites as well as among villages, descent groups, and regions. Some homogeneity among economic specialties. See table 6.1	*Considerable;* linear rank-ordering of political and religious groupings, economic specialties, kin groups, villages, regions, and slaves. See table 6.2
Agrarian societies	*Low to Moderate;* individuals, descent groups, occupational groups can be mobile	*Considerable;* high degrees of homogeneity among political and religious elites, bureaucratic officials, warriors, traders/merchants, craft specialists, slaves, peasants. Some homogeneity by town/villages, region, and descent group. See table 6.1	*Very Clear;* linear- and rank-ordering of population into levels, with political and religious elites at the top, followed by military and administrative leaders, bureaucratic personnel, economic specialties (which have their own ranking), peasants and slaves. Also some ranking by kin groups, town and region. See table 6.2
Industrial societies	*High;* individuals are often mobile, typically to or from the next adjacent ranked subpopulation	*Some;* homogeneity among manual/nonmanual workers, among ethnic populations, among elites, and among poor. Some homogeneity by region, national origin, and economic specialties. See table 6.1	*Considerable;* rank-ordering of elites, some professions, some economic specialties, and some ethnic populations. But much ambiguity in rankings within many economic specialties as well as among many subpopulations. See table 6.2

NP	CP	C_{OR}	C_{IR}
Few; age and sex major bases of differentiation in societies of 50 to 100 individuals	*Rare;* except when external conditions (famine, conquest by agricultural populations, etc.) disrupt old patterns	*Low;* there are virtually no organizational resources, except for nuclear units, social cliques, and secret societies, and these are dispersed	*Low;* all individuals can perform most tasks. Some differences in abilities with respect to hunting, gathering, and religious activites
Few; division by age, sex, occupational specialties, kin affiliation in society of 200 to 2,000 members	*Rare;* except when external forces intervene (conquest, war, ecological disruption) in system	*Some;* descent groups reveal different levels of resources, as do villages and regions. Certain individuals, such as chief and shaman, control resources. Yet, organizational resources remain widely available to all members of the society	*Some;* some individuals reveal more talent in occupational, domestic, warrior, religious, and political roles
Many; division by age, sex, and numerous occupational specialties in populations of 500 to 100,000	*Slow;* except when outside forces (conquest, war, ecological disruption) intervene in system	*Some;* descent groups, age groups, occupational specialties, villages represent organizational resources which are widely dispersed, although some individuals are more able to use them than others	*Considerable;* there is high concentration of individual resources in leadership, religious activity, and warfare because of ascriptive processes
Very Many; extensive division of labor by sex, age, vocation, numerous economic specialties in populations of 100,00 to many millions	*Slow;* except when outside forces (war, ecological disruption, conquest, disease, famine) intervene in system	*Considerable;* there are vast differences in the access of individuals and subgroups to the organizatinal resources of the society. This access is highly concentrated in the hands of a few individuals and groupings	*Considerable;* there is high concentration of individual resources in leadership, religious activity, and warfare because of ascriptive processes
A Great Many; extensive division of labor by vocation, profession, and a myriad of economic specialties in societies of 1 million to many millions	*Rapid;* change in the nature and types of productive roles is endemic to the structure of industrially based economic and social organization	*Some;* almost all members of the society have access to multiple organizational resources. There is, therefore, a wide dispersion of organizational resources, although only a few individuals and groupings have access to some of the more powerful organizations	*Some;* informal ascription, and discrimination, operate to concentrate individual resources, although skills and talents are widely dispersed

positions, which provide opportunities for individuals and groupings of individuals.

Industrial systems reveal considerable mobility, because the number and type of productive positions are constantly changing and because organizational and individual resources are widely dispersed. Most of this mobility involves movements to, and from, the next adjacent ranked subpopulation, but at times, more dramatic mobility occurs. Yet, the rate and distance of mobility are limited by virtue of exclusionary, ascriptive, and discriminatory processes by identifiable subpopulations. Thus, industrial systems reveal high rates of mobility only in relation to the rather low degree of mobility in nonindustrial societies.

In figure 10.6, the weights of the variables are summarized for societies at different stages of development. Comparatively low rates of mobility exist in nonindustrial systems because the opportunities for mobility created by the increasing number of positions and changes

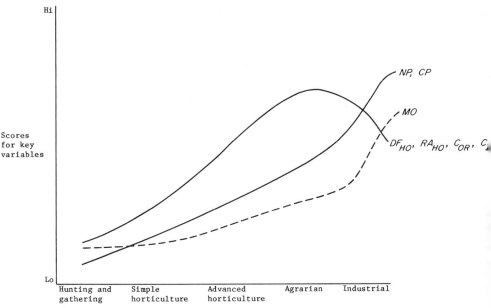

Figure 10.6 Relative Slopes for DF_{HO}, RA_{HO}, NP, CP, C_{OR}, C_{IR} During Societal Evolution

in their composition are countered by the even greater increase in subpopulation formation, ranking, and concentration of organizational and individual resources. It is only where the two sets of curves in figure 10.6 intersect that the weights for the variables in equation (10.1a) move in a direction facilitating an increase in rates of mobility. This intersection typically occurs with the industrialization of a previously agrarian-based economy.

A Concluding Comment

As I noted earlier, mobility MO has consumed too much of our time in the analysis of stratification. Other processes—C_{MW}, C_{PO}, C_{PR}, DF_{HO} and RA_{HO}—are more central. Mobility is only one critical process implicated in DF_{HO}. I am not asserting, of course, that (MO) is unimportant, in many contexts other than stratification.

When we perform the exercise of this chapter for each term in all the equations presented in previous chapters, we will have gone a long way toward developing a theoretical understanding of human social organization. We will be closer to Auguste Comte's dream of a "social physics"; and we will have come closer to a natural science of society. Let me review these implications in the closing chapter.

Chapter Eleven TOWARD A NATURAL SCIENCE OF SOCIETY

Out of the Shadows of Giants

In this chapter, a review of the theoretical approach advocated in this book is perhaps in order, especially since we now have an illustration of that strategy.

I argued in chapters 1 and 2 that sociologists have become reluctant to theorize about the social universe. Indeed, our fears of "grand theory" have been translated into an almost myopic interpretation of R. K. Merton's advocacy of middle range theory. We seem to fear abstraction, and we shrink from ideas that are not corroborated by hordes of statistically sanitized "facts." We decry theory as mere "armchair speculation" or as "off-the-wall thinking." My main point in this book has been to assert that sociologists need to climb back into their armchairs and to bounce more ideas off the wall. And we need to stop letting methodologists tell us how to think; on the contrary, in any mature science, it is the other way around. Theoretical speculation stimulates the methodologically inclined to develop ways to test the implications of theory.

The curious irony in all this is that at a time when contemporary theorists are viewed with suspicion, we continue to worship our early masters: St. Marx, St. Durkheim, St. Weber, St. Mead, and others who are close to being canonized. The problem with this ancestor worship is that we appear reluctant to move on, to digest these scholars' ideas and to build on them. Rather, we play scholastic games, much like medieval church scholars, in which we debate over what St. Marx really meant, or over whether or not this or that interpretation of our forebears is correct. In all this activity, there is clearly a craving for theory. Somehow, theory is proper when done in the tradition of one of these early masters,[1] but it is "grand theory" when we try to look at social reality for ourselves. Only in a discipline which has lost its vision could this occur. The "metatheoretical"— one of those words like "paradigm" that we use to hide our atheoretical bent—goal of this book has been to rekindle our theoretical fires, not just by advocacy but by demonstration. My theoretical ideas may be incorrect, but at least there is theory that represents more than mere recapitulation of the masters and that is not shackled by the intellectual tyranny of methodologists.

One Useful Strategy

My proposal has been very simple: (1) suspend excessive *initial* concern with causality and operationalization; (2) attempt to isolate the most fundamental and generic properties of the social universe; (3) seek to determine the general form and pattern of relationship among these properties; (4) state this relationship as a simple principle; and then, (5) attempt to specify the causal processes and underlying mechanisms that connect basic properties of the universe. I am not asserting that this strategy is the only way to build theory; I am only suggesting that it represents one useful approach. Let me now review in more detail the five elements of this strategy.

1. As I have argued, sociology has been too concerned with "causes" and "functions." Our love affair with functionalism gave way to an obsession with causality.[2] Neither functional nor causal analysis in itself is "bad"; their limitations are only severe when these approaches are viewed as *theoretical explanations* of events. Since the deficiencies of functional analysis are well documented,[3] I will concentrate here on causal modeling.[4] Causal analysis must, by its nature, be empirical and often idiographic. If explanation involves accounting for measurable variance in some empirical event, then variations in other empirial events are going to be viewed as the

"causes of" this event. Hence, causal explanations are intercorrelations among specific empirical variables. If we try to make these causal explanations more abstract, we must remove empirical content, and hence the capacity to explain variance, since we can no longer assign correlation coefficients to the causal links among abstractly stated variables. I have argued that this is not the way *to begin* theorizing; it is only a useful procedure for testing theory.

2. How do we isolate the most basic and generic features of the universe? There is no formula for this process; it is a creative act and involves some combination of deduction from explicitly and implicitly held theoretical constructs and familiarity with some of the relevant empirical facts.[5] Fortunately, much of this creative work has been done for us by our intellectual forefathers whose totems we still venerate. What is required, then, is to extract their insights and couple them with our implicit deductions and inductions.

3 and 4. With the isolation of basic properties of the universe, our goal is to understand the pattern—only the general form—of their relationship. Causal modeling with correlation coefficients obscures this goal; rather, we need to work with simple equations (or words) to describe the general form of relationship among variables. Such relational statements are also creative acts. They involve "eyeballing" the universe (that implicit synthesizing of inductive and deductive mental processes); and then, they require that we risk some speculation about the relationship which, no doubt, will be decried as off-the-wall fantasy.

5. Only at this point should be begin to try and construct a model of the processes that "connect" the generic properties and that give them their form as described in an equation. Too often, we create the models first—often highly sophisticated ones. But the model is useful only when it tells us *why* and *how* important, basic, and generic social phenomena are connected. Most of our models in social science do not do this, since they involve an elegant treatment of nongeneric phenomena.

The Nature of Social Theory

As I have argued, we cannot have "a" or "the" theory of a phenomenon. Rather, we can have an elementary principle(s) on a phenomenon, but this principle is not a theory. Rather, it is one of many principles that we will have in an inventory of theoretical propositions. These will not constitute a fully integrated whole—at least not at the present state of theory. For the present, they will be a somewhat eclectic mix of abstract statements that we combine in ad hoc ways to understand some empirical event. Thus, in our inventory we should have principles on such generic properties of the social universe as production; hierarchical, spatial, and temporal differentiation; subgroup homogeneity; ranking; the concentration of power, prestige, and material wealth; rates of interaction; and so on.

The number of such principles will, I suspect, be small. Their power to explain varied and diverse phenomena will come from the ways in which they are combined. But our initial task, I think, is to articulate these elementary principles; later, we can begin to use them (as well as test and revise them) to understand wide arrays of data. Thus, the form of sociological theory will be somewhat inelegant in the short run. In fact, our desire for elegance that, on the surface, emulates that in the "real sciences" has often involved short-circuiting more fundamental work: isolating generic (as opposed to easily modeled or measured) variables and stating in rough form (as opposed to precise but phenomenally irrelevant form) their relationship to each other.

We must also recognize that, since we work in natural and open systems where knowledge of and control over many variables are both impossible, we cannot be a predictive science. Our principles will rarely be able to provide accurate predictions, because diverse social forces (each understandable in its own right) intersect and interact in ways that cannot be precisely known in advance, or measured with our crude methodological technologies. Yet, our principles along with their accompanying models can help us understand *how* and *why* events in the social universe occur. Ecologists, biologists, geologists, and even at times chemists and physicists must work in realms where they must accept this limitation. But unlike so many sociologists, these other natural scientists do not view the lack of prediction as a barrier to knowledge and understanding of fundamental processes. They accept this inability to predict in natural empirical systems as a challenge to construct better measuring instruments, to develop a relevant experiment, or to wait for a "natural event" to occur in order that they may better understand the process under investigation. Sociologists should not be dismayed over these same realities of working in natural empirical systems; they do not preclude the possibility of a science of society any more than they do for other sciences of natural phenomena.

Elementary Principles of Stratification

It is with this orientation to social theory that I began the analysis of societal stratification. I have not sought to articulate, nor do the previous chapters pretend to be, "a" or "the" theory of stratification. Rather, I began this inquiry by asking: what basic properties of the social universe are implicated in the phenomenon that sociologists and anthropologists term "stratification"? In answering this question, I borrowed ideas from our enshrined early masters as well as from the work of my contemporaries. I also inducted in an unsystematic and implicit way from the large research literature and my own experiences (the last source of information is, as I noted in early chapters, not to be viewed as a handicap but as one of the *advantages* that social theorists have over their counterparts in other natural sciences). From this process of induction-deduction, or what Willer and Webster have termed "abduction,"[6] I isolated three generic social processes which compose a system of stratification when they operate concurrently. These processes are (1) the unequal distribution of valued resources (I), particularly the degree of concentration (C) in material wealth (MW), power (PO), and prestige (PR); (2) the differentiation of homogeneous subpopulations (DF_{HO}); and (3) the ranking of these homogeneous subpopulations (RA_{HO}).

These processes have been conceptualized as variables, and the goal of this book has been to discover the conditions in human societal systems that influence their variation. It is important to stress again that each of these variables denotes a social process which occurs in contexts other than societal stratification. The elementary principles developed for each of these variables are statements about social organization in general; they become principles of stratification only when they are combined. They can be separated and combined with other principles to explain other societal phenomena of interest to sociologists. My view of theory, then, is that it is a repository of elementary principles used in varying ad hoc combinations to explain phenomena of interest to sociologists and other social scientists.

As I suggested in the early chapters, there may be other processes involved in stratification. If such is the case, then we need to develop an elementary principle for each process and combine them with those that I have developed in previous chapters. Or, if one of my principles is considered inappropriate, then we can extract it and place it back into our repository of principles for use when trying to understand other basic social processes. It is in this strategic context, then, that these principles developed in this book should be viewed. The principles and their respective definitions of concepts are summarized below:

$$(1)\ C_{MW} = W_1(P^{\exp}) + \left[W_2(NH^{-\exp}) \times W_3(NO^{-\exp})\right]$$

where:

C_{MW} = the degree of concentration in material wealth, with material wealth defined as those material objects, or the capacity to purchase such objects with money, that people in a society value and perceive to be gratifying

P = productivity, or the total volume of products and services generated by the members of a society, with products defined as material objects created by the conversion of environmental resources and with services defined as activities that facilitate the production and distribution of material objects

NO = the number of subunits in a society that organize people's activities

NH = the number of hierarchies that link organizational subunits in a society, with hierarchies defined as the vertical organization of units in terms of power

and where:

$$W_1 > W_2 > W_3$$

$$(2)\ C_{PO} = W_1\left[\log(ET)\right] + \left[W_2(P^{\exp}) \times W_3(IC^{\exp}) \times W_4(IT^{\exp})\right]$$

where:

C_{PO} = the degree of concentration of power in a society

P = the level of productivity in a society (see above)

IC = the total level of internal conflict among subunits of a society

IT = the total volume of internal transactions among the subunits of a society

ET = the level of perceived threat from sources external to a society

and where:

$$W_1 > W_2 > W_3 > W_4$$

$$(3)\ C_{PR} = \left\{ W_1\left[-\log\left(\frac{Po}{N}\right) \right] \times W_4\left[\left(\frac{Mw}{N}\right)^{-\exp} \right] \right\}$$
$$+ \left\{ W_2\left[\left(\frac{SK}{N}\right)^{-\exp} \right] \times W_3\left[\left(\frac{FI}{N}\right)^{-\exp} \right] \right\}$$

where:

C_{PR} = the degree of concentration of prestige in a society

N = the number of people in a society

Po = the number of people in status positions which are *perceived* by members of the society to possess high levels of power

SK = the number of poeple in status positions which are *perceived* by members of a society to possess high levels of skill

FI = the number of people in status positions which are *perceived* by members of a society to possess a high degree of functional importance

Mw = the number of people in status positions which are *perceived* by members of a society to bring a high level of material wealth

and where:

$$W_1 > W_2 > W_3 > W_4$$

$$(4)\ DF_{HO} = \left\{ W_1\left[\log(N) \right] \times W_4(DF_P^{\exp}) \times W_5(MO^{-\exp}) \right\}$$
$$+ \left\{ W_2(I^{\exp}) \times W_3\left[\log(D) \right] \right\}$$

where:

DF_{HO} = the degree and extent to which subsets of members in a society reveal common behavioral tendencies and similar attitudes so that they can be distinguished from other subsets of members in a society

N = the total number of people in a society

I = the degree of inequality in the distribution of rewards

D = the rate and intensity of discriminatory actions in a society against selected minority populations

DF_P = the degree of differentiation of productive positions in a society

MO = the movement of individuals or collectivities from one subpopulation to another

and where:

$$W_1 = W_2 > W_3 > W_4 > W_5$$

$$(5) \quad RA_{HO} = W_1\big[\log(CN_{VS})\big] \times W_2(DF_{HO}{}^{\exp})$$

where:

RA_{HO} = the degree to which homogeneous subsets of members in a society are differentially evaluated and lineally rank-ordered

CN_{VS} = the degree of consensus among members of a population over value standards

DF_{HO} = the degree and extent to which subsets of members in a society reveal common behavioral tendencies and similar attitudes so that they can be distinguished from other subsets of members in a society

and where:

$$W_1 > W_2$$

As I have delineated for each of these equations, there are processes that help us understand *why* and *how* the variables on the right-hand side of the equation are connected to each other in their effects on the variable to be explained. That is, by modeling the processes underlying the relations among these variables, I have been able to specify the dynamics that connect properties of the social universe. Indeed, this discussion of dynamics has helped in establishing the relative weights and the form of interrelation among the variables.

I am sure that many will consider the variables in these equations as "too vague" and "imprecise." Perhaps this criticism is justified, since I make no claims about having a final answer to the problem at hand. But I suspect that much of the criticism involves the imposition of an empiricist's bias. As I have argued, theory is abstract and it is *not* the job of theorists to operationalize concepts. That is the task of methodologists, when they are not too busy handing out questionnaires. I think that with a little bit of creative work, a methodologist can operationalize each concept in the equations above. I am asserting, then, that the elementary principles listed above are testable and that they are not vague (abstract, yes; but not vague).

In sum, these five elementary principles represent my best effort to theorize about societal stratification. If my statements seem incorrect, someone can rewrite these principles in light of empirical evidence and/or new conceptual reasoning. I will feel little shame if such turns out to be the case; indeed, like any scientist, I wrote these equations as a challenge to others to prove them wrong. Only in this way will we begin to build a natural science of society.

Toward Additional Principles on Social Organization

As I have emphasized, a proposal for developing sociological theory has been presented in the pages of this book. One of the problems with confronting the social universe—or any universe, for that matter—is its seeming complexity. Theory is, of course, to reduce this complexity by extracting those fundamental properties of the universe and by developing principles that explain their dynamics. But it is still hard to know where to start building theory and how to go about its articulation. The enormity of the task, I think, has often led theorists into speculative philosophy or the history of ideas. Or, scholars have retreated behind Robert Merton's plea for middle range theory by elevating empirical generalizations in a delimited empirical realm to the lofty status of theory. I propose to avoid either of these extremes, but I have also borrowed a page from each.

I share the conviction of most sociologists that our first masters have uncovered some of the fundamental properties of the universe.[7] Accordingly, I have used their insights, but I do not feel an obligation to dissect in detail all their ideas or even to keep their ideas in context. Too much of social theory is, in reality, hero worship. I also share Merton's recognition that the "grand theoretical" schemes of Talcott Parsons and others are not particularly useful in building theory. We do not need grand metaphysical schemes. Rather, we need to start building theory about specific processes that occur in our universe; later, these can be consolidated and/or subsumed by ever more abstract principles. There was nothing terribly wrong with Merton's advocacy[8] in itself, but its execution by sociologists has propagated a mindless empiricism and a fear of abstraction. Thus in borrowing a page from Merton and from my colleagues who continue to genuflect at the Temple of the Great Masters, I have not wanted to fall into the trap of confusing empirical generalizations, history of ideas, and philosophical speculation with theory.

My alternative is to select a basic social process, human stratification in societies. Then I have sought to determine its constituent processes and to develop equations for each of these. The next step is to take each term on the right-hand side of each equation and develop a principle which delineates the dynamics of the processes denoted by this term. Once this step is taken, we have moved beyond stratification to more general processes of social organization. We have begun, in essence, to wedge our way into the complexity of our universe without a corresponding retreat into philosophy or empirical details.

It is for this reason that I have suggested for each term in the elementary principles presented in the preceding chapters some of the generic properties of the universe that influence their variability. I illustrated this approach by examining mobility (MO)—a term in the equation on DF_{HO}—in detail. All the terms in the equations presented can and will be similarly analyzed; in this way, I hope to begin accumulating an inventory of elementary principles of human social organization.

A Final Comment

At times, I have written polemically, because theory in sociology must overcome well-entrenched and, I feel, destructive biases. On the empirical side of the bias, critics will decry, no doubt, the lack of operationalization, the lack of an extensive literature review of empirical findings, the seeming vagueness of abstract concepts, the lack of attention to historical and contextual details, and so on. To these critics, I simply say that attention to all these issues has prevented sociology from developing interesting theory. To be consumed by these details when one begins to develop theory will increase the probabilities of failure. We will never see the forest for the trees, and hence, never develop as a theoretically informed science.

On the conceptual side of the bias, critics will be dismayed by the failure to offer a metatheory, the refusal to cite in reverent footnotes every great thinker, the willingness to pull out of context others' ideas and use them in my own way, and the general reluctance to worship at the Temple of the Masters. As I have emphasized, we must come out of the shadows of these giants; and as a few scholars[9] have sought to do in recent decades, we must climb onto shoulders. Only in this way will we develop a respectable "natural science of society."[10]

NOTES

1. Theoretical Problems and Prospects

1. A. R. Radcliffe-Brown, *A Natural Science of Society* (Glencoe, Ill.: Free Press, 1957).

2. For example, see Herbert Blumer, *Symbolic Interactionism: Perspective and Method* (Englewood Cliffs, N.J.: Prentice-Hall, 1969); Thomas P. Wilson and Don H. Zimmerman, "Ethnomethodology, Sociology, and Theory," *Humbolt Journal of Social Relations* (Fall–Winter 1979–80), 7:52–88; Ellsworth R. Fuhrman and William E. Snizek, "Some Observations on the Nature and Content of Critical Theory," *ibid.*, 7:33–35; Max Harkheimer, *Critical Theory* (New York: Herder and Herder, 1972).

3. See, for summaries and illustrations of diverse approaches: Jonathan H. Turner, *The Structure of Sociological Theory*, 3d ed. (Homewood, Ill.: Dorsey Press, 1982), and special issue on theoretical strategies, *Humbolt Journal of Social Relations* (Fall–Winter 1979–80), vol. 7; George Ritzer, *Sociology: A Multiple Paradigm Science* (Boston: Allyn and Bacon, 1975); Scott G. McNall, ed., *Theoretical Perspectives in Sociology* (New York: St. Martin's Press, 1979).

4. See my earlier statements on this issue: Jonathan H. Turner, "Towards a Social Physics: Reducing Sociology's Theoretical Inhibitions," *Humbolt Journal of Social Relations* (Fall–Winter 1979–80), 7:140–55, and "Returning to Social Physics: Illustrations from the work of G. H. Mead," *Current Perspectives in Social Theory* (1981), 2:150–63.

5. Radcliffe-Brown, *A Natural Science*, pp. 13–14.

6. Edmund Husserl, *Phenomenology and the Crisis of Western Philosophy* (New York: Harper and Row, 1965) and *Ideas: General Introduction to Pure Phenomenology* (London: Collier-Macmillan, 1969).

7. Blumer, *Symbolic Interactionism*.

8. George Herbert Mead, *Mind, Self and Society*, ed. by C. W. Morris (Chicago: University of Chicago Press, 1934).

9. See my "Returning to Social Physics"; and Jonathan H. Turner and Leonard Beeghley, *The Emergence of Sociological Theory* (Homewood, Ill.: Dorsey Press, 1980), pp. 502–14 for a summary of Mead's "laws" of action and interaction. See also my *The Structure of Sociological Theory*, pp. 322–43 for an analysis of Blumer's adaptation of G. H. Mead's ideas.

10. For example, Norman K. Denzin, *The Research Act: A Theoretical Introduction to Sociological Methods* (Chicago: Aldine, 1979).

11. Herbert Blumer, "What Is Wrong with Social Theory?" *American Sociological Review* (August 1954), 19:146–58.

12. At least we can see with our senses what we are studying.

13. Max Weber, *The Methodology of the Social Sciences,* trans. by E. A. Shils and H. A. Finch (Glencoe, Ill.: Free Press, 1949; originally published 1904).

14. This dualism is often taken to ridiculous and confusing extremes, as is the case with Marvin Harris' use of the "etic" and "emic" distinction in his *Cultural Materialism: The Struggle for a Science of Culture* (New York: Random House, 1979), pp. 32–45.

15. Herbert Blumer, *Symbolic Interactionism;* Randall Collins, *Conflict Sociology* (New York: Academic Press, 1975), "Micro-Translation as a Theory-building Strategy," in K. Knorr and A. Cicourel, eds., *Advance in Social Theory and Methodology: Toward an Integration of Micro- and Macro-Sociology* (London: Routledge and Kegan Paul, 1982), and "The Microfoundations of Macrosociology," *American Journal of Sociology* (March 1980), 86:984–1014.

16. See Turner and Beeghley, *The Emergence of Sociological Theory,* pp. 270–308 for an analysis of Simmel's work in these terms.

17. See, for illustrations, Samuel Leinhardt, ed., *Social Networks: A Developing Paradigm* (New York: Academic Press, 1977); Paul W. Hollander and Samuel Leinhardt, *Perspectives in Social Network Analysis* (New York: Academic Press, 1979).

18. Richard Emerson, "Exchange Theory, Part II: Exchange Relations and Network Structures," in J. Berger, M. Zelditch, and B. Anderson, eds., *Sociological Theories in Progress* (Boston: Houghton Mifflin, 1972), 3:58–87.

19. James Grier Miller, *Living Systems* (New York: McGraw-Hill, 1978).

20. For benchmark works in this sequence, see Talcott Parsons, *The Structure of Social Action* (New York: McGraw-Hill, 1937), *The Social System* (Glencoe, Ill.: Free Press, 1951), and *Action Theory and the Human Condition* (New York: Free Press, 1978). Obviously, there are many intermediate works; for a summary of these, see my *Structure of Sociological Theory.*

21. Peter M. Blau, *Exchange and Power in Social Life* (New York: Wiley, 1967).

22. Peter M. Blau, *Inequality and Heterogeneity: A Primitive Theory of Social Structure* (New York: Free Press, 1977).

23. In particular, the work of Erving Goffman has done much to increase our insight into the basic interactive process.

24. See my "Towards a Social Physics" for a review of these kinds of intellectual activities.

25. Ibid.

26. Max Weber's penchant for ordering empirical events with "ideal types" has, I feel, encouraged a taxonomic view of theory in sociology. This penchant for taxonomy is unfortunate. See T. Burger's *Max Weber's Theory of Concept Formation: History, Laws, and Ideal Types* (Durham, N.C.: Duke University Press, 1976).

27. Lee Freese, "Formal Theorizing," *Annual Review of Sociology* (1980), 6:187–212.

28. For the details of this line of argument, see Herbert L. Costner and R. K. Leik, "Deductions from Axiomatic Theory," *American Sociological Review* (December 1964), 29:819–35; Lee Freese, "Formal Theorizing," pp. 201–3.

29. Freese, "Formal Theorizing," p. 202.

30. See, for example, Lee Freese and Jane Sell, "Constructing Axiomatic Theories in Sociology," in L. Freese, ed., *Theoretical Methods in Sociology* (Pittsburgh: University of Pittsburgh Press, 1980), pp. 263–368. This is a well-reasoned argument which is as strong a case for axiomatic theory as can be made. It just does not convince me that we would be able to do much theorizing about a wide range of phenomena if the guidelines proposed were followed.

31. See, for example, Herbert M. Blalock, *Theory Construction: From Verbal to Mathematical Formulations* (Englewood Cliffs, N.J.: Prentice-Hall, 1969); Roger Maris, "The Logical Adequacy of Homans' Social Theory," *American Sociological Review* (December 1970), 35:1069–81; Robert L. Hamblin, R. B. Jacobsen, and J. L. Miller, *A Mathematical Theory of Social Change* (New York: Wiley, 1973).

2. A Proposal for Developing Sociological Theory

1. Auguste Comte, *The Course of Positive Philosophy* (originally published between 1830 and 1842 in several volumes). Most accessible now in Harriet Martineau's 1854 condensation, entitled: *The Positive Philosophy of Auguste Comte*, 3 vols. (London: George Bell and Sons, 1896).

2. Ibid., 1:5–6.

3. Ibid., 1:23.

4. For example, see Herbert Blumer, "What Is Wrong with Social Theory?" *American Sociological Review* (August 1954), 19:146–58.

5. See Melvin Tumin, *Social Stratification: The Forms and Functions of Inequality* (Englewood Cliffs, N.J.: Prentice-Hall, 1967), pp. 19–46.

6. Robert K. Merton, *Social Theory and Social Structure* (New York: Free Press, 1968), pp. 4–16. Merton's eloquent advocacy, though he probably did not intend this to be the case, became the legitimating pronouncement for "theories of" almost any empirical area of inquiry—from gang delinquency to marital stability. Theoretical explanation became a game of empirical description; that is, the once lowly empirical generalization was elevated to the status of theory.

7. For example, see Gerhard Lenski, *Power and Privilege: A Theory of Social Stratification* (New York: McGraw-Hill, 1966), esp. pp. 43–47, 434–46.

8. For example, see Talcott Parsons, "A Revised Analytical Approach to the Theory of Stratification," in R. Bendix and S. M. Lipset, eds., *Class, Status, and Power* (Glencoe, Ill.: Free Press, 1953), pp. 92–128.

9. Note for both Lenski and Parsons, they talk about "a" and "the" theory of stratification, respectively. This mode of theorizing is too well engrained in our thinking.

10. See, for example, Jonathan H. Turner, *The Structure of Sociological Theory* (Homewood, Ill.: Dorsey Press, 1974, 1978, 1982); Jonathan H. Turner and Leonard Beeghley, *The Emergence of Sociological Theory* (Homewood, Ill.: Dorsey Press, 1980).

11. Peter M. Blau, *Inequality and Heterogeneity: A Primitive Theory of Social Structure* (New York: Free Press, 1977).

12. For example, Jonathan H. Turner, "Toward a Social Physics," *Humboldt Journal of Social Relations* (Fall–Winter 1980), 7:140–55; "Durkheim's Theory of Integration in Differentiated Social Systems," *Pacific Sociological Review* (1981), 24(4):187–208.

13. Randall Collins, *Conflict Sociology: Toward an Explanatory Social Science* (New York: Academic Press, 1975).

14. Contrary to what may seem desirable, I consider my own ignorance of mathematics an enormous advantage, since I am not likely to become fascinated with the elegance of the mathematics per se. Also, I feel more comfortable bending conventional notation a bit in order to communicate with a larger sociological audience.

15. Technically, I suppose, one does not have a negative log, but the signs that I wish to describe can be constructed $Y = 1 - W \log X$, where $W > 0$. As I said in the preface, I am taking some liberties with mathematical notation. My concern is with the general shape of the curve describing relations among variables, not with the sophistication of the notation used to signify this shape.

3. Stratification Theory

1. Karl Marx, *Capital: A Critical Analysis of Capitalist Production* (New York: International Publishers, 1967).

2. Marshall D. Sahlins, *Social Stratification in Polynesia* (Seattle: University of Washington Press, 1958).

3. Gerhard Lenski, *Power and Privilege: A Theory of Social Stratification* (New York: McGraw-Hill, 1966).

4. Talcott Parsons, *Societies: Evolutionary and Comparative Perspectives* (Englewood Cliffs, N.J.: Prentice-Hall, 1966), and *The System of Modern Societies* (Englewood Cliffs, N.J.: Prentice-Hall, 1971).

5. Immanuel Wallerstein, *The Modern World System: Capitalist Agriculture and the Origins of the European World Economy in the Sixteenth Century* (New York: Academic Press, 1974).

6. Max Weber, *Economy and Society* (New York: Bedminister Press, 1968).

7. Pitirim Sorokin, *Social Mobility* (New York: Harper and Bros., 1927).

8. Peter M. Blau, *Inequality and Heterogeneity: A Primitive Theory of Social Structure* (New York: Free Press, 1977).

9. Marx, *Capital;* and any contemporary Marxist or critical theorist.

10. Ralf Dahrendorf, *Class and Class Conflict in Industrial Society* (Stanford: Stanford University Press, 1967).

11. See, for example, Lenski, *Power and Privilege* and Parsons, *Societies.*

12. See, for example, Peter M. Blau and Otis D. Duncan, *The American Occupational Structure* (New York: Wiley, 1967).

13. See, for example, K. Hope, "Models of Status Inconsistency and Social Mobility Effects," *American Sociological Review* (June 1975), 40:322–43.

14. For example, Dahrendorf, *Class and Class Conflict.*

15. For examples, see Robert A. Dahl, *Who Governs?* (New Haven: Yale University Press, 1961) and William G. Domhoff, *Who Really Rules* (Santa Monica: Goodyear, 1978).

16. For example, Wallerstein, *The Modern World System,* and "World Networks and the Politics of the World Economy," in A. Hawley, ed., *Societal Growth* (New York: Free Press, 1979), pp. 269–78.

17. For an example of the typical critique that I have received for doing this, see Richard P. Applebaum, "Marx's Theory of the Falling Rate of Profit: Towards a Dialectical Analysis of Structural Social Change," *American Sociological Review* (February 1978), 43:75–84.

18. Jonathan H. Turner, *The Structure of Sociological Theory* (Homewood, Ill.: Dorsey Press, 1978), pp. 121–42. See also Jonathan H. Turner and Leonard Beeghley, *The Emergence of Sociological Theory* (Homewood, Ill.: Dorsey Press, 1981), pp. 170–92.

19. These equations are more refined versions of discursive propositions in the works cited in note 18, as well as in Jonathan H. Turner, "Marx and Simmel Revisited," *Social Forces* (June 1975), 53:618–26.

20. See Turner and Beehgley, *The Emergence of Sociological Theory.*

21. See ibid., pp. 256–59.

22. Herbert Spencer, *Principles of Sociology* (New York: D. Appleton, 1885; originally published between 1874 and 1896).

23. Ibid., pp. 577–85.

24. Actually, this line of argument has been totally obscured in discussions of Spencer because of the terminology—"militant" and "industrial"—that he used to describe the processes of centralization and decentralization of power. Too often these states are viewed as an evolutionary sequence, when in fact, Spencer saw them as phases in a cycle. See Turner and Beeghley, *The Emergence of Sociological Theory;* and Jonathan H. Turner, "The Forgotten Giant," *International Journal of the Social Sciences* (1981), 19(59):79–98.

25. Pitirim Sorokin, *Social Mobility.*

26. A notable exception is Randall Collins' work in *Conflict Sociology* (New York: Academic Press, 1975), but this work is too phenomenological in its emphasis for my purposes. See my discussion in *The Structure of Sociological Theory.*

27. Ralf Dahrendorf, *Class and Class Conflict.* See Turner, *The Structure of Sociological Theory,* pp. 143–58, and "From Utopia to Where," *Social Forces* (December 1975), 52:236–44 for my analysis and critique of Dahrendorf's approach.

28. Kingsley Davis and Wilbert E. Moore, "Some Principles of Stratification," *American Sociological Review* (April 1945), 10:242–49.

29. See, for example, Walter Buckley, "On Equitable Inequality," *American*

Sociological Review (October 1963), 28:799–801, and "Social Stratification and the Functional Theory of Social Differentiation," *American Sociological Review* (August 1958), 23:369–75; George A. Huaco, "The Functionalist Theory of Stratification: Two Decades of Controversy," *Inquiry* (Autumn 1966), 9:215–40; Melvin M. Tumin, "Some Principles of Stratification: A Critical Analysis," *American Sociological Review* (August 1953), 18:387–94; Dennis H. Wrong, "The Functional Theory of Stratification: Some Neglected Considerations," *American Sociological Review* (December 1959), 24:772–82.

30. Talcott Parsons, "A Revised Analytical Approach to the Theory of Stratification," in R. Bendix and S. M. Lipset, eds., *Class, Status, and Power* (Glencoe, Ill.: Free Press, 1953), pp. 92–128.

31. Lenski, *Power and Privilege.*

4. Properties of Stratification

1. Melvin M. Tumin, *Social Stratification: The Forms and Functions of Inequality* (Englewood Cliffs, N.J.: Prentice-Hall, 1967).

2. Gerhard Lenski, *Power and Privilege: A Theory of Social Stratification* (New York: McGraw-Hill, 1966).

3. Ibid.; Kingsley Davis and Wilbert E. Moore, "Some Principles of Stratification," *American Sociological Review* (April 1945), 10:242–49.

4. Pitirim Sorokin, *Social Mobility* (New York: Harper and Bros. 1927).

5. Ralf Dahrendorf, *Class and Class Conflict in Industrial Society* (Stanford: Stanford University Press, 1967).

6. T. B. Bottomore, *Classes in Modern Society* (New York: Pantheon, 1966).

7. Davis and Moore, "Some Principles of Stratification."

8. Actually, Bernard Barber did something much like this in "Inequality and Occupational Prestige: Theory, Research, and Social Policy," *Sociological Inquiry* (1978), 48(2):75–88; see also, Keith Hope, "A Liberal Theory of Prestige," *American Journal of Sociology* (March 1982), 87:1011–31.

9. Jonathan H. Turner and Robert A. Hanneman, "Some Elementary Principles of Societal Stratification," *Sociological Theory* (1984), vol. 2.

10. Max Weber, *Economy and Society,* ed. by G. Roth and C. Wittich (Berkeley: University of California Press, 1968), pp. 302–10, 901–40.

11. In particular, Peter M. Blau, *Exchange and Power in Social Life* (New York: Wiley, 1966).

12. These comparisons are typically made in terms of Gini coefficients.

13. Consulting a variety of introductory or stratification textbooks reveals a plethora of diverse definitions.

14. I am borrowing, and adapting, here from Talcott Parsons' "A Revised Analytical Approach to the Theory of Social Stratification," in R. Bendix and S. M. Lipset, eds., *Class Status, and Power* (Glencoe, Ill.: Free Press, 1953).

15. And virtually anything that scholars can dream up.

16. Randall Collins, *Conflict Sociology: Toward An Explanatory Science* (New York: Academic Press, 1975), p. 51.

17. The psychological dynamic underlying this process is probably related to Leon Festinger's social comparison process.

18. We have spent, I feel, too much time worrying about how power elites push us all around, give us false consciousness, and in other ways shape our definitions of the world. These processes occur; there can be no doubt about this. But our concern with this process has been to the exclusion of other processes.

19. For but one example of this debate, see Robert A. Nisbet, "The Decline and Fall of Social Class," *Pacific Sociological Review* (Spring 1959), 11–17; Rudolf Heberle, "Recovery of Class Theory," ibid., pp. 18–24; Bernard Barber and Otis D. Duncan, "Discussion of Papers by Nisbet and Heberle," ibid., pp. 25–28.

5. The Unequal Distribution of Material Wealth

1. Not all services are economic in this definition. Only those services that facilitate the gathering of material resources, their conversion to usable commodities, and their distribution are involved in *P,* or productivity. See my *Patterns of Social Organization* (New York: McGraw-Hill, 1972) for a more detailed justification for this argument.

2. Recall my earlier warning that I am only trying to do what Comte advocated: to "connect" properties of the social universe to each other. We must first see what forces hang together before we can fine-tune our propositions. I am not attempting to fine-tune at this point; I only wish to state in a rough way those most generic forces that go together and account for important properties of our universe.

3. This idea of "surplus" has been trenchantly criticized by a number of scholars. For one of the best critiques, see Martin Orans, "Surplus," *Human Organization* (Spring 1966), 25:24–32. While much of this argument is well taken, I think that the concept of surplus is still useful.

4. Karl Marx, *Capital: A Critical Analysis of Capitalist Production* (New York: International Publishers, 1967).

5. Gerhard Lenski, *Power and Privilege: A Theory of Social Stratification* (New York: McGraw-Hill, 1966). See also Gerhard and Jean Lenski, *Human Societies: An Introduction to Macro Sociology* (New York: McGraw-Hill, 1982).

6. Lenski, *Power and Privilege*.

7. Marx, *Capital*.

8. Ralf Dahrendorf, *Class and Class Conflict in Industrial Society* (Stanford: Stanford University Press, 1967).

9. Ibid.

10. Randall Collins, *Conflict Sociology: Toward An Explanatory Social Science* (New York: Academic Press, 1975).

11. Robert Michels' *Political Parties: A Sociological Study of Oligarchal Tendencies in Modern Democracy* (New York: Dover, 1959) has firmly cemented this

idea into our conceptual approach to complex organization. This idea, of course, is much older and can be found in many nineteenth- and eighteenth-century works.

12. A number of recent studies have found a logarithmic relationship between GNP and income inequality. The argument is that income inequality $= \ln$ (GNP), or in my terms, log (P). Others have noted that the relationship is actually somewhat curvilinear, with very high levels of P decreasing inequality. This argument is expressed: $I = \log (P) + [\log (P)]^2$. The problem with these other equations is that the data set they describe is cross-sectional and does not include data on hunting-gathering or horticultural systems. Hence, the curve appears logarithmic because it begins with the agrarian-to-industrial transition. If one looks at only this portion of the curve that I have drawn in figure 5.4, it is evident that my conclusions and those of this literature are much the same. See, for relevant discussion, Steven Stack, "The Effect of Direct Government Involvement in the Economy on the Degree of Income Inequality: A Cross-National Study," *American Sociological Review* (December 1978), 43:880–88; Erich Weede, "Beyond Misspecification in Sociological Analysis of Income Inequality," *American Sociological Review* (June 1980), 45:497–501; Volker Bornschier and Thanh-Huyen Ballmer-Cao, "Income Inequality: A Cross-National Study of the Relationship Between MNC-Penetration, Dimensions of the Power Structure, and Income Distribution," *American Sociological Review* (June 1979), 44:487–506.

Another issue raised in these and related articles is the effect of governmental involvement in economic productivity. Some, such as Stack (see above) argue that direct governmental involvement lowers income inequality, whereas others emphasize the relationship between democracy and lowered income inequality. For this latter argument, see Robert W. Jackman, "Political Democracy and Social Equality," *American Sociological Review* (August 1974), 39:29–45. Still others question such conclusions on methodological grounds, as is the case for Richard Rubinson and Dan Quinlan, "Democracy and Social Inequality: A Reanalysis," *American Sociological Review* (August 1977), 42:611–23. My sense is that the variable *NH* captures the essence of these arguments and allows us to avoid dealing with hard-to-measure concepts like "democratization" and "government involvement." Both of these are, in my view, specific manifestations of the more generic variable *NH*. See my later discussion on the causal effects among *P* and *NH* for further clarification of this point.

13. I should note that both the exponential and logarithmic curves in my equations are probably Gompertz functions, but I have chosen to lop off the ends of the curves, since they represent extreme values and are less interesting than the portions of the curves described in my equations.

14. In this and subsequent tables, I have drawn from many sources. I have used my own analysis of these societies in *Patterns of Social Organization*. Equally important, I have drawn from other compilations of data on different types of societies. The most important of these are: Gerhard Lenski, *Power and Privilege;* Bernard Barber, *Social Stratification: A Comparative Analysis of Structure and Process* (New York: Harcourt, Brace, 1957); James L. Gibbs, ed., *Peoples of Africa* (New

York: Holt, 1965); Walter Goldschmidt, *Man's Way: A Preface to the Understanding of Human Society* (New York: Holt, 1959); Lucy Mair, *Primitive Government* (Baltimore: Penguin, 1962); Bronislaw Malinowski, *A Scientific Theory of Culture* (Chapel Hill: University of North Carolina Press, 1944); Robert M. Marsh, *Comparative Sociology* (New York: Harcourt and Brace, 1967); Julian Steward, ed., *Handbook of South American Indians* (Washington, D.C.: Smithsonian, 1948); George P. Murdock, *Africa: Its Peoples and Their Culture History* (New York: McGraw-Hill, 1959); Meyer Fortes and E. E. Evans-Pritchard, eds., *African Political Systems* (London: Oxford University Press, 1948); Sidney Painter, *The Rise of the Feudal Monarchies* (Ithaca, N.Y.: Cornell University Press, 1951); I. Schapera, *Government and Politics in Tribal Societies* (London: Watts, 1956); Elman Service, *Primitive Social Organization: An Evolutionary Perspective* (New York: Random House, 1962); Paul Bohannan, *Africa and Africans* (Garden City: American Museum of Science, 1964); H. H. Fried, *The Evolution of Political Society* (New York: Random House, 1959); Manning Nash, *Primitive and Peasant Economic Systems* (San Francisco: Chandler, 1966); Talcott Parsons, *Societies: Evolutionary and Comparative Perspectives* (Englewood Cliffs, N.J.: Prentice-Hall, 1966) and *The System of Modern Societies* (Englewood Cliffs, N.J.: Prentice-Hall, 1971); Elvin R. Service, *The Hunters* (Englewood Cliffs, N.J.: Prentice-Hall, 1966); R. F. G. Spier, *From the Hand of Man: Primitive Preindustrial Technologies* (Boston: Houghton Mifflin, 1970); Marshall Sahlins, *Stone Age Economics* (Chicago: Aldine, 1972) and *Social Stratification in Polynesia* (Seattle: University of Washington Press, 1958); M. G. Bicchieri, ed., *Hunters and Gatherers Today* (New York: Holt, 1972); D. B. Grigg, *The Agricultural Systems of the World: An Evolutionary Approach* (Cambridge: Cambridge University Press, 1974); Richard Lee and Irwin DeVore, eds., *Man the Hunter* (Chicago: Aldine, 1968) and *Kalahari Hunter-Gatherers* (Cambridge: Harvard University Press, 1976); James L. Gibbs, Jr., ed., *Peoples of Africa* (New York: Holt, 1965); Robert McC. Adams, *The Evolution of Urban Society: Early Mesopotamia and Prehispanic Mexico* (Chicago: Aldine, 1966); Fred Eggan, ed., *Social Anthropology of North American Tribes*, 2d ed. (Chicago: University of Chicago Press, 1955); Lucy Mair, *African Societies* (Cambridge: Cambridge University Press, 1974); Ronald Cohen and John Middleton, eds., *Comparative Political Systems: Studies in the Politics of Pre-industrial Societies* (Garden City, N.Y.: American Museum of Natural History, 1967).

15. See my *Patterns of Social Organization* for details on the justification of this classification.

16. Some of the apparent C_{MW} is dispersed because of a redistributive ethic in these societies. See discussion in chapter 6.

17. The degree of centralization in a feudal system varies with transportation and communication technologies, since these influence the capacity to monitor territories.

18. Lenski, *Power and Privilege.*

19. Max Weber, *Economy and Society* (Berkeley: University of California Press, 1978), esp. vol. 2.

6. The Unequal Distribution of Power

1. From my view, power is the capacity of one social unit to control the actions of another. This definition implies that power can vary with respect to such issues as: (1) what degree of control does one unit exercise over another? and (2) how many units are under control of a unit? My goal in this chapter, however, is not to develop a precise conceptualization of power but to understand its unequal distribution in societal social systems.

2. For discussion of these and related issues, see Gerhard Lenski, *Power and Privilege: A Theory of Social Stratification* (New York: McGraw-Hill, 1960); Randall Collins, *Conflict Sociology: Toward an Explanatory Social Science* (New York: Academic Press, 1975); Edward W. Lehman, "Toward a Macrosociology of Power," *American Sociological Review* (August 1969), 34:453–63; Dennis H. Wrong, "Some Problems in Defining Social Power," *American Journal of Sociology* (May 1968), 73:673–81.

3. There is a consistent misinterpretation of this distinction. Too often, secondary commentators view it as an evolutionary distinction, similar to mechanical and organic solidarity, Gemeinschaft and Gessellschaft, folk and urban, and the like. Actually, Spencer saw it as a distinction between centralized and decentralized power and felt that either state could exist in any type of society. See Jonathan H. Turner and Leonard Beeghley, *The Emergence of Sociological Theory* (Homewood, Ill.: Dorsey Press, 1981), pp. 88–89, for clarification of this issue. See also my "The Forgotten Giant: Spencer's Models and Principles," *International Journal of the Social Sciences* (1981), 19(59):79–98.

4. Herbert Spencer, *Principles of Sociology* (New York: D. Appleton, 1898; originally published 1874–96), vol. 1, pt. 2, pp. 569–80.

5. For example, the relations in equation (6.1a) have been discussed in the following sample of more recent conceptual and empirical works: Lenski, *Power and Privilege;* Collins, *Conflict Sociology;* Bernard J. Siegel, "Defensive Structuring and Environmental Stress," *American Journal of Sociology* (July 1970), 76:11–26; Mark Abrahamson, "Correlates of Political Complexity," *American Sociological Review* (October 1969), 34:690–701; Dietrich Rueschemeyer, "Structural Differentiation, Efficiency, and Power," *American Journal of Sociology* (July 1977), 83:1–25; Jack P. Gibbs and Harley L. Browning, "The Division of Labor, Technology: The Organization of Production in Twelve Countries," *American Sociological Review* (February 1966), 31:81–93; Theodore R. Anderson, "Organizational Size and Functional Complexity: A Study of Administration in Hospitals," *American Sociological Review* (February 1961), 26:23–27; Grant W. Childers, Bruce H. Mayhew, Jr., and Louis N. Gray, "System Size and Structural Differentiation in Military Organizations," *American Journal of Sociology* (March 1971), 76:813–30.

6. Spencer, *Principles of Sociology.*

7. Georg Simmel, "Conflict," in *Conflict and the Web of Group Affiliations,* trans. by R. Bendix (Glencoe, Ill.: Free Press, 1955), pp. 48–50, 88–91. For a

more recent statement of this idea, see Bernard J. Siegel, "Defensive Structuring and Environmental Stress."

8. Spencer, *Principles of Sociology.*

9. See, for example, Seymour Melman, *Pentagon Capitalism: The Political Economy of War* (New York: McGraw-Hill, 1970).

10. Lewis A. Coser, "The Termination of Conflict," in L. A. Coser, *Continuities in the Study of Social Conflict* (New York: Free Press, 1967), pp. 37–52.

11. See my "A Cybernetic Model of Economic Development," *The Sociological Quarterly* (Spring 1971), 12:191–203, for a more detailed analysis of these dynamics; see also Lenski, *Power and Privilege.* For more empirical efforts in different contexts, see: Anderson, "Organizational Size"; Gibbs and Browning, "The Division of Labor."

12. Spencer, *Principles of Sociology;* Vilfredo Pareto, *The Rise and Fall of Elites: An Application of Theoretical Sociology* (Totowa, N.J.: Bedminister Press, 1968; originally published in 1901). For a similar analysis at the organizational level, see Peter M. Blau, "A Formal Theory of Differentiation in Organizations," *American Sociological Review* (April 1970), 35:201–18.

13. See Ralf Dahrendorf's "Toward a Theory of Social Conflict," *Journal of Conflict Resolution* (June 1958), 2:170–83; and *Class and Class Conflict in Industrial Society* (Stanford: Stanford University Press, 1967) for an alternative way to state this idea. For additional conceptualizations of how resources are used to mobilize political power, see John D. McCarthy and Meyer N. Zald, "Resource Mobilization and Social Movements: A Partial Theory," *American Journal of Sociology* (May 1977), 86:1212–41.

14. A more general theory of conflict is needed to state the conditions under which these conflicts of interests lead to varying forms of conflictual interaction. As illustrative of efforts along these lines, see ibid.; Collins, *Conflict Sociology;* Jonathan H. Turner, "The Future of Conflict Theory," in *The Structure of Sociological Theory* (Homewood, Ill.: Dorsey Press, 1982), pp. 175–93. For another overview, see Anthony Oberschall, "Theories of Social Conflict," *Annual Review of Sociology* (Palo Alto: Annual Reviews, 1978), pp. 291–315.

15. For examples see Jonathan Kelley and Herbert S. Klein, "Revolution and the Rebirth of Inequality: A Theory of Stratification in Postrevolutionary Society," *American Journal of Sociology* (July 1977), 83:78–99.

16. Spencer, *Principles of Sociology;* Blau, "A Formal Theory"; Abrahamson, "Correlates of Political Complexity"; Paul Goldman, "Size and Differentiation in Organizations," *Pacific Sociological Review* (January 1973), 16:89–106; Gibbs and Browning, "The Division of Labor"; James R. Lincoln, "Organizational Differentiation in Urban Communities," *Social Forces* (March 1979), 57:915–30; Anderson, "Organizational Size"; Childers, Mayhew, and Gray, "System Size and Structural Differentiation . . ."

17. As with figure 5.3 in the last chapter, the slopes should not be compared to each other, since their shapes will vary somewhat under different empirical circumstances. My intent is to show the general nature of the relationship *between* each

variable (*ET, P, IC, IT*), on the one hand, and C_{PO} on the other. I am not addressing the issue of relationships among *ET, P, IC,* and *IT*.

18. See note 14 to chapter 5 for a list of sources used in illustrating this principle.

19. Simmel, "Conflict"; see also Lewis A. Coser, *The Functions of Social Conflict* (Glencoe, Ill.: Free Press, 1951).

20. Spencer, *Principles of Sociology*.

21. See my "Cybernetic Model of Economic Development."

22. For a review of the various definitons, see Clinton F. Fink, "Some Conceptual Difficulties in the Theory of Social Conflict," *Journal of Conflict Resolution* (December 1968) 12:429–31; and Turner, *The Structure of Sociological Theory*, pp. 176–81.

7. The Unequal Distribution of Prestige

1. For an interesting discussion of these, see Randall Collins, *Conflict Sociology* (New York: Academic Press, 1975); and Erving Goffman, *Interaction Ritual* (Garden City, N.Y.: Anchor, 1967).

2. For a detailed analysis of occupational prestige in industrial systems, see Donald Treiman, *Occupational Prestige in Comparative Perspective* (New York: Academic Press, 1977).

3. Kingsley Davis and Wilbert E. Moore, "Some Principles of Stratification," *American Sociological Review* (April 1945), 10:242–49.

4. Bernard Barber, "Inequality and Occupational Prestige: Theory, Research, and Social Policy," *Sociological Inquiry* (1978), 48(2):75–88. Keith Hope's "A Liberal Theory of Prestige," *American Journal of Sociology* (March 1982), 87:1911–31, supports the analysis in this chapter, although it emphasizes *MW/N* and *FI/N* variables. My sense is that the *Po/N* and *SK/N* variables needed to be added to Hope's analysis, especially with respect to my argument that *MW/N* and *Po/N* form one cluster while *FI/N* and *SK/N* form another.

5. Indeed, wealth alone is likely to be stigmatizing and the subject of resentment.

6. See note 14 to chapter 5 for a complete list of references used to construct table 7.1.

7. See Treiman, *Occupational Prestige*.

8. In chapter 3, this was defined as the concentration of the capacity for ideological manipulation. A Marxian version of equation (7.3) might read as follows:

$$\frac{Mw}{N} = h(C_{MW}) \circ i(C_{PO}) \circ j(C_{IM})$$

9. Gerhard Lenski, *Power and Privilege: A Theory of Social Stratification* (New York: McGraw-Hill, 1960), p. 437.

8. The Formation of Subpopulations

1. Randall Collins, *Conflict Sociology: Toward an Explanatory Social Science* (New York: Academic Press, 1975), p. 51.

2. Herbert Spencer, *Principles of Sociology, Part II* (New York: D. Appleton, 1898; originally published in 1874). For Spencer, this relationship can be simply expressed as $DF = \log (N)$.

3. Émile Durkheim, *The Division of Labor in Society* (Glencoe, Ill.: Free Press, 1933; originally published in 1893). For Durkheim the relationship was more complicated but in its most elementary form it can be expressed as $DF = (N^{\text{exp}}) \times (ES^{-\text{exp}})$, where ES = degree of ecological space. Increases in the size and concentration of the population were seen by Durkheim to increase "dynamic" and "moral density" which caused "competition" that, in turn, resulted in increased differentiation. See my "Émile Durkheim's Theory of Integration in Differentiated Social Systems," *Pacific Sociological Review* (1981), 24(4):187–208, for a more thorough discussion of this aspect of Durkheim's thinking.

4. See Collins, *Conflict Sociology,* for some interesting propositions on this score.

5. See note 14 in chapter 5 for a complete list of references used in compiling these data.

6. Spencer, *Principles of Sociology;* Georg Simmel, "Quantitative Aspects of the Group," in *The Sociology of Georg Simmel,* trans. by Kurt H. Wolff (Glencoe, Ill.: Free Press, 1950).

7. See, for example, John Skvoretz and Bruce H. Mayhew, "A Structural Theory of Vertical Mobility" (working paper, University of South Carolina); Bruce H. Mayhew, "A Structural Theory of Rank Differentiation," in Peter M. Blau and Robert K. Merton, eds., *Continuities in Structural Inquiry* (London: Sage, 1981), pp. 287–325; Peter M. Blau, *Inequality and Heterogeneity* (New York: Free Press, 1977), and "Hierarchical Differentiation in Imperatively Coordinated Associations," in Wolfgang Sodeur, ed., *Mathematische Analyse von Organizsationsstrukturen und-Prozessen* (March 1981), 5(7):177–98.

9. The Ranking of Subpopulations

1. Leon Festinger, "A Theory of Social Comparison Processes," *Human Relations* (March 1954), 7:117–40.

2. Talcott Parsons, "A Revised Analytical Approach to the Theory of Social Stratification," in R. Bendix and S. M. Lipset, eds., *Class, Status, and Power* (Glencoe, Ill.: Free Press, 1953), pp. 92–128.

3. Kingsley Davis and Wilbert E. Moore, "Some Principles of Stratification: A Critical Analysis," *American Sociological Review* (April 1945), 10:242–49.

4. Émile Durkheim, *The Division of Labor in Society* (Glencoe, Ill.: Free Press, 1933; originally published in 1893).

5. Ibid., pp. 168–73.

6. Talcott Parsons, *Societies: Evolutionary and Comparative Perspectives* (Englewood Cliffs, N.J.: Prentice-Hall, 1966).

7. See my discussion in *The Structure of Sociological Theory* (Homewood, Ill.: Dorsey Press, 1981).

8. Durkheim, *The Division of Labor*. See also Leonard Beeghley's and my discussion in *The Emergence of Sociological Theory* (Homewood, Ill.: Dorsey Press, 1982), chapters 15, 16, and 17. See also my "Durkheim's Theory of Integration in Differentiated Social Systems," *Pacific Sociological Review* (1981), 24(4):187–208.

9. When such generalization of the collective conscience occurred *without* compensatory normative specification, then Durkheim visualized the "pathological" state of "anomie" to exist.

10. Mobility Processes

1. Pitirim Sorokin, *Social Mobility* (New York: Harper and Bros., 1927).

2. For a summary of the results of this vast literature, see William T. Bielby, "Models of Status Attainment," *Research in Social Stratification and Mobility* (Summer 1980), 1:8–24.

3. Most typically, the SES index in Peter M. Blau's and Otis Dudley Duncan's work is employed. See their *The American Occupational Structure* (New York: Wiley, 1967).

4. For example, see Ralf Dahrendorf, *Class and Class Conflict in Industrial Society* (Stanford: Stanford University Press, 1959) and "Toward a Theory of Social Conflict," *Journal of Conflict Resolution* (June 1958), 2:170–83.

5. Ibid.; Eliot R. Smith and James R. Kluegal, "Ideological and Structural Determinants of Attitudes Toward Income Equality" (working paper, University of California at Riverside), and "Beliefs about Stratification," in A. Inkeles, et al., eds., *Annual Review of Sociology* (Palo Alto: Annual Reviews Inc., 1981), 7:29–56.

6. Peter M. Blau, *Inequality and Heterogeneity: A Primitive Theory of Social Structure* (New York: Free Press, 1977).

7. Robert K. Merton, *Social Theory and Social Structure* (New York: Free Press, 1968), pp. 279–334.

8. Yet, Sorokin, *Social Mobility,* clearly stressed the importance of examining mobility per se as a process. Only in the area of demography and human ecology has there been a long-term and consistent conceptual effort to understand mobility in its own right.

9. John Skvoretz and Bruce H. Mayhew, "A Structural Theory of Vertical Mobility" (working paper, University of South Carolina, 1980).

10. Sorokin, *Social Mobility*.

11. See note 14 in chapter 5 for the works used to construct table 10.1.

11. Toward a "National Science of Sociology"

1. Even the most cursory review of sociology's journals will reveal the extent to which the Old Masters are analyzed and reanalyzed. I would hazard a guess that Old Master–type articles outnumber new theoretical pieces five to one, at least.

2. Comte would turn over in his grave if he saw what had occurred to "sociology." See chapter 2.

3. For a summary, see Jonathan H. Turner and Alexandra Maryanski, *Functionalism* (Menlo Park: Benjamin-Cummings, 1978).

4. My views owe much to David and Judith Willer, *Systematic Empiricism* (Englewood Cliffs, N.J.: Prentice-Hall, 1973).

5. David Willer and Murray Webster, Jr., "Theoretical Concepts and Observables," *American Sociological Review* (August 1970), 35:748–57 term this simultaneous process "abduction."

6. Ibid.

7. I sought to explicate these principles in my and Leonard Beeghley's *The Emergence of Sociological Theory* (Homewood, Ill.: Dorsey Press, 1981).

8. Robert K. Merton, *Social Theory and Social Structure* (New York: Free Press, 1968).

9. For example, Peter M. Blau, *Inequality and Heterogeneity* (New York: Free Press, 1977); George C. Homans, *Social Behavior: Its Elementary Forms* (New York: Harcourt, 1974); Bruce H. Mayhew and Roger L. Levinger, "On the Emergence of Oligarchy in Human Interaction," *American Journal of Sociology* (1970), 81:1017–49; Randall Collins, *Conflict Sociology* (New York: Academic Books, 1974); Ralf Dahrendorf, "Toward a Theory of Social Conflict," *Journal of Conflict Resolution* (June 1958), 2:170–83; Richard Emerson, "Exchange Theory, Part II," in J. Berger, M. Zelditch, and B. Anderson, *Sociological Theories in Progress, Volume II* (New York: Houghton Mifflin, 1972); Ralph Turner, "Strategy for Developing an Integrated Role Theory," *Humbolt Journal of Social Relations* (Fall–Winter 1980), 7:123–39. There are other efforts along these lines; I am simply citing some of my favorite works.

10. To use, once again, A. R. Radcliffe-Brown's terms. See his *A Natural Science of Society* (Glencoe, Ill.: Free Press, 1948).

INDEX OF NAMES

INDEX OF SUBJECTS